# The Philosophy of History in Our Time

## AN ANTHOLOGY

HANS MEYERHOFF was born in Germany in 1914 and has lived in the United States since 1934. He received his Ph.D. in Philosophy from the University of California, where he is now Professor of Philosophy. During World War II he served as a political analyst in the Office of Strategic Services and afterward in the Department of State. In 1955 he was Visiting Professor of Philosophy at the University of Michigan and from 1957 to 1958 at the Massachusetts Institute of Technology. He has written numerous articles on philosophy, literature, psychology, and politics for *Partisan Review*, *Commentary*, and other journals, and has published a book entitled *Time in Literature*.

# THE
# Philosophy of History
## IN OUR TIME:

*An Anthology Selected,*
*and with an Introduction*
*and Commentary by*
*Hans Meyerhoff*

DOUBLEDAY ANCHOR BOOKS
DOUBLEDAY & COMPANY, INC.
GARDEN CITY, NEW YORK
1959

Pablo Picasso, *Guernica*, 1937, on loan from the artist to the Museum of Modern Art, New York. Cover by Diana Klemin. Typography by Edward Gorey.

# PREFACE

An anthology presents a selection; and every selection reflects a personal point of view. Some of the considerations that have guided me in choosing the selections contained in this volume are as follows:

1. I decided to use only writings that are contemporary in the sense that they are, roughly, of our own century. This restriction does not express a personal preference. On the contrary, I tend to believe that the philosophical reflections about history during the eighteenth and nineteenth centuries are still, in their total impact, superior to what has been produced in our own age. I have chosen to stay within contemporary confines partly because it would have been impossible to do justice to both earlier and recent writings in a volume of this size, partly because I also believe, as I explain in the general introduction, that the contemporary situation in the philosophy of history merits a survey and re-thinking in its own right.

2. I have tried to achieve a balance of contributions from professional historians and from professional philosophers.

3. I have also tried to present selections from different national communities.

4. I have organized the material in terms of topics rather than in chronological sequence; and I have divided the material into four parts, each dealing with a general topic. I have written brief introductory comments to the different selections in each part. These comments are designed primarily to weave the individual contributions together and to explain some of the problems that arise in connection with each topic. I have, however, departed from certain standard practices in anthologies by not giving detailed

biographical or bibliographical information about each contributor. References to various works and authors may be found throughout the text; and I have added some bibliographical comments and apologies as a postscript.

5. I decided to exclude any writings that had already found their way into some other anthology. To anthologize anthologies seemed supererogatory. Since there is no rule without exception, I have granted myself special dispensation in the case of the essay by Ernest Nagel.

6. I have tried, as far as possible, to reprint separate articles or relatively complete sections from books. I have had to deviate from this policy in a few cases; but I have been pleased to discover that, on the whole, the separate, individual pieces form a kind of unity. Thus, while any anthology is piecework in the literal sense, the essays collected in this volume are, as it were, variations on a common theme.

Numerous friends and colleagues have helped me at various stages of this work, and I am grateful to them even though I cannot name them individually. I am indebted to my wife for improvements in the introductory essay; and I am pleased to have this opportunity to thank the Department of Humanities at the Massachusetts Institute of Technology for the cordial hospitality extended to a visitor and for the resourceful secretarial assistance rendered by Mrs. Ruth Dubois and Mrs. Mary Lou Joyner.

H.M.

Cambridge, Massachusetts
Los Angeles, California

# CONTENTS

# The Philosophy of History in Our Time

# HISTORY AND PHILOSOPHY:
# AN INTRODUCTORY SURVEY

## I

The writing of history is an ancient and honorable profession. What is more, like the arts and unlike the sciences, it reached a degree of pefection early in the ancient world which, in a sense, it has never surpassed. Thucydides is as supreme a figure in the art of history as Sophocles in the art of tragedy. Only science and technology have progressed, steadily, encouragingly, and frighteningly, since the days of Thales and Aristotle.

Again like the arts, history—I mean, the writing and study of history—achieved this triumph without leaning upon philosophy. There were, of course, writers like Herodotus and Plato who advanced speculative ideas—that history was a vast Ferris wheel of ups and downs, a succession of cycles or spirals; and Thucydides knew his Sophist contemporaries and set out to explain how and why the methods he used in writing the history of the Peloponnesian War differed from those of his predecessors. Polybius, too, laid down definite rules by which he was guided in telling the story of Rome's conquest of the ancient world; and we find methodological hints and philosophical or moral presuppositions in the works of Sallust, Livy, Tacitus, and Josephus. But we do not find anywhere in the ancient world a philosophy of history—either in the speculative sense, as there were philosophies of nature, man, and society; or in the analytic sense, as there were logical inquiries into the nature of knowledge in science, ethics, politics, or art. Plato's *Critias*, possibly an attempt to construct a mythology, or philosophy, of history analogous to his philosophy of nature in the *Timaeus*, does not get beyond a fragmentary beginning; and there is no ancient treatise that deals with the logic of historical knowledge as, say, Aristotle's *Posterior Analytics* does with the logic of science.

Thus we often hear it said that Israel and Christianity were responsible for the birth of a historical consciousness in the Western world. This is true in one sense, but misleading in another. Other ancient peoples, beside the Hebrews, kept historical records and produced historico-religious narratives. And, surely, the people of Rome, deeply imbued as they were with a consciousness of their past *ab urbe condita* and distinguished by the eminence of their historians, did not lack a sense of history. It is true that Plato and Aristotle were more interested in an eternal realm of Being than in the historical world of Becoming; but this does not mean that the Greeks were an unhistorical people. The Sophists showed a distinct awareness of the historical and cultural world around them; and the cyclical view of history which we find in Herodotus and Plato is nonhistorical only if we judge it from the Jewish and Christian conception of history.

Israel and Christianity, therefore, did not awaken the ancient world from its unhistorical slumber. What they did was (a) to charge history with a religious significance which it had not had previously and (b) to read the progression of history as a clue to the design and direction imposed upon it by God's will. The historical world assumed a new significance because certain events in it, such as Israel's covenant with God or the temporal existence of Jesus, were imbued with a crucial symbolic meaning. Moreover, these events and others were interpreted as part of an over-all pattern of history which exhibited a meaningful movement and direction from its obscure origins in the Book of Genesis to a redemptive, eschatological goal in or beyond history. In both these respects, the Jewish and Christian tradition expressed a new type of historical consciousness, which has become the characteristic conception of history in the Western world.

At the end of the Roman Empire, this religious tradition produced a great theological interpretation of history, *The*

*City of God* by St. Augustine. The influence of this monumental work extends into our own times.

History, according to this view, is one aspect of the
world created by God. It encompasses the life of all mankind; it is "universal history," not only the history of local,
regional, or national units as for Greek and Roman historians. As a work of creation, history has a beginning; and
in its beginning are contained, by Divine Providence, the
seeds of its development and its end. In short, history has
an origin and goal and moves in a linear progression.

Next, the movement of history is subject to law. History
is not an arbitrary succession, a meaningless conglomeration
of events, but it is an intelligible process guided by an inherent law or the transcendent design of a Divine Intelligence. The design may be obscure in secular history
where it is constantly thwarted by man's sinfulness; but it
is lucid and luminous in the pages of sacred history. It discloses a course that runs through certain crucial phases or
stages: from paradise to the fall of man; from the fall to
the incarnation of Christ; and from the incarnation to redemption.[1] In the course of secular history, Augustine
recognized a fourfold division, marked by the rise and fall
of the four great empires in the ancient world: Assyria,
Persia, Macedonia, and Rome.

Rome was the first universal empire. Its tragic fall finds
a proper place in the general schema of history, because
a universal empire, though conceived in sin and culminating in despair, was needed to make possible the establishment of the Universal Church. Ancient Israel anticipated
the City of God; Christianity has come to fulfill it. Thus
the goal of history will make good the evil of history. It
is not the mere ending of vast temporal sequences, not a
disaster like the sacking of Rome; but it is a goal which will
see the Church triumphant and which will redeem the
promise of the resurrection of the body and life everlasting
for the community of believers united in the faith of Christ.
In short, the goal of history is a condition of man *beyond*
history. If, in the words of Arnold J. Toynbee, a contem-

[1] In the twelfth century, Joachim de Flore used this threefold
division for an elaborate and imminent Christian eschatology.

porary Augustinian, history is "a vision of God's creation
on the move, from God its source to God its goal,"[2] it is
also correct to say that the secular history of mankind is a
vast detour, as it were, in the transhistorical drama of human salvation.

A *Study of History* as much as *The City of God* is a
work of Christian apologetics. St. Augustine defended
Christianity against the charge that it was responsible for
the fall of Rome (410) and he rested his defense primarily
on the distinction between secular and sacred history. Professor Toynbee is more hard pressed because he must defend the possible breakdown of a Christian civilization,
namely ours; in the concluding volume of his study, however, he also appeals, as did St. Augustine, to the "faith"
that ordinary events in secular history are but obscure
shadows of God's inscrutable design and intelligible only
if viewed from the transhistorical perspective of the Chris-
tological myth.

This Christian transmutation of history into a theodicy
dominated Western thought for more than a thousand
years. It was discarded only when the Renaissance challenged religious authority in history as in other areas of
life and culture; but after an eclipse of a few hundred
years, the Christian view has come back strongly in our
own century.

The liberation of history from theology began in Italy
with the works of Machiavelli and Guicciardini; it reached
its fullest development in the historical and philosophical
works of the eighteenth century. When Voltaire, as one
writer has said,[3] "shattered tradition," it was the Augustinian tradition as then represented in France by Bossuet's
*Universal History* (1681) which he ridiculed and rejected.
And Hume's skepticism in philosophy was fully matched
by Gibbon's in history. The spirit of his great work was

[2] Arnold J. Toynbee, *A Study of History*, Vol. X (London and
New York 1954), p. 3.
[3] Emery Neff, *The Poetry of History* (New York 1947), heading of Chapter I. I am also indebted to this study for the brief
passages from Voltaire and Herder quoted below without special
acknowledgment.

the very antithesis of St. Augustine's defense of Christianity.
For Gibbon the Roman Empire was a symbol of civilization succumbing to the joint assault of barbarism and religion (Christianity). In addition to these historical works,
the eighteenth century produced a number of straight
philosophical theories which completed the emancipation
of history from theology. They discovered history as an
autonomous, self-sufficient domain. They created a historical consciousness which was predominantly immanent, not
transcendent; and they employed rational, not religious,
concepts.

Vico's *New Science* (1725) revived the Greek conception
that history was subject to cyclical phases. Voltaire, Herder,
Kant, Condorcet, and Humboldt discovered some sort of
inherent evolutionary tendencies in historical change and
progress.[4] Vico still used the concept of "Providence," but
in such a way, as Löwith puts it,[5] that "nothing remains
of the transcendent and miraculous operation" of Providence in St. Augustine or Bossuet. "With Vico, Providence
has become as natural, secular, and historical as if it did
not exist at all." Voltaire, of course, like Hume, had no use
for the "Providence with which God governs human affairs" and ridiculed the superstitious belief in miracles by
which God, according to Bossuet, overthrows his laws
"when He pleases." Herder, who had no use for Voltaire's
enlightened rationalism, nevertheless shared and expanded
the belief that history was an immanent, autonomous process, "a purely natural history of human forces, actions, and
instincts, according to time and place." And Hegel's famous
*Lectures on the Philosophy of History* (1836), the culmination of this new secular philosophical tradition, represent,

---

[4] Herder's major work is the vast study called *Ideas for a
Philosophical History of Mankind,* which prompted Kant's review article (1874) entitled "The Idea of a Universal History
from a Cosmopolitan Point of View." Condorcet's Outlines of a
*Historical View of the Progress of the Human Mind* (1793) had
a special influence upon Comte. Humboldt's essay "Ueber die
Aufgabe des Geschichtsschreibers" (1822), published in the
annals of the Royal Academy of Science, marks the transition to
an empirical historiography and influenced Ranke.

[5] Karl Löwith, *Meaning in History* (Chicago 1949), p. 123.

as it were, the self-realization of the historical consciousness
that St. Augustine had bequeathed to the Western world.
Both he and Marx discovered the dimension of pure historicity; for both there is no escape from time into a realm
of eternal essences or into a faith beyond history. They are
the foremost precursors of the characteristic mood of our
own age that the historical condition determines the human situation. Man's existence is history; or "life and reality
are history, and history alone," as Croce said. Thus history, and not any City of God, is the key to a philosophy
of man and society.

Despite these radical differences, however, there are distinct formal analogies between philosophical and religious
historiographies which indicate that both express the same
type of historical consciousness. Sometimes, as in the case
of Hegel, these parallels are striking in detail. His system
throughout reflects the Augustinian model; only it elimi-
nates the dimension of faith and translates the religious concepts into a rationalistic vocabulary. The Johannine concept of *logos*—the word, or Holy Spirit, made flesh—
reappears as the Objective Spirit. History is the rational,
not the divine, spirit objectified. It depicts the creations and
manifestations of Reason "on the move." What is, is rational—from the dim, hidden dawn of Reason to its luminous clarity in the French Revolution and in German
idealism, from the sacking of Rome to the storming of the
Bastille. Again, there are critical phases and junctures in
the movement of history: the famous law of three stages,
which Marx and Comte adopted, too, is a secular revision
of the religious dialectic in St. Augustine and Joachim de
Flore. The crucial, decisive individual in world history,
Napoleon, for example, is an "incarnation" of the World
Spirit. History is intelligible because it is a product of
Reason, instead of Divine Providence; but the rational pattern is often seen through a glass, darkly. Hegel's concept
of "the cunning of Reason" is a substitute for the mysterious
and inscrutable ways of God in history. His assertion that
the Whole, or the Absolute, is the Truth corresponds to
the belief that the ultimate truth is with God, or hidden
in God. Even his so-called immoralism, more precisely, his

moral neutrality, is a concession to the religious tradition; for it means that what looks evil and irrational in human eyes is due to the fragmentary and limited vision of man. Viewed in the rational light by which the Objective Spirit shineth in the darkness, the obscurities and contradictions of history vanish. The temporal trials and tragedies of mankind appear as necessary and insignificant by-products of the self-realization of Reason. And philosophical truth, instead of religious faith, will set man free. It sublimates his sorrows and sufferings by assigning a meaningful place to them in the rational structure of the Whole. In the end, history fulfills itself by reaching a stage in which all the irrational, paradoxical, and evil forces encountered on its long road are transcended. For Hegel history was as unmistakably a theodicy as for St. Augustine; only he used reason, instead of faith, to justify the ways of God.

In other philosophical works, these parallels are not so close as in the case of Hegel; yet all of them have an essential formal element in common with the religious tradition going back to St. Augustine. This common heritage shows in their search for a meaning of history. To say that history has a meaning was to assert that the story of mankind showed continuity and unity from beginning to end; that history, as well as nature, was subject to law, divine or rational; and that either faith or reason would reveal this inherent structure. The nature of these "iron laws" of history, of course, differed: according to the religious tradition, they were imposed by Divine Providence; according to the secular philosophies of history, they might be the laws of dialectics; or they might reflect the sad spectacle of the eternal return of the same, the inevitable succession of rise and fall, flowering and decline, *corso* and *ricorso;* or they might be more gentle and vague as in the application of a progressive, evolutionary law to history. But whether imposed or immanent, both views assumed that some kind of metaphysical determinism provided a clue to the meaning of history.[6]

The search for meaning, however, invariably contained

---

[6] Cf. the analysis of "historical inevitability" in the excerpt from Professor Berlin's work; p. 249 ff. below.

a strong teleological component as well. Temporal progression also spelled moral progress. World history was the world's, or God's, court of justice. And the goal of history atoned for the crimes of history. A golden future loomed at the end of history as its origins lay hidden in some golden age of the past. The goal might be derived from the Book of Daniel, from the second Isaiah, or from the Apostolic Creed; it might be envisaged, in a nonreligious context as the triumph of reason, the leap into freedom, or the birth of the *Übermensch;* it might be the regaining of Paradise Lost, Rousseau's state of nature, the founding of a rational state or the classless society; it might signify the achievement of freedom or self-consciousness—the underlying schema in all these variations was very similar: theoretical and moral ideas fused in a beatific vision of the end of history which would vindicate human hopes and aspirations, resolve moral ambiguities, and redeem the sufferings and tragedies that are inscribed in the pages of history.

Ordinary expressions like "what is the meaning of history?" or "does history have a meaning?" make sense only against this religious and philosophical background. This is worth remembering in particular, since the rational, philosophical theories have suffered a decisive decline during the last hundred years. Speculative philosophy, in history or elsewhere, is bad metaphysics; and we rejoice at having swept the metaphysical ghosts from the closets of history; but this decline of rationalism has had another consequence as well. For these theories did more than engage in idle, armchair speculation about history. By eliminating the mysterious concept of Divine Providence, they also established the sovereignty of history as a rational domain. And by affirming that the meaning of man's history lies in this world, not beyond, they also made this domain accessible to human mastery. Just as the discovery of natural laws had opened the world of nature to human conquest and control, so man would master the world of history by diagnosing and "obeying" its immanent laws. By repudiating divine necessity, he would be free to remake history in his own image. By exploiting the necessities of history, he would gain his freedom from history. By "understanding" both nature and history, man would cease being their victim and establish his own kingdom of rational ends. He would, at last, be owner and master of his own history.

The failure of this secular faith, therefore, has left a deep mark upon modern culture in general. Man seems to have lost both the rational key to, and the practical mastery over, his own history; and this twofold loss has contributed to the prevailing mood of our age that history is full of sound and fury signifying nothing.

The eclipse of speculative reason is a general phenomenon of modern thought; and a variety of causes, social as well as intellectual, have contributed to it. In the field of history, two factors were pre-eminently influential: a movement known as "historicism" and the rise of an empirical, scientific historiography. Both trends combined, in the nineteenth century, to defeat the traditional philosophical approach to history.

## II

Historicism opens a new chapter in the study of history. Friedrich Meinecke, who wrote the classic work on its origins,[7] described historicism as "the greatest spiritual revolution of the Western world." He compared it to the Reformation; Lord Acton, to the Copernican revolution. These judgments are hyperbolical, but there is no doubt that the contemporary situation in the theory of history, and culture in general, is unintelligible without an appreciation of the meaning and the consequences of historicism. "Today none of us, no matter where our particular interests may lie, can escape its all-pervasive influence."[8]

Historicism is a by-product of the romantic revolt against enlightenment and rationalism. Thus it marks a crucial departure from the type of philosophical theories that we

[7] Friedrich Meinecke, *Die Entstehung des Historismus*, 2 vols. (Munich 1936).

[8] Geoffrey Barraclough, *History in a Changing World* (Oxford 1955), p. 2; reprinted on p. 28 below.

have just discussed. Herder, one of its first and foremost spokesmen, was an ardent advocate of history as a key to an understanding of mankind; but he passionately rejected any rationalistic, philosophical approach to history. He satirized the follies of the intellect, or "the mole's eye of this most enlightened century"; and he composed his first essay, *Still Another Philosophy of History for the Culture of Humanity*, as a specific reply to the "exceedingly hasty reasoning à la Voltaire." He thought that a historical work like Voltaire's was a shallow distillation of the "heart, warmth, humanity, and life" that were the essence of history and reality.

The basic thesis of historicism is quite simple: The subject matter of history is human life in its totality and multiplicity. It is the historian's aim to portray the bewildering, unsystematic variety of historical forms—people, nations, cultures, customs, institutions, songs, myths, and thoughts —in their unique, living expressions and in the process of continuous growth and transformation. This aim is not unlike the artist's; at any rate, it differs from the systematic, conceptual approach of the philosopher. The abstract concepts employed in philosophy are not adequate for rendering the concrete realities of history. Such abstract concepts are static and catch the common properties of things and people, not their specific differences. *Individuum est ineffabile* is the motto of Meinecke's work, expressing an aesthetic rather than a philosophic sentiment. Thus the special quality of history does not consist in the statement of general laws or principles, but in the grasp, so far as possible, of the infinite variety of particular historical forms immersed in the passage of time. The meaning of history does not lie hidden in some universal structure, whether deterministic or teleological, but in the multiplicity of individual manifestations at different ages and in different cultures. All of them are unique and equally significant strands in the tapestry of history; all of them, in Ranke's famous phrase, are "immediate to God."

In short, history cannot be cast into a rational system; nor are its methods entirely rational. Reason is often a poor guide to the deeply hidden, irrational strata from which many of the richest manifestations of human life draw their meaning and sustenance. Herder was the first historian to appeal to the principle of empathy. One must *feel* oneself, he wrote, into a period, into life, and into history as a whole. The historian, not unlike the artist, must recreate a character, the sense of a meeting, the atmosphere on the eve of a battle, the spirit of the Renaissance; he must re-enact, in the words of R. G. Collingwood, a contemporary historicist, past experience in the living thought of the present; he must draw upon imagination and sympathy in order to bring back to life, as Stendhal did in *The Charterhouse of Parma* or Tolstoi in *War and Peace,* past shadows of people and movements, conflicts and victories, landscapes and physical hardships, secret passions and social forces, in their specific and unique characteristics—instead of enshrining them in dry-as-dust categories of philosophy.

Thus historicism, from its beginnings, carried a strong plea for the autonomy of Clio as a muse. Perhaps history was simply a "branch of literature," as Macaulay said, urging that a "truly great historian would reclaim the materials which the novelist has appropriated." Ranke did not subscribe to such an aesthetic outlook, but strongly insisted that the historian's imagination, unlike the artist's, be disciplined by, and subordinated to, factual evidence and criticism. Yet, in his philosophical approach to history, he was a true heir of Herder's and an antagonist of Hegel's. "The spirit manifesting itself in this world is not of a conceptual nature." It is impossible, he continued, to force the wealth of historical life into the poverty of rational concepts, to "subsume it under abstractions . . . Life disappears in [Hegelian] scholasticism."

Process and individuality, change, the transiency of time and the concreteness of historical facts have remained the cornerstones of historicism; "Instead of trying to constrain reality within a system, we have dismissed the empty figment of one linear history and learnt appreciation of the subtle shades of individuality, respect for irreducible particularity, acceptance of the untold multitude of facts, and awareness of endless formation and transformation, of achievement without end."[9]

The present situation, however, is made more complex and confusing because, during the nineteenth century, historicism itself passed through two distinct phases, one predominantly scientific and positivistic, the other "pure and complete," in Croce's words.

The scientific phase coincided with the rise of history as an empirical discipline. Thus it reinforced by empirical arguments the romantic revolt against philosophy. This was, of course, not the first empirical protest against philosophical distortions of history. As Thucydides or Polybius in the ancient world, so Machiavelli, Guicciardini, Mabillon, and Hume, in the modern period, departed from a speculative approach to history and advocated empirical methods and critical standards; but none of them worked these principles out in a systematic way. Descartes specifically excluded history from his *Discourse on Method;* and this choice prevailed among his philosophical successors, including Kant. Thus logical, analytic studies of the nature of historical knowledge, in contrast to philosophical historiographies, were as rare in modern philosophy as in the ancient world. They did not become of serious concern to either historian or philosopher until the great awakening of history as an empirical and/or scientific discipline in the nineteenth century.

It was Ranke, together with his contemporaries and successors of the Prussian Historical School, who made a signal advance in the scientific approach to history. Ranke, of course, was not a positivist; on the contrary, he was deeply steeped in the romantic origins of historicism. But by his indefatigable research and his monumental works he created a new conception of history which meant to be strictly empirical and which, in the hands of some of his successors, was turned into a positive science. As a result of the opening of diplomatic archives and in conjunction with the "auxiliary sciences" of biblical scholarship, mythology,

[9] Cf. p. 30 below; cf. also Dwight E. Lee and Robert N. Beck, "The Meaning of Historicism," *The American Historical Review,* Vol. LIX, no. 3 (pp. 568–77).

philology, numismatics, and archaeology,[10] history, too, began to develop logical tools and analytic techniques of its own. Critical methods were devised for sifting, testing, collating, and evaluating documentary sources; rigorous standards were employed for judging the impartiality, objectivity, and truthfulness of a historical work; and the new techniques were taught and applied in the academic seminars of the Historical School, to which students flocked from all over the world. Thus the training of a new generation of "scientific" historians, in the image of their great teachers —Niebuhr, Ranke, Droysen, or Mommsen in Germany, Taine and Fustel de Coulange in France, Lord Acton and Bury in England—nourished the hope that history would, at last, take its place as an equal partner in the universe of science. Methodology was discovered as the cure—and may have become the curse—of historical scholarship.

"To history," Ranke wrote in the preface of his first work,[11] "has been assigned the office of judging the past, of instructing the present for the benefit of future ages. To such high offices this work does not aspire: it wants to show only what really happened (*wie es eigentlich gewesen*)." This last phrase became the manifesto of modern empirical historiography. It signified that history was neither philosophical speculation, nor a substitute for art, entertainment, or morality. "The strict presentation of the facts is . . . the supreme law of historiography." The new *Historische Zeitschrift* (1859) announced to its contributors and readers that "this periodical should, above all, be a scientific one. Its first task, therefore, should be to represent the true method of historical research and to point out the deviations therefrom." And, in 1902, J. B. Bury reaffirmed these intentions in his Inaugural Lecture as Regius Professor of Modern History: "So long as history was regarded as an art, the sanctions of truth and accuracy could not be

[10] Cf. the essay by Henri Pirenne; p. 87 ff. below.

[11] The passage is reprinted in *The Varieties of History*, ed. by Fritz Stern (New York: Meridian Books 1956). I am also indebted to this volume for the following passages from the *Historische Zeitschrift* and from J. B. Bury quoted without special acknowledgment.

severe . . . A new transfiguring conception of her scope and limits was needed, if she was to become an independent science . . . The systematized method which distinguishes a science was beyond the vision of all . . . Erudition has now been supplemented by scientific method, and we owe this change to Germany." Thus great achievements, and even greater expectations, kindled the conviction that history had arrived at last as a legitimate scientific discipline.

These hopes faded quickly. History had just begun to make a good claim for its status as a science (and produced its own methodological compendia[12]) when a reaction set in against this scientific trend. A generation after Ranke, Burckhardt—who had declined succession to Ranke's chair in Berlin—expressed this reaction in the somber and paradoxical reflections that "history is the most unscientific discipline; yet it contains much worth knowing."

What caused this reversal? In general, it was the result of an increasing awareness that the scientific conception, "the systematized method which distinguishes a science," was as incompatible with history as the rational method which distinguished traditional philosophy. For whether the historical system was philosophical or scientific, it was a system; and the system, as Kierkegaard argued against Hegel, was static and abstract, the very antithesis of life, movement, and individual existence. Yet the recapture of these "essences" was precisely the meaning which a romantic historicism had assigned to history.

What happened in the nineteenth century, however, was much more complex and resulted in a critical situation, of which Burckhardt's pessimistic reflections were but one symptom.[13] A host of factors co-operated to produce the conviction that history could be accommodated neither in the traditional framework of rationalistic philosophies nor in the new framework of the empirical sciences.

[12] The best-known compendia of this kind are E. Bernheim, *Lehrbuch der Historischen Method* (1894), and C. V. Langlois and C. Seignobos, *Introduction aux Études Historiques* (1897; English translation 1898).

[13] For Burckhardt's pessimism, see the essay reprinted below; p. 272 ff.

The last century witnessed a succession of assaults upon the traditional assumption that the "essence" of man or society rested on solid rational foundations. The belief in the primacy and autonomy of "reason," whether in the Greek sense or in the sense of philosophers of the enlightenment, was increasingly challenged and gradually replaced by a belief in the primacy of the "will" or "vital" powers.

There was Kierkegaard's lonely existential revolt against systematic thought in general and his leap into faith on the wings of absurdity. There were the residues of romanticism gathered up in Schopenhauer's doctrine that a "blind will" beat at the heart of Being. There was the emergence of vitalism and pragmatism. Nietzsche, Bergson, William James, and a host of other minds under the impact of Darwinism upon philosophy, all discovered a realm of secret, irrational powers and undercurrents behind the stream of consciousness, the ineluctable presence of attitudes, interests, purposes, and unconscious drives behind the façade of reason. Rationality, whether in science or philosophy, was at best a limited practical instrument, at worst, a form of self-deception. Other thinkers reinforced and expanded this conclusion that emotive and irrational factors—class interests, social stereotypes, dogmas, myths, residues, ideologies, and illusions—permeated history and society. This, in part, is the intellectual heritage of Marx, Comte, Burckhardt, Pareto, Sorel, and Freud.

The combined force of these tendencies seemed to dispel any hope for an objective, universal conceptual system in science or society. The quest for objective truth succumbed to the *élan vital*, the struggle for existence, the will to power, or the will to believe. The theory of knowledge turned into a sociology of knowledge; rationality into rationalization.

Historicism itself contributed to the rise of relativism and sociologism; for it revealed, in Dilthey's words, "the relativity of every metaphysical and religious doctrine." All of them were immersed in and swept away by the stream of history; all of them were but different interpretations of and perspectives on the process of life. "Historical consciousness," Dilthey wrote, "shatters the last chains which philosophy and natural science could not break. Man has now achieved freedom."[14] This final freedom of modern man, however, came at a time when the traditional foundations and institutions of the liberal, bourgeois society were giving way to new forms and modes of thought characteristic of a predominantly industrial and technological world. The new social conditions jeopardized the idea of freedom itself. Dilthey's freedom, which existential thinkers have rediscovered in our times as the last refuge of man, is, at best, an inner, spiritual condition divorced from reality, at worst, a dreadful burden to be exchanged for the blessings of conformism.

Against these formidable trends stood Ranke's claim that the historian was an impartial spectator and objective recorder of what really happened; Bury's assertion that history was "simply a science, no less and no more"; and Lord Acton's advice that "a historian is seen at his best when he does not appear."

Thus, at the end of the century, a crucial dilemma was shaping up for modern historicism. One horn of the dilemma reminded the historian that he must tell the truth and nothing but the truth; that personal integrity, impartiality, and objectivity are the marks of dignity and the standards of ethics in any intellectual discipline; that bias, prejudice, conformism, and subservience to the ideology of the powers that be are incompatible with the high office of the historian as the guardian of the past. The other horn of the dilemma reminded the historian of what he would rather forget: namely, that this ideal may be unobtainable; that there are barriers, insuperable barriers, which separate him from his co-workers in other scientific disciplines; that, upon closer inspection, history sets definite limits to any claims of truth and objectivity; that it is affected by subjective, emotional, or irrational factors in its subject matter and in the mind of the historian himself; and that a historical work seems to be constructed according to a peculiar logic of its own which makes it difficult to say whether it is a work of science or art, both or neither.

This disturbing situation set the stage for the historicism

[14] Cf. Wilhelm Dilthey, "The Dream," p. 37 ff. below.

of Wilhelm Dilthey and his successors. Dilthey was not, as Ortega y Gasset believed, "the greatest thinker of the second half of the nineteenth century"; but he has been an extremely influential thinker because he set out to save the heritage of historicism; or more precisely, to reformulate and reconstruct its theoretical foundations in the light of the serious difficulties at the turn of the century. He did not complete the "Critique of Historical Reason" on which he worked throughout his life; but what he envisaged was a "Critique" in Kant's sense: i.e., an epistemology of history which would be a refutation of both speculative philosophy and scientific empiricism.

The result was an elaborate inquiry into the methodological problems of a modern historicism, which greatly expanded and transformed the relatively simple heritage of the eighteenth century. It was no longer merely a question of vindicating the autonomy of history; it was the much more difficult task of disentangling, from the bewildering crosscurrents of thought in the nineteenth century, the specific logical problems that distinguished history from other sciences and of justifying, so far as possible, the distinct features of historical knowledge in its own context. In other words, it was a matter of discovering a "logic" of history which would be neither philosophical nor scientific in the traditional sense, yet would promise to save the "appearance" of history as an empirical, objective discipline.

Dilthey pursued his inquiries in two directions: First, he proposed that a new kind of psychology was needed for history. He criticized "scientific" psychology, by which he meant an associationist and sensationalist analysis in the tradition of Mill, Spencer, Taine, and Herbart. In its place, he tried to develop a "descriptive and analytic psychology." This meant, in brief, that Dilthey originated what we now call a phenomenological approach, with special emphasis upon the dynamic interconnections of psychological processes, upon meaningful patterns in perception, thought, and behavior, and upon structural units and types as the characteristic modes of the mind. These aspects, not abstract sense data, he believed, were the "realities" of the psychic life. And this work has greatly influenced, not only subsequent developments in *Gestalt* and typological psychology, but also studies in many other areas; e.g., phenomenology, existentialism, aesthetics, the history of ideas, and even sociology. Secondly, Dilthey tried to formulate a set of concepts and categories which, he believed, distinguished a logic of the cultural sciences (*Geisteswissenschaften*) from a logic of the natural sciences (*Naturwissenschaften*). And this distinction has become an integral part of modern historicism in the works of Rickert, Croce, Collingwood, Troeltsch, Weber, Beard, Becker, Mannheim, Huizinga, and other writers.[15]

### III

Whether this work was fruitful or useless is a question that exceeds the scope of these introductory remarks. It is enough to note that the problems and difficulties which Dilthey tried to solve in a "Critique of Historical Reason" still haunt the modern historical consciousness. Since they go to the heart of the contemporary debate between historians and philosophers, as we shall encounter it in the selections of this volume, I shall indicate briefly—in the form of questions, not answers—some of the significant areas in which history reveals disturbing and difficult features.

1. The *subject matter* of history presents a problem. It is so vast and complex that it can hardly be subsumed under a single concept. What, then, is history? Chronicles or interpretative narratives? The history of diplomacy or the history of place names in Great Britain? The monograph written for the Ph.D. or a study of universal history like Toynbee's? The biography of Washington, the day Lincoln was shot, the drama of Virginia City—or deep-level analyses

---

[15] For the best brief presentation of Dilthey in English see Hajo Holborn, "Wilhelm Dilthey and the Critique of Historical Reason," *Journal of the History of Ideas*, Vol. XI, no. 1 (pp. 93–118). *Consciousness and Society* by H. Stuart Hughes (New York: Knopf, 1958) includes a detailed and thoughtful analysis of Dilthey, Croce, Meinecke, and the problems of contemporary historicism.

of economic trends, cultural patterns, conflicting ideologies, and institutional changes?

2. The *facts* of history are peculiar, as historicism has insisted all along. They are individual, concrete, unrepeatable events and entities: persons, killings, invasions, land reforms, revolutions, settlements, sales, barters and marriages, edicts, decrees, customs, manners, industrial techniques, popular novels, the *Zeitgeist*, classes, religious practices, and the doctrines of the *philosophes*. All these and the inexhaustible multitude of other historical facts are unique events of the past that are accessible to us, not through direct experience or experimental repetition (as the facts in the sciences), but only through memory or through the indirect evidence of physical remains, verbal reports, and written documents.

3. The *primary aim* of a historical narrative is to reconstruct these events in their unique individuality, not to formulate general laws, to bring out the particular differences rather than the common properties of the events included in the historical portrait. In this respect, a historical work seems to resemble a literary work much more than a scientific treatise.

4. The *language* of history is different. Again, a historical narrative reads much more like a novel than a scientific text—unless it be a dull history which reads like a tract in sociology. By what "logic," then, is this narrative put together? What rational factors determine "the judicious selection, rejection, and arrangement" by which, as Macaulay said, the historian "gives to truth those attractions which have been usurped by fiction"? What makes him choose between those facts that are "relevant" and those that are not? What enables him to say that *his* judicious selection and arrangement "truly" represents what "really" happened?

5. *Fact, theory, and interpretation* form a closely knit complex in a historical narrative. The simple facts of history are not simple at all; or insofar as they are simple and elicit universal agreement among historians—dates, names, places, and the innumerable pieces of factual knowledge we learn in school—they seem to be trivial and only rein-

force the demand for an interpretation. The strict presentation of the facts may be the supreme law of historiography, as Ranke said; and a historian violates his professional code when he makes a factual error or tells an actual falsehood; but what difference does the "presentation" make to the facts that are simon-pure and simple? The facts of history invariably appear in a context of interpretation. There is no narration without interpretation; and there is no interpretation without theory. How, then, do we disentangle this complex web of facts and theory, narration, and interpretation?

6. The *methods* of history are often dubious and suspect. Some, to be sure, follow ordinary scientific procedures of evidence and inference; others, however, are quite extraordinary—whether they be called insight, introspection, empathy, imagination, or "understanding" in Dilthey's sense. Yet these unorthodox methods seem to be quite indispensable; for how else can we even begin to get close to the character of a person, the motives for an action, the climate of an opinion, the overt behavior of which we can no longer observe?

7. *Explanations* in history raise extremely puzzling questions. The historian shares the ordinary belief that to know means to know the causes of things. But what are causes in history? How do they "determine" the course of events? How many causes do we need for a historical explanation? How do we distinguish between secondary and primary, proximate and ultimate causes? What determines the order and hierarchy of causes in terms of which a historian constructs his narrative? How far does this order correspond to objective causal relations; how far does it reflect a subjective point of view? All these questions are very difficult, and are not solved by disposing of the historical determinism of Marx and Comte, or by stretching historical laws and explanations over the same lathe as scientific laws and explanations. Moreover, the historian employs the concept of causality not only in the ordinary sense in which we say that Thomas More died because he was decapitated; he must also deal with the motives and purposes behind these actions; and he ascribes motives and goals not only to in-

dividuals but to whole groups, or even nations (i.e., strange collective entities). Thus, in addition to explanations in ordinary causal terms, a historical narrative cannot dispense with teleological explanations.

8. *Freedom* is a special problem for history. There may not be any historical necessity; but, no doubt, there is a necessity of nature, environment, heredity, conditioned reflex, social pressure, legal restrictions, and perhaps even unconscious motivations. Yet there must also be a sense of freedom; otherwise the behavior of human beings transcending these objective limits does not make any sense. What, then, are the lines that separate freedom from necessity? And who would dare draw them and claim objective validity for his personal decision?

9. *Values*, emotive meanings, and ideological concepts invariably enter into the study of history. They are, in turn, as historicism has shown, subject to change and social climate. Relativism and the sociology of knowledge are common to all the antirationalistic modes of thought which we have inherited from the nineteenth century. Historical interpretations differ even when the experts agree on the facts. The only safe generalization about history is still that it is being, and always will be, rewritten, not only because new facts come to light, but because every age, and every historian, looks upon the past from a different perspective. The question arises whether a historian can—or should—ever divest himself completely from the preconceptions of his age, class, or personal *Weltanschauung*. Moreover, this relativistic trend has challenged not only the status of absolute truths, but that of moral absolutes as well. How, then, do we dare judge history from a moral point of view and claim that our moral judgments are legitimate and objective, that they express more than social convention or the exercise of a private privilege?

10. *Meaning* has receded, or vanished, from history in the sense of the philosophical theories discussed above. Instead of a single theoretical law or a universal rational principle, the modern historian operates with a plurality of laws and principles, the logical status of which is often very obscure. Instead of a coherent, unified pattern of world his-

tory, he discloses a great variety of different historical forms
and patterns of culture. Instead of a single linear direction,
he discovers multiple and incompatible directions in history
—or no direction at all.

Sometimes, these dramatic consequences of historicism
—the twilight of all absolutes and the vanishing horizons of
meaning—are singled out as its most characteristic features;
but they are only parts of a much larger whole. In fact,
a complete statement of a modern historicism would be a
"Critique of Historical Reason" in Dilthey's sense, or an inquiry into the philosophy of history which would move beyond two traditional assumptions: (1) that history must
find a haven either in theology or in metaphysics; (2) that
history must either conform to the logic of the general
sciences or suffer banishment into the realms of art and entertainment. Such an inquiry still remains to be written.

Our age has witnessed the climax of the difficulties that
took shape in the nineteenth century; and a modern historicism must find its way out of a distressing and quixotic
situation. There are still those who "see in history the most
exhilarating testimony to the creative vigour, the splendid
variety, of the human spirit";[16] but it is doubtful whether
many people subscribe to this vigorous reaffirmation of
historicism. For most people the contemporary situation
seems to be much more depressing. "History," as Stephen
Dedalus says, "is a nightmare from which I am trying to
awaken." It seems to present a gigantic jigsaw puzzle for
which there is no solution, or resemble a powerhouse in
which "the past is being ground to pieces and senselessly
used up as so much raw material in the fabrication of an
unthinkable future."[17] Thus the brilliant conquest of the
most distant frontiers of historical knowledge also coincides
with an increasing awareness of the meaninglessness of history. This awakening, in turn, has produced a strange loss
of historical appetite. There is a deep craving for an escape
from the nightmare of history into a mode of existence beyond history: art, mythology, religion, or apathy. "Man
lives in world history but history is such that man prevails

[16] Cf. p. 30 below.
[17] Philip Rahv in *Partisan Review* (Nov.–Dec. 1953) p. 642.

only if he does not know anything about it nor about his place in it."[18] Or, as Auden said; "Leave history to itself."

This is a far cry from Dilthey's rejoicing at the final liberation of man from "philosophy and natural science" through history. This freedom, as we now know, is a dubious blessing. It is gained at the price of losing any universal conceptual system which would render history as a whole either theoretically intelligible or morally reassuring. This situation may be a comfort to positivistic and existentialistic minds. Both have announced that history has no meaning; and both rejoice at these glad tidings; for now the "meaning" of history depends entirely upon the meaning we give it. But whose meaning? Or, who can still make sense out of history either as a theoretical system or in its impact upon the life of the individual. For most people the succession of events in history is so rapid, paradoxical, and unintelligible, the powers that guide them so obscure, irrational, and uncontrollable that they feel lost in this world of history which they did not make. The only alternatives they seem to face are either to abdicate and leave history to the historians or to escape, as many historians choose to do, from the burdens of history into a faith beyond history.

Christian interpretations of history, in the Augustinian tradition, have reasserted themselves strongly after a lapse of a few hundred years. The names of contemporary religious thinkers—like Berdyaev, Barth, Niebuhr, Tillich, Butterfield, Löwith, Pieper, Dawson, and Toynbee—form a long and impressive list. Their impact indicates that a Christian solution of the problem of history again finds a remarkable response, not only among specialists, but also among the public at large. This, of course, is in keeping with the revival of antirational modes of thought in general; but it also suggests, I think, that these writers still seem to satisfy the demand for a "meaning" of history in the traditional sense that has otherwise been lost.

Yet, ultimately, their solution expresses the same mood of defeat and despair before the reality of history; for, in

[18] Cited by Theodor Litt, *Die Wiedererweckung des geschichtlichen Bewusstseins* (Heidelberg 1956).

the words of one religious spokesman, "the problem of history is unanswerable within its own perspective. Historical processes as such do not bear the least evidence of a comprehensive and ultimate meaning. History as such has no outcome. There never has been and never will be an immanent solution to the problem of history, for man's historical experience is one of steady failure. Christianity, too, as a historical *world* religion, is a complete failure."[19] In a strange alliance, logical positivism, atheistic existentialism and dialectical theology join forces in reviving and supporting antihistorical tendencies in the modern world. In fact, both positivism and existentialism unwittingly help the religious cause; for if philosophy forsakes the search for a conceptual structure that might render the totality of history intelligible, both for theoretical and for practical mastery by man, then, indeed, there is no immanent solution to the problem of history. And if "history proves to be impenetrable"[20] to rational comprehension and reconstruction, the natural way out of such an impasse has always been an escape into the irrational paradoxes of faith.

Thus these introductory comments cannot but conclude on an open question. The theoretical situation confronting modern historicism is as critical as it is unresolved.

1. The Hegelian tradition of a philosophical theory that set out to discover a meaning *in* history, rational as well as teleological, has suffered a virtual eclipse.

2. The Augustinian tradition of a religious theory that discovered a meaning in history only through a faith beyond history again finds considerable support in our times as an antidote against the general despair at the limits and failures of human reason. Yet this solution is incompatible with historicism because it is essentially antihistorical, a reversal of the emancipation of history from theology.

3. The question whether history is a science is still being

---

[19] Karl Löwith, op. cit., p. 191.
[20] Gerhart Krueger, "Die Geschichte im Denken der Gegenwart," in *Grosse Geschichtsdenker*, ed. by R. Stadelmann (Tübingen und Stuttgart 1949). Krueger's essay is a thoughtful analysis and critique of the contemporary situation. He, too, ends up with a leap into faith.

debated actively, as we shall see in Part II below. It is difficult to defend the simple thesis that history is a science, no more and no less, in the light of the multiple criticisms leveled against this conception during the last century; and without prejudging the issue I think it is fair to say that the actual application of scientific techniques to history has met great obstacles and limitations.

4. Thus there remains the open question: in what sense is history a legitimate intellectual discipline—though different from, and independent of, theology, philosophy, and science? And there remain a score of unsolved problems, of which I have tried to give a brief sketch, which modern historicism has inherited from its own methodological awakening in the nineteenth century.

The theory of history, as Morris R. Cohen said, is "the most neglected province of philosophy." Fortunately, the inconclusive, unsatisfactory state of the theoretical foundations of history does not impede the writing and study of history. The historiography of our times descends from an ancient and honorable lineage. It has achieved great triumphs and a high degree of maturity. It is only the philosophy of history that is again in its infancy.

# PART I

# The Heritage of Historicism

**1.**

*The brief, introductory selection is in the nature of a prelude. It is important for what follows because it is a reminder of some of the general features of historicism such as: (1) the denial of a "systematic" approach to history; (2) the repudiation of any single, unified interpretation of history; and (3) the positive assertions (a) that the basic concepts of history are change and particularity, (b) that the historian has a special way of explaining things by telling a story, and (c) that history is all-pervasive, that historical categories permeate all aspects of human life, including morality and philosophy.*

*Mr. Barraclough, who is Professor of Modern History in the University of Liverpool, takes an ambivalent attitude toward historicism. On the one hand, he endorses the thesis that history is "the most exhilarating testimony to the creative vigour, the splendid variety, of the human spirit." On the other hand, he deplores the relativistic consequences of historicism for knowledge and moral judgments—two crucial issues which are discussed in Parts II and III.*

## GEOFFREY BARRACLOUGH

## THE HISTORIAN IN A CHANGING WORLD[*]

One of the pressing needs of to-day is a new vision of the course of modern history. Ever since the end of the war we have laboured under a sense of the inadequacy of our inherited view of the past. As Alfred Weber wrote in 1946,[1] we feel that we stand at the end and outside of the traditional history of the schools and universities, the history which has western Europe at its centre; and it is obvious to us, in the new constellation of world-affairs, that an interpretation which surveys the background to the present almost exclusively from the point of view of western Europe has little relevance to our current problems. It is not here, in the painstaking examination of the diplomacy of Bismarck or of the origins of the First World War, or even in the history of international relations in the inter-war years, that we can hope to find the essential clues to the dilemmas of the present; and we are beset by a sense of uncertainty because we feel ourselves on the threshold of a new age, to which previous experience offers no sure guide.

One result of this new situation is that history itself is losing, if it has not already lost, the hold it once exercised over the best minds as a key to present living. For a century and a half, from the time of the French Revolution, historical principles and historical conceptions dominated, shaped and determined the character of European thought. It was during this period that the underlying assumption took hold 'that the nature of anything is entirely comprehended in its development', and that most of the spheres

[*] In *History in a Changing World* (Norman, Oklahoma: University of Oklahoma Press, 1956), pp. 1–7; reprinted by permission of the University of Oklahoma Press. The excerpt represents only the first section of Professor Barraclough's essay; and I have deleted a few footnotes referring to later essays. H.M.

[1] *Abschied von der bisherigen Geschichte* (1946), 10. (An English translation of this work, under the title: *Farewell to European History*, appeared in 1947.)

of intellectual, and often also of active life, are permeated by history.[2] The result was that history was raised up to a perilous eminence as the ultimate *magistra vitae*, and an imperious, self-confident Clio displaced religion and philosophy as the deity before which we bowed.

The cult of historicism which was thus established, meant, in the words of Guido de Ruggiero, 'the evaluation of reality as a historical process of spiritual formation'.[3] It implied the rejection of the rationalism of the eighteenth-century Enlightenment, a total break with the outlook of Voltaire and Turgot and Condorcet.[4] It substituted the concepts of development and individuality for belief in the stability of human nature and in reason; and this revaluation constituted, in the judgement of Friedrich Meinecke, 'the greatest spiritual revolution which western thought has undergone'.[5] To-day none of us, no matter where our particular interests may lie, can escape its all-pervasive influence. The reason is not merely that, before the end of the nineteenth century, history had become a principal branch of study; far more important is the fact that 'human thought in every field seemed to run to history', and that 'it affected all other departments of mental activity'.[6] We think of ourselves as living in a scientific age; but in a profounder sense, we live—all of us, including, from Darwin's time, the natural scientists—in an historical age, or an age of historicism; and this is perhaps the ultimate reason and justification for concerning ourselves with history: it has be-

[2] Cf. D. E. Lee and R. N. Beck, 'The Meaning of "Historicism",' *American Historical Review* LIX (1954), 568–69.

[3] *Encyclopedia of the Social Sciences* VII (1932), 569. Addressing the Tenth International Congress of the Historical Sciences on 7 September, 1955, His Holiness Pope Pius XII described it as 'un système philosophique, celui qui n'aperçoit dans toute réalité spirituelle, dans le connaissance du vrai, dans la religion, la moralité et le droit, que changement et évolution, et rejette par conséquent tout ce qui est permanent, éternellement valable et absolu'.

[4] Cf. M. J. A. N. C. de Condorcet, *Sketch for a Historical Picture of the Progress of the Human Mind* (tr. J. M. Barraclough, 1955).

[5] F. Meinecke, *Die Entstehung des Historismus* I (1936), 1.

[6] H. Butterfield, *History and Human Relations* (1951), 159.

come, whether we like it or not, an inseparable part of our mental processes and of our being.

Who would deny that the result has been to enrich our experience, to increase beyond measure our perceptions of reality, if not, indeed, our very capacity for perception? Instead of trying to constrain reality within a system, we have dismissed the 'empty figment of one linear history' and learnt appreciation of the subtle shades of individuality, respect for irreducible particularity, acceptance of the untold 'multitude of facts', and awareness of 'endless formation and transformation', of 'achievement without end'; we see in history 'the most exhilarating testimony to the creative vigour, the splendid variety, of the human spirit'.

And yet who, to-day, would dare to claim that historicism provides an ultimate view of reality, an adequate philosophy either for thinking or for living? 'The more we try to sound the inexhaustible meaning of the particular', it has been well said,[7] 'the more devoid everything seems to be of any meaning in particular'. That historicism is the progenitor of relativism, is too obvious a fact to require demonstration. Everything is related, judged and evaluated in relation—and far too often solely in relation—to time, place, context and environment; there are no absolutes; there is no transcendent sanction for man's action; morality itself is atomized, particularized, pulverized, until in the end it is held to be 'impossible to think one man essentially more wicked than another'.[8] The historian is taught to discover, not whether Charles I—or Hitler—was right or wrong, but 'how his action was historically conditioned', to disengage 'the structural features of a conflict which was inherent in the dialectic of events'.[9] If this is truly his function, the only function which the material to his hands permits him to undertake, then we can only conclude that his view of reality is so limited and circumscribed that it sidetracks the very problems which touch us, as individuals, most nearly. It does not abolish the moral issue; for, assuming

[7] Cf. P. Leon, 'The Terror of History,' The Listener LIV (1955), 16.
[8] Butterfield, op. cit., 108.
[9] Ibid., 14, 70.

that our knowledge is insufficient for condemnation, it is evidently by the same token insufficient for exoneration. In fact, the only conclusion we can reasonably draw is that historicism, as a key to present living, is inadequate; but who can blame the ordinary man, his modes of thought permeated through and through by unquestioned assumptions springing from historicist premisses, if he acts and thinks as though historical judgements are final and sufficient in themselves, and that the criteria upon which historical judgements are based are applicable to all human problems? And who has the right to blame him if, finding as a result of an overdose of history that he has no standards left, except to judge everything in the light of circumstances, he either uses history as a comfortable pretext for cynicism, or (more likely) rejects it in disgust?

What I have tried in these few words to sketch, is, I imagine, the fundamental deficiency of the historicist myth, the direction in which—precisely because it was the dominant mode of thought of more than one generation—its effects, as they passed into wider currency under the coarsening impact of popularization, were most nefarious. But it is becoming apparent, also, that as an explanation of historical change and of historical processes the doctrine of historicism has done almost as much to obscure and bewilder as it has to enrich and enlighten our perceptions; or at least it is clear—in terms of its own relativism—that as a theory it was *zeitgebunden*, in the sense that it expressed the appropriate outlook of one particular period, and of that period alone, and is no longer appropriate to a changing world in which conditions are radically different. It may be that Friedrich Meinecke, the leading exponent of historicism, recognized this fact when, at the end of his life, he transferred his allegiance from Ranke to Burckhardt, thereby turning away from the tradition in which he had been bred and to which he, more than any other, had given conscious shape and expression.[10] Periods of ad-

[10] F. Meinecke, *Burckhardt und Ranke* (Deutsche Akademie, Vorträge u. Schriften, no. 27, 1948); I cite the English translation in *German History. Some New German Views* (ed. H. Kohn, 1954), 141–56.

vance, security, quiet enjoyment—such as was, all in all, the
nineteenth century for the professional writer of history—
produce one attitude to the past; times of defeat and col-
lapse, as Meinecke observed, produce another, and involve
the necessity of searching out new paths.[11]

In the first place, the very concentration on development
and continuity, which is fundamental to historicism, may
well have been natural, and seemed well founded, a century ago; but to-day we are in a position to realize more
clearly that such assumptions are at best partial views, and
probably (more bluntly) deceptive half-truths. The historian who observed, over thirty years ago, that 'continuity
is by no means the most conspicuous feature of history',[12]
put his finger unerringly on one central fallacy of historicism; and since that time we ourselves have experienced
enough of discontinuity to feel renewed sympathy with all
those historians who, from the time of Augustine and
Orosius, have been more impressed by the cataclysmic than
by the continuous in human affairs. Nor is it easy, any
longer, to believe that 'the nature of anything is entirely
comprehended in its development'. This plausible view
leaves too little room for the impact of the fortuitous and
the unforeseen, for the new, the dynamic and the revolutionary, which breaks through untrammelled by the past,
at every great turning-point in human history. The influences and ingredients of a given age and environment—
which, in earlier historical thought, were considered, too
often, as an adequate explanation of the course of events
—are, in fact, 'by no means sufficient in themselves to explain the next stage of the story';[13] for no present-day issue
is, or ever was, intelligible in terms of its history. In the
end the historian's search for causes and origins only brings
us up against the ultimate mysteries. Who would suppose,
for example, after all that has been written on the 'causes'
of the French Revolution, or on the 'causes' of the Reformation, that we are as a result really much nearer to an

[11] Ibid., 155–56.
[12] F. J. C. Hearnshaw, *Mediaeval Contributions to Modern
Civilisation* (1921), 18.
[13] Butterfield, op. cit., 94.

explanation of these two great upheavals? The doctrine of continuity is serviceable, provided that it is not pressed too far; but development and continuity are not a total explanation of the historical process.

Furthermore they may, unduly emphasized, be misleading and dangerous because they produce in the treatment of history an evenness, an illusion of steady flow, which is both at variance with experience and detrimental to all perspective. We all, in our own lives, recognize turning-points, moments of crisis, decisions which in some sense have been determinative of our future actions. For the historian, on the contrary, it is one of the cherished platitudes of historical thinking that the garment of Clio is a seamless web, that every age is an age of change, and that the world which comes within the historian's vision is in a permanent state of flux. When, long ago, the great German historian, Ranke, proclaimed that all ages are 'immediate to God',[14] the implication was that all possess equal significance in the perspective of eternity, and that all are worthy of, and will repay, equal treatment at the hands of the historian.[15] No one will deny the element of truth in this view. We realize to-day, for example, that the seventh century or the ninth century has as much to tell us, and as much ultimate importance in the human story—as well as equal intrinsic interest—as the more spectacular Carolingian era which separates them. To pick out 'important' or 'decisive' phases or periods—'creative centuries', they have been called,[16] as though all centuries are not creative—does not merely create the danger of false emphasis; it also means that we shall miss the peculiar contribution which each generation makes

[14] In his famous lectures 'On the Epochs of Modern History', delivered before king Maximilian of Bavaria in 1854, and printed in vol. IX of Ranke's *Weltgeschichte* (1888).

[15] Therefore, after the famous statement: 'I maintain that every epoch is immediate to God and that its value rests in no way upon what it produces, but upon the very fact of its existence' (ibid., 5), Ranke specifically continues: 'before God all generations of humanity appear as having equal right, and this is the way in which the historian also must look at the matter' (p. 6).

[16] H. J. Randall, *The Creative Centuries* (1944).

to the problem of living, its answers to questions which are
eternal. As that fine historian, A. G. Little, once observed,[17]
'the most valuable function of the historian' is not

> to trace back the institutions and ways of thought which
> have survived, as though we were at the end and climax
> of history. It is at least as important to retrieve the treas-
> ures that have been dropped on the way and lost, which,
> if restored, would enrich our civilisation.

No one, to-day, would maintain that any age of the past
was unproductive, a mere halting-place in time, or that at
any period of the past new impulses were not stirring under
the surface. We are aware, for example, that the apparent
tranquillity of the years after 1815, the 'Indian summer'
following the French Revolution and the Napoleonic Wars,
was illusory, and that the words 'conservatism' or 'reaction'
only typify the most superficial aspects of the age of Met-
ternich. Similarly the old view that Germany fell back, exhausted, into stagnation after the Thirty Years' War, until
Frederick the Great of Prussia awakened it from its leth-
argy, has been dispelled by closer observation of the German scene after 1648. And yet who, granted all this, would
deny that, at certain times, the impetus of change gathered
pace, the tempo was suddenly accelerated? Troeltsch once
observed that an original system of thought, a revolution
in the modes of thinking, is only possible every couple of
hundred years, after the preliminary stages have been thoroughly worked over.[18] The implication is that some ages
are periods of preparation, others periods of fulfilment. It
is not necessary (nor is it logically possible) to argue that
the one is more 'important' than the other; it is enough to
see that they are different, both in their implications and
in their effects, and in their relation to us. For this reason
it is, I think, legitimate to describe certain periods as
turning-points, when European society swung upwards, out
of its existing course, on to a new plane. All ages, it is true,
are ages of change, all periods are transitional periods; but

[17] The passage is cited by F. M. Powicke, *Modern Historians
and the Study of History* (1955), 95.
[18] E. Troeltsch, *Gesammelte Schriften* III (1922), 110.

we are not suffering from an illusion or hallucination when we feel, and say, that we to-day live in an age of change so great that the older preoccupations—of historians, but not of historians alone—no longer correspond to living needs, their inherited assumptions no longer fit the reality we have experienced.

An age which has undergone great upheavals—which has seen, for example, tens and hundreds of thousands of men, women and children uprooted, first by one side and then by the other, and thrust from their homes in a vast new *Völkerwanderung*—will not be impressed when it is told that history is a story of continuity, governed by a law not of revolution but of evolution. An age which has seen morality pitchforked out of politics, and has experienced the results of that experiment, will not be satisfied when it is given an historical explanation of what has taken place, and why. It is easy, at a distance of one and a half centuries, to adopt towards Napoleon I an attitude of detached relativism—and every schoolboy to-day (it would seem) has learnt to speak and write of Napoleon or Frederick the Great without falling into the vulgar error of moral approbation or disapprobation—but how many of us would adopt the same attitude towards Hitler or Mussolini? We may perhaps say—as I have ventured to say elsewhere—that how a thing was accomplished, and at what cost, 'does not concern us here and now', provided that we put due emphasis on the words 'here and now'. But 'when we are told that it is foolish to judge Charlemagne, or Napoleon, or Genghis Khan, or Hitler, or Stalin, for their massacres', or that such judgements are beside the point, we can only answer that 'to accept this doctrine is to do violence to the basic notions of our morality, to misrepresent our sense of the past, and to ignore the most general concepts of normal thought'.[19] A doctrine which leads, as historicism does, in this direction, is unacceptable: it is time for reconsideration of the foundations, and of the fundamental postulates, of historical thought.

[19] Cf. I. Berlin, *Historical Inevitability* (1954), 76–77. See below pp. 249–69.

## 2.

*The selections that follow are a cross section of recent European historicism. Wilhelm Dilthey (1833–1911) has been identified before. Benedetto Croce (1866–1952) was the most influential Italian philosopher and man of letters of his age; he was also a practicing historian and an active political figure. José Ortega y Gasset (1883–1956) enjoyed as great a reputation and influence in Spain and the Spanish-speaking world as Croce did in Italy. R. G. Collingwood (1889–1943) did not occupy as eminent a place in his country as these men did in theirs, but he was the most original and stimulating historical mind in recent English philosophy.*

*All these men, despite individual differences, subscribed to some form of historicism; all of them also tended to combine historicism with some kind of idealism in the tradition of Kant and Hegel. History was a "spiritual" realm, by which they meant that the ultimate constituents of the historical world were human thoughts, purposes, motives, and actions, not natural, social, or institutional factors, and that the aim of a genuine historical work was to reconstruct these "spiritual" facts in their original meaning.*

*"It is time," Mr. Barraclough concluded, "for a reconsideration of the foundations of historical thought." It was Dilthey's ambition, as I have said, to reconsider these foundations. "The Dream"—a lecture delivered at the occasion of his seventieth birthday—does not, of course, give an idea of his work along these lines or of the profound influence Dilthey has had on modern thought. Unfortunately, no major work of his is available in English. Yet brief and "poetic" as the dream is, it repays a close reading. It is a mild intellectual nightmare, "a philosophically engendered anxiety." And it conveys two significant strands of Dilthey's mind: (1) Historicism as the key to the final liberation of man from theology, philosophy, and natural science; and (2) the failure to work out a universal conceptual system for history or philosophy.*

*Philosophy is split into three major factions represented by the three groupings appearing in the dream: (1) materialism or positivism, (2) the idealism of freedom, and (3) classical or objective idealism. (In the arts, this division would roughly correspond to the three types of naturalism or realism, romanticism, and classicism.) Nothing can heal this split. "We see the pure light of truth only in various broken rays." What remains is to see the "truth" in different perspectives, to work out a typology of the human mind in history, or to achieve a semblance of synthesis by viewing the three major types in different historical contexts. "To contemplate all the aspects in their totality is denied to us."*

*The dream also reveals the transitional place which Dilthey occupies in recent intellectual history: his link with the Hegelian tradition of "surrendering to the great objective forces" in history and his break-through to the existentialist thesis that "what man is, only his history tells."*

## WILHELM DILTHEY

## THE DREAM*

I have endeavored to present methods of research to my students and have attempted to develop in them the ability to analyze reality. This power of analysis is the key to all philosophizing and historical thinking. I have no solution for the enigma of life; what I would like to transmit to my students is the temper of life which has developed in me as a result of my reflecting on the meaning of historical consciousness. This tone or temper of life I would like to express again today. But every expression is either too difficult or too cold. My friend Wildenbruch, however, has shown me a way. How deeply honored a man feels when praised by a poet! The poet Wildenbruch has called forth the poet in me and therefore he is responsible, if the ashheap begins

* In William Kluback, *Wilhelm Dilthey's Philosophy of History* (New York: Columbia University Press, 1956) pp. 103–9; reprinted by permission of the Columbia University Press.

to glow again and I attempt to express my consciousness
of life which has evolved out of many years of philosophical
concern. I shall not express my thoughts in verse; nevertheless, allow me some poetic license.

This happened more than a decade ago. One clear summer evening I arrived at my friend's castle, Klein-Oels. As
usual our philosophical conversation lasted deep into the
night, and still resounded in my mind when I undressed in
the old familiar bedroom. I faced Volpato's fine etching of
the School of Athens which hung over the bed. It was grati-
fying to visualize how the harmonious spirit of the divine
Raphael blended the life and death struggle of hostile philosophical systems into a peaceful discourse. About these
gentle, related figures there hovered an atmosphere of
peace which, for the first time at the dawn of ancient culture, strove to harmonize powerfully conflicting thoughts.
In the noblest intellects of the Renaissance the same atmosphere was present.

Tired, I fell asleep. Instantly an alert dream life possessed
me. I dreamed of Raphael's picture and of our conversation. In my dream, the figures of the philosophers came to
life; in the distance, I saw on the left a long line of men,
in varied garments of succeeding centuries, approach the
temple of the philosophers. Whenever a philosopher
passed and turned his face toward me, I tried to recognize
him. There was Bruno, Descartes, Leibniz, and so many
others just as I had imagined them in the light of their
portraits. They ascended the steps and, as they did so, the
barriers of the Temple collapsed. The newcomers mixed
with the Greek philosophers. Then something happened
which I did not expect even in a dream. As if driven by
an inner necessity, they hastened toward each other to assemble themselves in groups. At first the movement pressed
to the right where the mathematician, Archimedes, drew
his circles and where the astronomer, Ptolemy, was recog-
nizable by the globe he wore. Then there gathered all those
thinkers, who based their explanation of the world upon
the material solidity of the universal physical nature. Pro-
ceeding from the lower to the higher, they tried to find a

single causality in the universe which could be derived from the dependent laws of nature; they subordinated the spirit to matter. They have limited our knowledge to what is known only through the methods of the natural sciences. In this group of materialists and positivists I also recognized d'Alembert with his fine features and ironic smile which seemed to mock the dreams of the metaphysicians. I also saw Comte, the systematizer of positivism, to whom a group of thinkers from all nations listened devotedly.

Another group pressed toward the center where Socrates and the noble figure of the old and god-like Plato were distinguishable. Socrates and Plato have tried to establish the knowledge of a supersensual world order based on the consciousness of the divine in the human. I also saw St. Augustine, whose heart was so passionately seeking God; around him clustered many philosophizing theologians. I listened to their conversation seeking to reconcile the idealism of personality, which is the essence of Christianity, with the teachings of the two venerable Greeks. Then Descartes separated himself from the mathematical naturalists—Descartes, whose delicate figure worn out by the power of thought was drawn as if by an inner force toward the idealists of freedom and personality. The whole circle opened as soon as the slightly stooped, slightly built Kant, his features hardened by the strain of thought, approached with his three-cornered hat and cane. This was the great Kant who elevated the idealism of freedom to the level of critical consciousness, thus reconciling it with empirical knowledge. Walking energetically toward Kant came Schiller, the poet of the idealism of freedom, whose melancholy face reflected deep thought, a poetic idealizing intuition, and the divination of his tragic fate. Fichte and Carlyle approached; Ranke, Guizot, and other great historians seemed to be listening attentively to them. A strange shudder seized me when I saw together with them a friend of my youth, Heinrich von Treitschke.

The two groups had hardly assembled when from the left converged thinkers of all nations around Pythagoras and Heraclitus, the first men to intuit the divine harmony of the universe. Giordano Bruno, Spinoza and Leibniz were also present. A wondrous spectacle, walking hand in hand as in the days of their youth, was the sight of Schelling and Hegel, our nation's greatest thinkers. All these philosophers were proclaimers of a comprehensive, spiritual divine power in the universe which lives in every object and every person, operating in them all according to the laws of nature, with the consequences that there is no transcendental order, no realm of free will. It seemed to me that all these thinkers hid poetic souls behind their furrowed faces. A commotion arose among them when, at last, with a measured step, arrived a majestic figure whose countenance was stern and composed. I was filled with reverence when I saw the large radiant eyes and the Apollonian head of Goethe. He was in the prime of life and all his creations—Faust, Wilhelm Meister, Iphigenie, and Tasso—appeared to encompass him with all his great thoughts about laws of evolution which extend from nature to the creations of man.

Amid these great men, some figures were standing, others lying down and still others restlessly moving about. These people wished to mediate: between positivism with its thorough rejection of life's enigma, and all metaphysics, but also between an all comprehensive determinism, and those who believed in the freedom of the individual. But in vain the mediators hastened to and fro among the groups. The distance between the groups increased with each moment. Now even the ground disappeared from under them and a hostile alienation enveloped them. A strange anxiety overcame me, a philosophically engendered anxiety caused by seeing philosophy divided and torn in three or even more directions. The unity of my being was torn asunder for I was deeply attracted at times to one group and at other times to the second or even to the third. I strove for the unity of thought, and in this struggle the cover of sleep became thinner and lighter, the figures of my dream faded away. And I awoke. The stars glimmered through the large windows of the room. The immeasurability and impenetrability of the universe overwhelmed me. How free I felt when I thought of the consoling ideas which I had offered to my friend in our previous evening's conversation.

This immeasurable, incomprehensible and unfathomable

universe mirrors itself palpably in founders of religion, in poets and in philosophers. These all stand under the influence of time and space. Every world-view is conditioned historically and therefore limited and relative. A frightful anarchy of thought appears. The very historical consciousness that has brought forth this absolute doubt, however, is able to set limits for it. The world views are divided by an inner law. Here my thoughts returned to the three groups of philosophers of my dream. These types of world views exist along side each other through the centuries. The liberating element here is that the world views are grounded in the nature of the universe and in the relationship between the finite perceptive mind and the universe. Thus each world-view expresses within its limitations one aspect of the universe. In this respect each is true. Each, however, is one-sided. To contemplate all the aspects in their totality is denied to us. We see the pure light of truth only in various broken rays.

Philosophy has a Janus face. The unquenchable metaphysical drive aims toward the solution of the world and the enigma of life. Up to this point the philosophers are related to the men of religion and the poets. However, the philosophers are distinguished from them by desiring to solve this life enigma by a universally valid knowledge. A solution based on this presupposition is no longer possible for us.

The highest aim of philosophy is that the objective thinking of an experimental science, which derives from appearances an order determined by laws, is raised to the consciousness of itself. There is an accessible reality given in appearances, an order according to laws. This order is truth, universally valid, although expressed in the figurative speech of our senses and our faculty of perception. This basis of our knowledge is the highest object of philosophical inquiry. Toward this end, all true philosophers have worked. Another result of philosophy is the organization of empirical sciences. A philosophical spirit is present where the basis of science is simplified or sciences are related to each other, where their relation to the idea of knowledge is established, or methods are tested according to their value for the attainment of knowledge. It seems to me, however, that the time is past when there can be an independent philosophy of art, religion, law, or of the state. The powerful cohesion which is thus constituted is the highest realization of philosophy and is destined to guide the human race. The natural sciences have transformed the outer world. In the great world epoch now evolving, the social sciences are winning an ever-increasing influence.

Beyond this universally valid knowledge lie questions which are of concern for each person so alone in life and in death. The answers to these questions are given only in the framework of the different world-views, in which our reason expresses in various forms the complexities of reality, all of which point to a single truth. This truth is hidden and each system is involved in antinomies. Historical consciousness shatters the last chains that philosophy and natural sciences could not break. Man has now achieved freedom. At the same time, however, historical consciousness saves the unity of man's soul; the glimpse into a final harmony, although otherwise incomprehensible, is revealed by the creative power of our essential being. Confidently we may recognize in each of these world views an element of truth. And if the course of our life brings us closer to a particular aspect of the incomprehensible harmony, if the truth of the world view which this particular aspect expresses fills us with creativity, then we may quietly surrender. For truth is present in them all.

These were the thoughts that arose again and again as I lay awake between dream and dream. For a long time I thought of these ideas, raising my eyes to the summer majesty of the stars. Finally a light slumber overcame me and dreams returned. The starry arches shone brighter and clearer, as the light of the morning flooded in. Light, blissful figures passed through the skies. When I awoke I strove in vain to recall the happy images of my dreams. I felt that surely these images were the expression of the bliss, of the highest freedom and of the creative activity of the soul.

This is the dream I have recorded for my friends. I hope that some of the tone and feeling of life in which my dream resounds can be transmitted to them. Stimulated more than ever, our generation seeks to read the mysterious face of life with its laughing mouth and its sad eyes. Yes, let us strive toward the light, toward freedom and beauty—but not with a new beginning, sloughing off the past. Into each new home we must take the old gods with us. In vain Nietzsche sought, in lonely self-meditation, the primordial nature and his own unhistorical existence. He peeled off one layer of skin after another, but what remained? Only an historically conditioned individual, the features of the supermen of the Renaissance. What man is, only his history tells. In vain others put the past behind them in order to begin life anew. They cannot shake off the gods of the past because they become haunting ghosts. The melody of our life is conditioned by the accompanying voices of the past. Only by surrendering to the great objective forces which history has engendered can man liberate himself from the pain of the moment and from ephemeral joy. Neither subjective caprice nor egotistic pleasure can reconcile man with life. Only surrender of his sovereign personality to the course of the world can affect this reconciliation.

3.

*Croce's essay is self-explanatory. It is the first chapter of* History: Its Theory and Practise, *the initial statement of Croce's criticism of rationalistic, scientific, or positivistic trends in modern historiography.*

*The essay makes a simple and absolutely valid point: that there is an essential difference between what happened and why it happened, between the chronicle-like records of past events and historical narrative in which these happenings are interpreted and/or explained. This distinction raises basic questions which any philosophy of history, whether speculative or analytic, must answer: What makes a historical narrative? Or, how are mere happenings transformed into history?*

*The chapter also shows Croce's idealism: history, for him, is "a spiritual act"; as for Hegel, "the spirit itself is history"; but these extreme metaphysical assertions become more empirical and reasonable when they are read in the context of Croce's ingenious reference to "the history of Hellenic painting" where we have chronicle-like reports, but no direct knowledge of the works; hence, no "history" in the ordinary sense of a history of art.*

*For the sequel, the most important passage is Croce's famous proposition that "every true history is contemporary history." It has been the most succinct and influential statement of his philosophy of history. It is the basis for a "pragmatic" interpretation of history; for it means that the past is dead except insofar as it is "unified with an interest of the present life." This sentiment—at odds with the attitude of the professional historian who is in love with the past for its own sake—recurs in numerous passages of the following selections; e.g., in Ortega y Gasset, Collingwood, Becker, Beard, and Dewey. It seems to correspond to the sentiments of the "general reader," who tends to feel that history is an archaic, dead discipline unless it has something to say to him which is pertinent to his own life and times. Nonetheless, this natural feeling gives rise to many technical problems as we shall see in the critical discussion of Part II below.*

## BENEDETTO CROCE

## HISTORY AND CHRONICLE*

### I

'Contemporary history' is wont to be called the history of a passage of time, looked upon as a most recent past, whether it be that of the last fifty years, a decade, a year, a month, a day, or indeed of the last hour or of the last

* In *History: Its Theory and Practise*, tr. by Douglas Ainslee (New York: Harcourt, Brace and Co., Inc., 1921), pp. 11–26; reprinted by permission of Harcourt, Brace and Co.

minute. But if we think and speak rigorously, the term 'contemporaneous' can be applied only to that history which comes into being immediately after the act which is being accomplished, as consciousness of that act: it is, for instance, the history that I make of myself while I am in the act of composing these pages; it is the thought of my composition, linked of necessity to the work of composition. 'Contemporary' would be well employed in this case, just because this, like every act of the spirit, is outside time (of the first and after) and is formed 'at the same time' as the act to which it is linked, and from which it is distinguished by means of a distinction not chronological but ideal. 'Non-contemporary history,' 'past history,' would, on the other hand, be that which finds itself in the presence of a history already formed, and which thus comes into being as a criticism of that history, whether it be thousands of years or hardly an hour old.

But if we look more closely, we perceive that this history already formed, which is called or which we would like to call 'non-contemporary' or 'past' history, if it really is history, that is to say, if it mean something and is not an empty echo, is also *contemporary*, and does not in any way differ from the other. As in the former case, the condition of its existence is that the deed of which the history is told must vibrate in the soul of the historian, or (to employ the expression of professed historians) that the documents are before the historian and that they are intelligible. That a narrative or a series of narratives of the fact is united and mingled with it merely means that the fact has proved more rich, not that it has lost its quality of being present: what were narratives or judgments before are now themselves facts, 'documents' to be interpreted and judged. History is never constructed from narratives, but always from documents, or from narratives that have been reduced to documents and treated as such. Thus if contemporary history springs straight from life, so too does that history which is called non-contemporary, for it is evident that only an interest in the life of the present can move one to investigate past fact. Therefore this past fact does not answer to a past interest, but to a present interest, in so far as it is unified with an interest of the present life. This has been said again and again in a hundred ways by historians in their empirical formulas, and constitutes the reason, if not the deeper content, of the success of the very trite saying that history is *magister vitæ*.

I have recalled these forms of historical technique in order to remove the aspect of paradox from the proposition that 'every true history is contemporary history.' But the justice of this proposition is easily confirmed and copiously and perspicuously exemplified in the reality of historiographical work, provided always that we do not fall into the error of taking the works of the historians all together, or certain groups of them confusedly, and of applying them to an abstract man or to ourselves considered abstractly, and of then asking what present interest leads to the writing or reading of such histories: for instance, what is the present interest of the history which recounts the Peloponnesian or the Mithradatic War, of the events connected with Mexican art, or with Arabic philosophy. For me at the present moment they are without interest, and therefore for me at this present moment those histories are not histories, but at the most simply titles of historical works. They have been or will be histories in those that have thought or will think them, and in me too when I have thought or shall think them, re-elaborating them according to my spiritual needs. If, on the other hand, we limit ourselves to real history, to the history that one really thinks in the act of thinking, it will be easily seen that this is perfectly identical with the most personal and contemporary of histories. When the development of the culture of my historical moment presents to me (it would be superfluous and perhaps also inexact to add to myself as an individual) the problem of Greek civilization or of Platonic philosophy or of a particular mode of Attic manners, that problem is related to my being in the same way as the history of a bit of business in which I am engaged, or of a love affair in which I am indulging, or of a danger that threatens me. I examine it with the same anxiety and am troubled with the same sense of unhappiness until I have succeeded in solving it. Hellenic life is on that occasion present in me; it solicits, it attracts and torments me, in the same way as the appearance of the adversary, of the loved one, or of the beloved son for whom one trembles. Thus too it happens or has happened or will happen in the case of the Mithradatic War, of Mexican art, and of all the other things that I have mentioned above by way of example.

Having laid it down that contemporaneity is not the characteristic of a class of histories (as is held with good reason in empirical classifications), but an intrinsic characteristic of every history, we must conceive the relation of history to life as that of *unity;* certainly not in the sense of abstract identity, but of synthetic unity, which implies both the distinction and the unity of the terms. Thus to talk of a history of which the documents are lacking would appear to be as extravagant as to talk of the existence of something as to which it is also affirmed that it is without one of the essential conditions of existence. A history without relation to the document would be an unverifiable history; and since the reality of history lies in this verifiability, and the narrative in which it is given concrete form is historical narrative only in so far as it is a *critical exposition* of the document (intuition and reflection, consciousness and auto-consciousness, etc.), a history of that sort, being without meaning and without truth, would be inexistent as history. How could a history of painting be composed by one who had not seen and enjoyed the works of which he proposed to describe the genesis critically? And how far could anyone understand the works in question who was without the artistic experience assumed by the narrator? How could there be a history of philosophy without the works or at least fragments of the works of the philosophers? How could there be a history of a sentiment or of a custom, for example that of Christian humility or of knightly chivalry, without the capacity for living again, or rather without an actual living again of these particular states of the individual soul?

On the other hand, once the indissoluble link between life and thought in history has been effected, the doubts that have been expressed as to the *certainty* and the *utility* of history disappear altogether in a moment. How could that which is a *present* producing of our spirit ever be *uncertain?* How could that knowledge be *useless* which solves a problem that has come forth from the bosom of *life?*

## II

But can the link between document and narrative, between life and history, ever be broken? An affirmative answer to this has been given when referring to those histories of which the documents have been lost, or, to put the case in a more general and fundamental manner, those histories whose documents are no longer alive in the human spirit. And this has also been implied when saying that we all of us in turn find ourselves thus placed with respect to this or that part of history. The history of Hellenic painting is in great part a history without documents for us, as are all histories of peoples concerning whom one does not know exactly where they lived, the thoughts and feelings that they experienced, or the individual appearance of the works that they accomplished; those literatures and philosophies, too, as to which we do not know their theses, or even when we possess these and are able to read them through, yet fail to grasp their intimate spirit, either owing to the lack of complementary knowledge or because of our obstinate temperamental reluctance, or owing to our momentary distraction.

If, in these cases, when that connexion is broken, we can no longer call what remains history (because history was nothing but that connexion), and it can henceforth only be called history in the sense that we call a man the corpse of a man, what remains is not for that reason nothing (not even the corpse is really nothing). Were it nothing, it would be the same as saying that the connexion is indissoluble, because nothingness is never effectual. And if it be not nothing, if it be something, what is narrative without the document?

A history of Hellenic painting, according to the accounts that have been handed down or have been constructed by the learned of our times, when closely inspected, resolves itself into a series of names of painters (Apollodorus, Polygnotus, Zeuxis, Apelles, etc.), surrounded with biographical anecdotes, and into a series of subjects for painting (the burning of Troy, the contest of the Amazons, the battle of Marathon, Achilles, Calumny, etc.), of which certain particulars are given in the descriptions that have reached us; or a graduated series, going from praise to blame, of these painters and their works, together with names, anecdotes, subjects, judgments, arranged more or less chronologically. But the names of painters separated from the direct knowledge of their works are empty names; the anecdotes are empty, as are the descriptions of subjects, the judgment of approval or of disapproval, and the chronological arrangement, because merely arithmetical and lacking real development; and the reason why we do not realize it in thought is that the elements which should constitute it are wanting. If those verbal forms possess any significance, we owe it to what little we know of antique paintings from fragments, from secondary works that have come down to us in copies, or in analogous works in the other arts, or in poetry. With the exception, however, of that little, the history of Hellenic art is, as such, a tissue of empty words.

We can, if we like, say that it is 'empty of determinate content,' because we do not deny that when we pronounce the name of a painter we think of some painter, and indeed of a painter who is an Athenian, and that when we utter the word 'battle,' or 'Helen,' we think of a battle, indeed of a battle of hoplites, or of a beautiful woman, similar to those familiar to us in Hellenic sculpture. But we can think indifferently of any one of the numerous facts that those names recall. For this reason their content is indeterminate, and this indetermination of content is their emptiness.

All histories separated from their living documents resemble these examples and are empty narratives, and since they are empty they are without truth. Is it true or not that there existed a painter named Polygnotus and that he painted a portrait of Miltiades in the Pœcile? We shall be told that it is true, because one person or several people, who knew him and saw the work in question, bear witness to its existence. But we must reply that it was true for this or that witness, and that for us it is neither true nor

false, or (which comes to the same thing) that it is true
only on the evidence of those witnesses—that is to say, for
an extrinsic reason, whereas truth always requires intrinsic
reasons. And since that proposition is not true (neither true
nor false), it is not useful either, because where there is
nothing the king loses his rights, and where the elements of
a problem are wanting the effective will and the effective
need to solve it are also wanting, along with the possibility
of its solution. Thus to quote those empty judgments is
quite useless for our actual lives. Life is a present, and that
history which has become an empty narration is a past:
it is an irrevocable past, if not absolutely so, καθ' αὐτό,
then certainly for the present moment.

The empty words remain, and the empty words are
sounds, or the graphic signs which represent them, and they
hold together and maintain themselves, not by an act of
thought that thinks them (in which case they would soon
be filled), but by an act of will, which thinks it useful for
certain ends of its own to preserve those words, however
empty or half empty they may be. Mere narrative, then,
is nothing but a complex of empty words or formulas asserted by an act of the will.

Now with this definition we have succeeded in giving
neither more nor less than the true distinction, hitherto
sought in vain, between *history* and *chronicle*. It has been
sought in vain, because it has generally been sought in a
difference in the *quality* of the facts which each difference
took as its object. Thus, for instance, the record of *individual* facts has been attributed to chronicle, to history that of
*general* facts; to chronicle the record of *private*, to history
that of *public* facts: as though the general were not always
individual and the individual general, and the public were
not always also private and the private public! Or else the
record of *important* facts (memorable things) has been attributed to history, to chronicle that of the *unimportant:*
as though the importance of facts were not relative to the
situation in which we find ourselves, and as though for a
man annoyed by a mosquito the evolutions of the minute
insect were not of greater importance than the expedition
of Xerxes! Certainly, we are sensible of a just sentiment in

these fallacious distinctions—namely, that of placing the difference between history and chronicle in the conception of what *interests* and of what does not *interest* (the general interests and not the particular, the great interests and not the little, etc.). A just sentiment is also to be noted in other considerations that are wont to be adduced, such as the close bond between events that there is in history and the *disconnectedness* that appears on the other hand in chronicle, the *logical* order of the first, the purely *chronological* order of the second, the penetration of the first into the *core* of events and the limitation of the second to the superficial or *external*, and the like. But the differential character is here rather metaphorized than thought, and when metaphors are not employed as simple forms expressive of thought we lose a moment after what has just been gained. The truth is that chronicle and history are not distinguishable as two forms of history, mutually complementary, or as one subordinate to the other, but as two different spiritual *attitudes*. History is living chronicle, chronicle is dead history; history is contemporary history, chronicle is past history; history is principally an act of thought, chronicle an act of will. Every history becomes chronicle when it is no longer thought, but only recorded in abstract words, which were once upon a time concrete and expressive. The history of philosophy even is chronicle, when written or read by those who do not understand philosophy: history would even be what we are now disposed to read as chronicle, as when, for instance, the monk of Monte Cassino notes: 1001. *Beatus Dominicus migravit ad Christum.* 1002. *Hoc anno venerunt Saraceni super Capuam.* 1004. *Terremotus ingens hunc montem exagitavit,* etc.; for those facts were present to him when he wept over the death of the departed Dominic, or was terrified by the natural human scourges that convulsed his native land, seeing the hand of God in that succession of events. This does not prevent that history from assuming the form of chronicle when that same monk of Monte Cassino wrote down cold formulas, without representing to himself or thinking their content, with the sole intention of not allowing those memories to be lost

and of handing them down to those who should inhabit
Monte Cassino after him.

But the discovery of the real distinction between chronicle and history, which is a formal distinction (that is to
say, a truly real distinction), not only frees us from the
sterile and fatiguing search after material distinctions (that
is to say, imaginary distinctions), but it also enables us to
reject a very common presupposition—namely, that of the
*priority* of chronicle in respect to history. *Primo annales*
[chronicles] *fuere, post historiæ factæ sunt*, the saying of
the old grammarian, Mario Vittorino, has been repeated,
generalized, and universalized. But precisely the opposite
of this is the outcome of the inquiry into the character and
therefore into the genesis of the two operations or attitudes:
*first comes history, then chronicle*. First comes the living
being, then the corpse; and to make history the child of
chronicle is the same thing as to make the living be born
from the corpse, which is the residue of life, as chronicle is
the residue of history.

## III

History, separated from the living document and turned
into chronicle, is no longer a spiritual act, but a thing, a
complex of sounds and of other signs. But the document
also, when separated from life, is nothing but a thing like
another, a complex of sounds or of other signs—for example,
the sounds and the letters in which a law was once communicated; the lines cut into a block of marble, which manifested a religious sentiment by means of the figure of a
god; a heap of bones, which were at one time the expression
of a man or of an animal.

Do such things as empty narratives and dead documents
exist? In a certain sense, no, because external things do not
exist outside the spirit; and we already know that chronicle,
as empty narrative, exists in so far as the spirit produces it
and holds it firmly with an act of will (and it may be
opportune to observe once more that such an act carries
always with it a new act of consciousness and of thought):
with an act of will, which abstracts the sound from the

thought, in which dwelt the certainty and concreteness of the sound. In the same way, these dead documents exist to the extent that they are the manifestations of a new life, as the lifeless corpse is really itself also a process of vital creation, although it appears to be one of decomposition and something dead in respect of a particular form of life. But in the same way as those empty sounds, which once contained the thought of a history, are eventually called *narratives,* in memory of the thought they contained, thus do those manifestations of a new life continue to be looked upon as remnants of the life that preceded them and is indeed extinguished.

Now observe how, by means of this string of deductions, we have put ourselves into the position of being able to account for the partition of historical *sources* into *narratives* and *documents,* as we find it among some of our modern methodologists, or, as it is also formulated, into *traditions* and *residues* or *remains (Überbleibsel, Überreste).* This partition is irrational from the empirical point of view, and may be of use as indicating the inopportunity of the introduction of a speculative thought into empiricism. It is so irrational that one immediately runs against the difficulty of not being able to distinguish what one wished to distinguish. An empty 'narrative' considered as a thing is tantamount to any other thing whatever which is called a 'document.' And, on the other hand, if we maintain the distinction we incur the further difficulty of having to base our historical construction upon two different orders of data (one foot on the bank and the other in the river)—that is to say, we shall have to recur to two parallel instances, one of which is perpetually referring us back to the other. And when we seek to determine the relation of the two kinds of sources with a view to avoiding the inconvenient parallelism, what happens is this: either the relation is stated to depend upon the superiority of the one over the other, and the distinction vanishes, because the superior form absorbs into itself and annuls the inferior form; or a third term is established, in which the two forms are supposed to become united with a distinction: but this is another way of declaring them to be inexistent in that abstractness. For this reason it does not seem to me to be without significance that the partition of accounts and documents should not have been adopted by the most empirical of the methodologists. They do not involve themselves in these subtleties, but content themselves with grouping the historical sources into those that are *written* and those that are *represented*, or in other similar ways. In Germany, however, Droysen availed himself of these distinctions between narratives and documents, traditions, etc., in his valuable *Elements of Historicism* (he had strong leanings toward philosophy), and they have been employed also by other methodologists, who are hybrid empiricists, 'systematists,' or 'pedants,' as they are looked upon in our Latin countries. This is due to the copious philosophical traditions of Germany. The pedantry certainly exists, and it is to be found just in that inopportune philosophy. But what an excellent thing is that pedantry and the contradictions which it entails, how it arouses the mind from its empirical slumbers and makes it see that in place of supposed things there are in reality spiritual acts, where the terms of an irreconcilable dualism were supposed to be in conflict, relation and unity, on the contrary, prevail! The partition of the sources into narratives and documents, and the superiority attributed to documents over narratives, and the alleged necessity of narrative as a subordinate but ineradicable element, almost form a mythology or allegory, which represents in an imaginative manner the relation between life and thought, between document and criticism in historical thought.

And document and criticism, life and thought, are the true *sources* of history—that is to say, the two elements of historical synthesis; and as such, they do not stand face to face with history, or face to face with the synthesis, in the same way as fountains are represented as being face to face with those who go to them with a pail, but they form part of history itself, they are within the synthesis, they form a constituent part of it and are constituted by it. Hence the idea of a history with its sources outside itself is another fancy to be dispelled, together with that of history being the opposite of chronicle. The two erroneous fancies converge to form one. Sources, in the extrinsic sense of the empiricists, like things, are equally with chronicle, which is a class of those things, not anterior but posterior to history. History would indeed be in a fix if it expected to be born of what comes after it, to be born of external things! Thing, not thought, is born of thing: a history derived from things would be a thing—that is to say, just the inexistent of which we were talking a moment ago.

But there must be a reason why chronicle as well as documents seems to precede history and to be its extrinsic source. The human spirit preserves the mortal remains of history, empty narratives and chronicles, and the same spirit collects the traces of past life, remains and documents, striving as far as possible to preserve them unchanged and to restore them as they deteriorate. What is the object of these acts of will which go to the preservation of what is empty and dead? Perhaps illusion or foolishness, which preserves a little while the worn-out elements of mortality on the confines of Dis by means of the erection of mausoleums and sepulchres? But sepulchres are not foolishness and illusion; they are, on the contrary, an act of morality, by which is affirmed the immortality of the work done by individuals. Although dead, they live in our memory and will live in the memory of times to come. And that collecting of dead documents and writing down of empty histories is an act of life which serves life. The moment will come when they will serve to reproduce past history, enriched and made present to our spirit.

For dead history revives, and past history again becomes present, as the development of life demands them. The Romans and the Greeks lay in their sepulchres, until awakened at the Renaissance by the new maturity of the European spirit. The primitive forms of civilization, so gross and so barbaric, lay forgotten, or but little regarded, or misunderstood, until that new phase of the European spirit, which was known as Romanticism or Restoration, 'sympathized' with them—that is to say, recognized them as its own proper present interest. Thus great tracts of history which are now chronicle for us, many documents now mute, will in their turn be traversed with new flashes of life and will speak again.

These revivals have altogether interior motives, and no wealth of documents or of narratives will bring them about; indeed, it is they themselves that copiously collect and place before themselves the documents and narratives, which without them would remain scattered and inert. And it will be impossible ever to understand anything of the effective process of historical thought unless we start from the principle that the spirit itself is history, maker of history at every moment of its existence, and also the result of all anterior history. Thus the spirit bears with it all its history, which coincides with itself. To forget one aspect of history and to remember another one is nothing but the rhythm of the life of the spirit, which operates by determining and individualizing itself, and by always rendering indeterminate and disindividualizing previous determinations and individualizations, in order to create others more copious. The spirit, so to speak, lives again its own history without those external things called narratives and documents; but those external things are instruments that it makes for itself, acts preparatory to that internal vital evocation in whose process they are resolved. The spirit asserts and jealously preserves 'records of the past' for that purpose.

What we all of us do at every moment when we note dates and other matters concerning our private affairs (chronicles) in our pocket-books, or when we place in their little caskets ribbons and dried flowers (I beg to be allowed to select these pleasant images, when giving instances of the collection of 'documents'), is done on a large scale by a certain class of workers called *philologists*, as though at the invitation of the whole of society. They are specially known as the *erudite* when they collect evidence and narrations, as *archæologists* and *archivists* when they collect documents and monuments, as the places where such objects are kept (the "silent white abodes of the dead") are called libraries, archives, and museums. Can there be any ill-feeling against these men of erudition, these archivists and archæologists, who fulfil a necessary and therefore a useful and important function? The fact remains that there is a tendency to mock at them and to regard them with compassion. It is true enough that they sometimes afford a hold for derision with their ingenuous belief that they have history under lock and key and are able to unlock the 'sources' at which thirsty humanity may quench its desire for knowledge; but we know that history is in all of us and that its sources are in our own breasts. For it is in our own breasts alone that is to be found that crucible in which the *certain* is converted into the *true*, and *philology*, joining with *philosophy*, produces *history*.

### 4.

*The selection from José Ortega y Gasset pays tribute to Dilthey and makes explicit the transition from historicism to existentialism. "Man, in a word, has no nature; what he has . . . is history."*[1] *The excerpt also shows Ortega's indebtedness to Croce's assertion that history is contemporary and invariably tied to "present interests." Ortega y Gasset, in my estimate, was a lesser figure than these two predecessors of his; but the passage I have selected makes a point which is crucial to the tradition of modern historicism. This is the contrast between two kinds of "reasoning"—or explanation: the generalizing type employed in the natural sciences and the historical type which "consists in narration."*

### JOSÉ ORTEGA Y GASSET

### HISTORY AS A SYSTEM*

. . . Let the reader . . . take note of what happens to him when, faced with the great political problems of the

[1] The same idea may be found in Sartre, Jaspers, and Heidegger. For Jaspers, cf. below, Part IV, p. 333 ff.; for Heidegger's discussion of Dilthey's conception of historicism, cf. *Sein und Zeit*, #77.

* In *Toward a Philosophy of History* (New York: W. W. Norton & Co., Inc., 1941), pp. 211–23; reprinted by permission of W. W. Norton & Co. I have omitted one long footnote and one sentence from this passage, which is only a brief excerpt from the whole chapter. H.M.

day, he desires to take up an attitude. First there arises in his mind a certain form of government, let us say, authoritarianism. In it he sees, rightly, a means of surmounting some of the difficulties of the public situation. But if this solution is the first or one of the first to occur to him it is not by chance. It thrusts itself upon him precisely because it already lay there to his hand, because he did not need to invent it for himself. And it lay to his hand not merely as a project, but as an experiment already made. The reader knows, from personal experience or from reference, that there have been absolute monarchies, Caesarisms, unipersonal or collective dictatorships. And he knows further that all these forms of authoritarianism, if they solve some difficulties, leave others unsolved and in fact bring new ones of their own. The reader is thus led to reject this solution and to essay another in his mind which will avoid the drawbacks of authoritarianism. But here the same thing happens over again, and so it goes on until he has exhausted all the obvious forms of government, those that lay already to his hand, those he knew about because they had already been tried. At the end of this intellectual journey through forms of government he finds that, if he is to be sincere and act with full conviction, there is only one he could accept: to wit, a new one, different from any that has been before, one invented by himself. He must either invent a new being of the state himself—even though it be only a *new* authoritarianism or a *new* liberalism—or search around for someone who has invented such or who is capable of inventing it. Here, then, may be seen how in our present political attitude, in our political being, there persists all the past of mankind that is known to us. That past is past not because it happened to others but because it forms part of our present, of what we are in the form of having been, because, in short, it is *our* past. Life as a reality is absolute presence: we cannot say that *there is* anything unless it be present, of this moment. If, then, *there is* a past, it must be as something present, something active in us *now*. And, in effect, if we analyze what we are now, if we take the consistency of our present and hold it up against the light in order to reduce it to its component elements as the chemist or the physicist may an object, we find to our surprise that this life of ours that is always this, the life of this present, actual moment, is *composed* of what, personally or collectively, we have been. And if we speak of *being* in the traditional sense as a *being already* what one is, as a fixed, static, invariable, and given being, we shall have to say that the only element of being, of "nature," in man is what he has been. The past is man's moment of identity, his only element of the thing: nothing besides is inexorable and fatal. But, for the same reason, if man's only Eleatic being is what he has been, this means that his authentic being, what in effect he is—and not mere "has been" —is distinct from the past, and consists precisely and formally in "being what one has not been," in non-Eleatic being. And since we cannot hope ever to rid the term "being" of its traditional static signification, we should be well advised to dispense with it. Man *is* not, he "goes on being" this and that. The concept "to go on being" is, however, absurd: under promise of something logical it turns out in the end to be completely irrational. The term we can apply, without absurdity, to "going on being" is "living." Let us say, then, not that man *is*, but that he *lives*.

. . . It is advisable to take due note of the strange mode of knowledge, of comprehension, represented by this analysis of what, concretely, our life, that of the present, is. In order to understand my conduct with regard to Hermione and to Christianity,[1] or the reader's with regard to public problems, in order to discover the reason of our being or, what comes to the same thing, *why* we are as we are, what have we done? What was it that made us understand, *conceive*, our being? Simply the telling, the narrating that *formerly* I was the lover of this and that woman, that formerly I was a Christian, that the reader in himself or through others he has heard of was an absolutist, a Caesarist, a democrat, etc. In short, the reasoning, the *reason*, that throws light here consists in a narration. Alongside

[1] This is a reference to an earlier section of this chapter in which the author asks two hypothetical questions: (1) What does it mean to say that I was, or might have been, somebody's— say, Hermione's—lover? (2) What does it mean to say that I once was a Christian, but now I am no longer one? H.M.

pure physico-mathematical reason there is, then, a narrative reason. To comprehend anything human, be it personal or collective, one must tell its history. This man, this nation does such a thing and is in such a manner, *because* formerly he or it did that other thing and was in such another manner. Life only takes on a measure of transparency in the light of *historical reason*.

The most disparate forms of being *happen* to man. To the despair of the intellectualist, *being* is in man mere *happening, happening to him:* it "happens to him to be" a Stoic, a Christian, a rationalist, a vitalist. It happens to him to be the paleolithic female and the Marquise de Pompadour, Jenghiz Khan and Stefan George, Pericles and Charles Chaplin. Man does not actively subscribe to any of these forms: he passes through them—he lives them—like Zeno's arrow, moving, in spite of Zeno, during the whole of its flight.

Man invents for himself a program of life, a static form of being, that gives a satisfactory answer to the difficulties posed for him by circumstance. He essays this form of life, attempts to realize this imaginary character he has resolved to be. He embarks on the essay full of illusions and prosecutes the experiment with thoroughness. This means that he comes to believe *deeply* that this character is his real being. But meanwhile the experience has made apparent the shortcomings and limitations of the said program of life. It does not solve all the difficulties, and it creates new ones of its own. When first seen it was full face, with the light shining upon it: hence the illusions, the enthusiasm, the delights believed in store. With the back view its inadequacy is straightway revealed. Man thinks out another program of life. But this second program is drawn up in the light, not only of circumstance, but also of the first. One aims at avoiding in the new project the drawbacks of the old. In the second, therefore, the first is still active; it is preserved in order to be avoided. Inexorably man shrinks from being what he was. On the second project of being, the second thorough experiment, there follows a third, forged in the light of the second and the first, and so on. Man "goes on being" and "unbeing"—living. He goes on accumulating being—the past; he goes on making for himself a being through his dialectical series of experiments. This is a dialectic not of logical but precisely of historical reason—the *Realdialektik* dreamt of somewhere in his papers by Dilthey, the writer to whom we owe more than to anyone else concerning the idea of life, and who is, to my mind, the most important thinker of the second half of the nineteenth century.

In what does this dialectic that will not tolerate the facile anticipations of logical dialectic consist? This is what we have to find out on the basis of facts. We must know what is this series, what are its stages, and of what nature is the link between one and the next. Such a discovery is what would be called history were history to make this its objective, were it, that is to say, to convert itself into historical reason.

Here, then, awaiting our study, lies man's authentic "being"—stretching the whole length of his past. Man is what has happened to him, what he has done. Other things might have happened to him or have been done by him, but what did in fact happen to him and was done by him, this constitutes a relentless trajectory of experiences that he carries on his back as the vagabond his bundle of all he possesses. Man is a substantial emigrant on a pilgrimage of being, and it is accordingly meaningless to set limits to what he is capable of being. In this initial illimitableness of possibilities that characterizes one who has no nature there stands out only one fixed, pre-established, and given line by which he may chart his course, only one limit: the past. The experiments already made with life narrow man's future. If we do not know what he is going to be, we know what he is not going to be. Man lives in view of the past.

*Man, in a word, has no nature; what he has is . . . history.* Expressed differently: what nature is to things, history, *res gestae*, is to man. Once again we become aware of the possible application of theological concepts to human reality. *Deus, cui hoc est natura quod fecerit . . .* says St. Augustine.[2] Man, likewise, finds that he has no nature other than what he has himself done.

[2] *De Genesi ad litteram*, vi, 13. 24 (*Patrologia Latina*, vol. 34).

It is comic in the extreme that "historicism" should be condemned because it produces or corroborates in us the consciousness that the human factor is changeable in its every direction, that in it there is nothing concrete that is stable. As if the stable being—the stone, for instance—were preferable to the unstable! "Substantial" mutation is the condition on which an entity as such can be progressive, the condition on which its being may consist in progress. Now concerning man it must be said, not only that his being is variable, but also that his being grows and, in this sense, that it progresses. The error of the old doctrine of progress lay in affirming *a priori* that man progresses towards the better. That is something that can only be determined *a posteriori* by concrete historical reason: it is precisely the great discovery we await from this, since to it we look for the clarifying of human reality and, along with this, for light on the nature of the good, the bad, the better, and the worse. But that our life does possess a simply progressive character, this we can affirm *a priori* with full evidence and with a surety very different from that which has led to the supposition of the improgressivity of nature, that is to say, the "invariability of its laws." The same knowledge that discovers to us man's variation makes patent his progressive consistency. The European of today is not only different from what he was fifty years ago; his being now includes that of fifty years ago. The European of today finds himself without a living faith in science precisely *because* fifty years ago he did believe wholeheartedly in it. That faith that held sway half a century ago may now be defined with reasonable precision; were this done it would be seen that it was such *because* about 1800 the same faith in science wore a different profile, and so successively until we come to the year 1700 or thereabouts, at which date faith in reason is constituted as a "collective belief," as something socially operative. (Earlier than 1700 faith in reason is an individual belief or the belief of particular small groups that live submerged in societies where faith in God, if already more or less inert, yet continues operative.) In our present "crisis," in our present doubt concerning reason, we find then included the whole of that earlier life. We are, that is to say, all those forms of faith in reason, and we are in addition the doubt engendered by that faith. We are other than the man of 1700, and we are more.

There is no cause, therefore, for weeping overmuch concerning the mutability of everything human. This is precisely our ontological privilege. Progress is only possible to one who is not linked today to what he was yesterday, who is not caught for ever in that being which is already, but can migrate from it into another. But this is not enough: it is not sufficient that man should be able to free himself from what he is already and take on a new form, as the serpent sloughs its skin and is left with another. Progress demands that this new form should rise above the old and to this end should preserve it and turn it to account, that it should take off from the old, climbing on its shoulders as a high temperature mounts on lower ones. To progress is to accumulate being, to store up reality. This increase of being, it is true, when referred only to the individual, might be interpreted naturalistically as the mere development or *enodatio* of an initial disposition. With the evolutionary thesis still unproved, whatever its probability, it can be said that the tiger of today is neither more nor less a tiger than was that of a thousand years ago: it is being a tiger for the first time, it is always a first tiger. But the human individual is not putting on humanity for the first time. To begin with, he finds around him, in his "circumstance," other men and the society they give rise to. Hence his humanity, that which begins to develop in him, takes its point of departure from another, already developed, that has reached its culmination: in short, to his humanity he adds other humanities. He finds at birth a form of humanity, a mode of being a man, already forged, that he need not invent but may simply take over and set out from for his individual development. This does not begin for him—as for the tiger, which must always start again—at zero but at a positive quantity to which he adds his own growth. Man is not a first man, an eternal Adam: he is formally a second man, a third man, etc. . . .

Let the reader reflect closely on his life, studying it against the light as one looks at a glass of water to study

its infusoria. If he asks himself why his life is thus and not
otherwise, it will appear to him that not a few details had
their origin in inscrutable chance. But he will find the broad
lines of its reality perfectly comprehensible once he sees
that he is thus because, in the last resort, the society—
"collective man"—in which he lives is thus. And in its turn
the mode of being of society will stand revealed, once there
is discovered within it what that society was—what it believed, felt, preferred—at an earlier stage. That is to say
that in his individual and fleeting today man will see, fore-
shortened, the whole of man's past still active and alive.
For we can only throw light on yesterday by invoking the
day before yesterday; and so with all yesterdays. History
is a system, the system of human experiences linked in a
single, inexorable chain. Hence nothing can be truly clear
in history until everything is clear. We cannot properly understand what this "rationalist" European is unless we know
what it was to be a Stoic: and so the process goes on. And
this systematism of *res gestae* becomes reoperative and potent in history as *cognitio rerum gestarum*. Every historic
term whatsoever, to have exactness, must be determined as
a function of all history, neither more nor less than each
concept in Hegel's *Logic* has value only in respect of the
niche left for it by the others.

History is the systematic science of that radical reality,
my life. It is therefore a science of the present in the most
rigorous and actual sense of the word. Were it not a science
of the present, where should we find that past that is commonly assigned to it as theme? The opposite—and customary—interpretation is equivalent to making of the past an
abstract, unreal something lying lifeless just where it happened in time, whereas the past is in truth the live, active
force that sustains our today. There is no *actio in distans*.
The past is not yonder, at the date when it happened, but
here, in me. The past is I—by which I mean my life.

5.

*The final essay marks a transition to Part II; for it deals di-
rectly with the problem of historical knowledge. R. G. Col-*

lingwood was an exceptional figure in recent English philosophy. He was Professor of Philosophy in the University of Oxford; but he was quite cut off from his philosophical contemporaries. "When I read their works . . . I find myself constantly haunted by the thought that their accounts of knowledge, based as they seem to be primarily on the study of perception and scientific thinking, not only ignore historical thinking but are actually inconsistent with their being such a thing."

Thus Collingwood was the first and most serious English thinker of our times to defend history as an autonomous branch of human knowledge and to plead for its respectability in philosophical circles.[1] As often happens with a man working in isolation and in protest against the prevailing winds of doctrine, he overshot his mark. Following Croce (and Hegel), he believed that, ultimately, history was philosophy, or philosophy was history, and nothing else. Moreover, like Croce, he staked his whole position on the controversial idealistic thesis that written history was nothing but the present re-enactment, in the mind of the historian, of past thought. This is an issue which will come up again in Part II.

Here I have chosen Collingwood's essay "The Historical Imagination," partly because it is an eloquent statement in defense of the uniqueness of history, partly because it singles out a problem which is frightfully difficult and obscure: the role of the imagination in the cognitive life. Collingwood assigns to the "productive imagination" as crucial a function in the mind as Kant did. Whether his solution of the problem of "historical truth" in terms of a self-justifying, a priori imagination is acceptable or not; whether it does justice to the role played by objective conditions in history; whether it dispels the shadow of historical relativism, or skepticism (as in the reference to Suetonius and Tacitus)—these questions must be left open.

Aside from its main theme, however, the essay makes a number of interesting comments on such difficult topics as sources, authorities, evidence, and inference in history, and

[1] Collingwood's special place in the intellectual life of his times is best described in his own Autobiography.

*puts the essence of historicism in a nutshell: History is "reasoned knowledge of what is transient and concrete."*

## R. G. COLLINGWOOD

## THE HISTORICAL IMAGINATION*

An inquiry into the nature of historical thinking is among the tasks which philosophy may legitimately undertake; and at the present time [1935] there are reasons, as it seems to me, for thinking such an inquiry not only legitimate but necessary. For there is a sense in which, at particular periods of history, particular philosophical problems are, as it were, in season, and claim the special attention of a philosopher anxious to be of service to his age. In part, the problems of philosophy are unchanging; in part, they vary from age to age, according to the special characteristics of human life and thought at the time; and in the best philosophers of every age these two parts are so interwoven that the permanent problems appear *sub specie saeculi,* and the special problems of the age *sub specie aeternitatis.* Whenever human thought has been dominated by some special interest, the most fruitful philosophy of the age has reflected that domination; not passively, by mere submission to its influence, but actively, by making a special attempt to understand it and placing it in the focus of philosophical inquiry.

In the Middle Ages theology was the interest that served in this way to focus philosophical speculation. In the seventeenth century it was physical science. To-day, when we conventionally date the beginnings of modern philosophy to the seventeenth century, we mean, I think, that the scientific interest which then began to dominate human life still dominates it. But if we compare the seventeenth-century mind, in its general orientation, with that of to-day, by comparing the subjects dealt with in their literature, we

* In *The Idea of History* (Oxford-New York: Oxford University Press, 1946), pp. 231–49; reprinted by permission of the Oxford University Press.

can hardly fail to be struck by one important difference. Since the time of Descartes, and even since the time of Kant, mankind has acquired a new habit of thinking historically. I do not mean that there were no historians worthy of the name until a century and a half ago; that would be untrue: I do not even mean that since then the bulk of historical knowledge and the output of historical books have enormously increased; that would be true but relatively unimportant. What I mean is that during this time historical thought has worked out a technique of its own, no less definite in its character and certain in its results than its elder sister, the technique of natural science; and that, in thus entering upon the *sichere Gang einer Wissenschaft,* it has taken a place in human life from which its influence has permeated and to some extent transformed every department of thought and action.

Among others, it has profoundly influenced philosophy; but on the whole the attitude of philosophy towards this influence has been more passive than active. Some philosophers are inclined to welcome it; others to resent it; comparatively few have thought philosophically about it. Attempts have been made, chiefly in Germany and Italy, to answer the questions: What is historical thinking? and What light does it throw on the traditional problems of philosophy? and by answering these questions to do for the historical consciousness of to-day what Kant's transcendental analytic did for the scientific consciousness of the eighteenth century. But for the most part, and especially in this country, it has been usual to ignore all such questions, and to discuss the problems of knowledge in seeming unawareness that there is such a thing as history. This custom can of course be defended. It may be argued that history is not knowledge at all, but only opinion, and unworthy of philosophical study. Or it may be argued that, so far as it is knowledge, its problems are those of knowledge in general, and call for no special treatment. For myself, I cannot accept either defence. If history is opinion, why should philosophy on that account ignore it? If it is knowledge, why should philosophers not study its methods with the same attention that they give to the very different methods of

science? And when I read the works of even the greatest
contemporary and recent English philosophers, admiring
them deeply and learning from them more than I can hope
to acknowledge, I find myself constantly haunted by the
thought that their accounts of knowledge, based as they
seem to be primarily on the study of perception and of
scientific thinking, not only ignore historical thinking but
are actually inconsistent with there being such a thing.

No doubt, historical thought is in one way like perception. Each has for its proper object something individual.
What I perceive is this room, this table, this paper. What
the historian thinks about is Elizabeth or Marlborough,
the Peloponnesian War or the policy of Ferdinand and
Isabella. But what we perceive is always the this, the here,
the now. Even when we hear a distant explosion or see a
stellar conflagration long after it has happened, there is
still a moment at which it is here and now perceptible, when
it is this explosion, this new star. Historical thought is of
something which can never be a this, because it is never a
here and now. Its objects are events which have finished
happening, and conditions no longer in existence. Only
when they are no longer perceptible do they become objects for historical thought. Hence all theories of knowledge
that conceive it as a transaction or relation between a subject and an object both actually existing, and confronting
or compresent to one another, theories that take acquaintance as the essence of knowledge, make history impossible.

In another way history resembles science: for in each of
them knowledge is inferential or reasoned. But whereas
science lives in a world of abstract universals, which are in
one sense everywhere and in another nowhere, in one sense
at all times and in another at no time, the things about
which the historian reasons are not abstract but concrete,
not universal but individual, not indifferent to space and
time but having a where and a when of their own, though
the where need not be here and the when cannot be now.
History, therefore, cannot be made to square with theories
according to which the object of knowledge is abstract and
changeless, a logical entity towards which the mind may
take up various attitudes.

Nor is it possible to give an account of knowledge by combining theories of these two types. Current philosophy is full of such combinations. Knowledge by acquaintance and knowledge by description; eternal objects and the transient situations into which they are ingredient; realm of essence and realm of matter; in these and other such dichotomies, as in the older dichotomies of matters of fact and relations between ideas, or truths of fact and truths of reason, provision is made for the peculiarities both of a perception which grasps the here and now, and of the abstract thought that apprehends the everywhere and always: the αἴσθησις and νόησις of philosophical tradition. But just as history is neither αἴσθησις nor νόησις, so it is not a combination of the two. It is a third thing, having some of the characteristics of each, but combining them in a way impossible to either. It is not partly acquaintance with transient situations and partly reasoned knowledge of abstract entities. It is wholly a reasoned knowledge of what is transient and concrete.

My purpose here is to offer a brief account of this third thing which is history; and I will begin by stating what may be called the common-sense theory of it, the theory which most people believe, or imagine themselves to believe, when first they reflect on the matter.

According to this theory, the essential things in history are memory and authority. If an event or a state of things is to be historically known, first of all some one must be acquainted with it; then he must remember it; then he must state his recollection of it in terms intelligible to another; and finally that other must accept the statement as true. History is thus the believing some one else when he says that he remembers something. The believer is the historian; the person believed is called his authority.

This doctrine implies that historical truth, so far as it is at all accessible to the historian, is accessible to him only because it exists ready made in the ready-made statements of his authorities. These statements are to him a sacred text, whose value depends wholly on the unbrokenness of the tradition they represent. He must therefore on no account tamper with them. He must not mutilate them; he must

not add to them; and, above all, he must not contradict
them. For if he takes it upon himself to pick and choose,
to decide that some of his authority's statements are important and others not, he is going behind his authority's
back and appealing to some other criterion; and this, on
the theory, is exactly what he cannot do. If he adds to them,
interpolating in them constructions of his own devising,
and accepting these constructions as additions to his knowledge, he is believing something for a reason other than the
fact that his authority has said it; and this again he has no
right to do. Worst of all, if he contradicts them, presuming
to decide that his authority has misrepresented the facts,
and rejecting his statements as incredible, he is believing
the opposite of what he has been told, and committing the
worst possible offence against the rules of his craft. The
authority may be garrulous, discursive, a gossip and a
scandal-monger; he may have overlooked or forgotten or
omitted facts; he may have ignorantly or wilfully mis-
stated them; but against these defects the historian has no
remedy. For him, on the theory, what his authorities tell
him is the truth, the whole accessible truth, and nothing
but the truth.

These consequences of the common-sense theory have
only to be stated in order to be repudiated. Every historian
is aware that on occasion he does tamper in all these three
ways with what he finds in his authorities. He selects from
them what he thinks important, and omits the rest; he in-
terpolates in them things which they do not explicitly say;
and he criticizes them by rejecting or amending what he
regards as due to misinformation or mendacity. But I am
not sure whether we historians always realize the consequences of what we are doing. In general, when we reflect
on our own work, we seem to accept what I have called
the common-sense theory, while claiming our own rights of
selection, construction, and criticism. No doubt these rights
are inconsistent with the theory; but we attempt to soften
the contradiction by minimizing the extent to which they
are exercised, thinking of them as emergency measures, a
kind of revolt into which the historian may be driven at
times by the exceptional incompetence of his authorities,

but which does not fundamentally disturb the normal peaceful régime in which he placidly believes what he is told because he is told to believe it. Yet these things, however seldom they are done, are either historical crimes or facts fatal to the theory: for on the theory they ought to be done, not rarely, but never. And in fact they are neither criminal nor exceptional. Throughout the course of his work the historian is selecting, constructing, and criticizing; it is only by doing these things that he maintains his thought upon the *sichere Gang einer Wissenschaft*. By explicitly recognizing this fact it is possible to effect what, again borrowing a Kantian phrase, one might call a Copernican revolution in the theory of history: the discovery that, so far from relying on an authority other than himself, to whose statements his thought must conform, the historian is his own authority and his thought autonomous, self-authorizing, possessed of a criterion to which his so-called authorities must conform and by reference to which they are criticized.

The autonomy of historical thought is seen at its simplest in the work of selection. The historian who tries to work on the common-sense theory, and accurately reproduce what he finds in his authorities, resembles a landscape-painter who tries to work on that theory of art which bids the artist copy nature. He may fancy that he is reproducing in his own medium the actual shapes and colours of natural things; but however hard he tries to do this he is always selecting, simplifying, schematizing, leaving out what he thinks unimportant and putting in what he regards as essential. It is the artist, and not nature, that is responsible for what goes into the picture. In the same way, no historian, not even the worst, merely copies out his authorities; even if he puts in nothing of his own (which is never really possible), he is always leaving out things which, for one reason or another, he decides that his own work does not need or cannot use. It is he, therefore, and not his authority, that is responsible for what goes in. On that question he is his own master: his thought is to that extent autonomous.

An even clearer exhibition of this autonomy is found in

what I have called historical construction. The historian's
authorities tell him of this or that phase in a process whose
intermediate phases they leave undescribed; he then inter-
polates these phases for himself. His picture of his subject,
though it may consist in part of statements directly drawn
from his authorities, consists also, and increasingly with every increase in his competence as an historian, of statements
reached inferentially from those according to his own criteria, his own rules of method, and his own canons of relevance. In this part of his work he is never depending on
his authorities in the sense of repeating what they tell him;
he is relying on his own powers and constituting himself
his own authority; while his so-called authorities are now
not authorities at all but only evidence.

The clearest demonstration of the historian's autonomy,
however, is provided by historical criticism. As natural
science finds its proper method when the scientist, in Bacon's metaphor, puts Nature to the question, tortures her
by experiment in order to wring from her answers to his
own questions, so history finds its proper method when the
historian puts his authorities in the witness-box, and by
cross-questioning extorts from them information which in
their original statements they have withheld, either because
they did not wish to give it or because they did not possess
it. Thus, a commander's dispatches may claim a victory;
the historian, reading them in a critical spirit, will ask: 'If
it was a victory, why was it not followed up in this or that
way?' and may thus convict the writer of concealing the
truth. Or, by using the same method, he may convict of
ignorance a less critical predecessor who has accepted the
version of the battle given him by the same dispatches.

The historian's autonomy is here manifested in its ex-
tremest form, because it is here evident that somehow, in
virtue of his activity as an historian, he has it in his power
to reject something explicitly told him by his authorities and
to substitute something else. If that is possible, the criterion
of historical truth cannot be the fact that a statement is
made by an authority. It is the truthfulness and the information of the so-called authority that are in question; and
this question the historian has to answer for himself, on his

own authority. Even if he accepts what his authorities tell him, therefore, he accepts it not on their authority but on his own; not because they say it, but because it satisfies his criterion of historical truth.

The common-sense theory which bases history upon memory and authority needs no further refutation. Its bankruptcy is evident. For the historian there can never be authorities, because the so-called authorities abide a verdict which only he can give. Yet the common-sense theory may claim a qualified and relative truth. The historian, generally speaking, works at a subject which others have studied before him. In proportion as he is more of a novice, either in this particular subject or in history as a whole, his fore-runners are, relatively to his incompetence, authoritative; and in the limiting case where his incompetence and igno-rance were absolute, they could be called authorities with-out qualification. As he becomes more and more master of his craft and his subject, they become less and less his au-thorities, more and more his fellow students, to be treated with respect or contempt according to their deserts.

And as history does not depend on authority, so it does not depend upon memory. The historian can rediscover what has been completely forgotten, in the sense that no statement of it has reached him by an unbroken tradition from eyewitnesses. He can even discover what, until he dis-covered it, no one ever knew to have happened at all. This he does partly by the critical treatment of statements con-tained in his sources, partly by the use of what are called unwritten sources, which are increasingly employed as his-tory becomes increasingly sure of its own proper methods and its own proper criterion.

I have spoken of the criterion of historical truth. What is this criterion? According to the common-sense theory, it is the agreement of the statements made by the historian with those which he finds in his authorities. This answer we now know to be false, and we must seek another. We cannot renounce the search. Some answer to the question there must be, for without a criterion there can be no criti-cism. One answer to this question was offered by the great-est English philosopher of our time in his pamphlet on *The*

*Presuppositions of Critical History*. Bradley's essay was an early work with which in his maturity he was dissatisfied; but, unsatisfactory though it certainly is, it bears the stamp of his genius. In it Bradley faces the question how it is possible for the historian, in defiance of the common-sense theory, to turn the tables on his so-called authorities and to say 'This is what our authorities record, but what really happened must have been not this but that'.

His answer to this question was that our experience of the world teaches us that some kinds of things happen and others do not; this experience, then, is the criterion which the historian brings to bear on the statements of his authorities. If they tell him that things happened of a kind which, according to his experience, does not happen, he is obliged to disbelieve them; if the things which they report are of a kind which according to his experience does happen, he is free to accept their statements.

There are many obvious objections to this idea, on which I shall not insist. It is deeply tinged with the empiricist philosophy against which Bradley was soon so effectively to rebel. But apart from this there are certain special points in which the argument appears to me defective.

First, the proposed criterion is a criterion not of what did happen but of what could happen. It is in fact nothing but Aristotle's criterion of what is admissible in poetry; and hence it does not serve to discriminate history from fiction. It would no doubt be satisfied by the statements of an historian, but it would be satisfied no less adequately by those of an historical novelist. It cannot therefore be the criterion of critical history.

Secondly, because it can never tell us what did happen, we are left to rely for that on the sheer authority of our informant. We undertake, when we apply it, to believe everything our informant tells us so long as it satisfies the merely negative criterion of being possible. This is not to turn the tables on our authorities; it is blindly to accept what they tell us. The critical attitude has not been achieved.

Thirdly, the historian's experience of the world in which he lives can only help him to check, even negatively, the statements of his authorities in so far as they are concerned not with history but with nature, which has no history. The laws of nature have always been the same, and what is against nature now was against nature two thousand years ago; but the historical as distinct from the natural conditions of man's life differ so much at different times that no argument from analogy will hold. That the Greeks and Romans exposed their new-born children in order to control the numbers of their population is no less true for being unlike anything that happens in the experience of contributors to the *Cambridge Ancient History*. In point of fact Bradley's treatment of the subject grew not out of the ordinary course of historical study but out of his interest in the credibility of the New Testament narratives, and in particular their miraculous element; but a criterion which only serves in the case of miracle is of sadly little use to the weekday historian.

Bradley's essay, inconclusive though it is, remains memorable for the fact that in it the Copernican revolution in the theory of historical knowledge has been in principle accomplished. For the common-sense theory, historical truth consists in the historian's beliefs conforming to the statements of his authorities; Bradley has seen that the historian brings with him to the study of his authorities a criterion of his own by reference to which the authorities themselves are judged. What it is, Bradley failed to discover. It remains to be seen whether, sixty years later, his problem, which in the meantime I believe no English-speaking philosopher has discussed in print, can be advanced beyond the point at which he left it.

I have already remarked that, in addition to selecting from among his authorities' statements those which he regards as important, the historian must in two ways go beyond what his authorities tell him. One is the critical way, and this is what Bradley has attempted to analyse. The other is the constructive way. Of this he has said nothing, and to this I now propose to return. I described constructive history as interpolating, between the statements borrowed from our authorities, other statements implied by them. Thus our authorities tell us that on one day Caesar was in

Rome and on a later day in Gaul; they tell us nothing about
his journey from one place to the other, but we interpolate
this with a perfectly good conscience.

This act of interpolation has two significant characteristics. First, it is in no way arbitrary or merely fanciful: it
is necessary or, in Kantian language, *a priori*. If we filled
up the narrative of Caesar's doings with fanciful details
such as the names of the persons he met on the way, and
what he said to them, the construction would be arbitrary:
it would be in fact the kind of construction which is done
by an historical novelist. But if our construction involves
nothing that is not necessitated by the evidence, it is a legitimate historical construction of a kind without which
there can be no history at all.

Secondly, what is in this way inferred is essentially something imagined. If we look out over the sea and perceive
a ship, and five minutes later look again and perceive it in
a different place, we find ourselves obliged to imagine it as
having occupied intermediate positions when we were not
looking. That is already an example of historical thinking;
and it is not otherwise that we find ourselves obliged to
imagine Caesar as having travelled from Rome to Gaul
when we are told that he was in these different places at
these successive times.

This activity, with this double character, I shall call *a
priori* imagination; and, though I shall have more to say of
it hereafter, for the present I shall be content to remark
that, however unconscious we may be of its operation, it is
this activity which, bridging the gaps between what our
authorities tell us, gives the historical narrative or description its continuity. That the historian must use his imagination is a commonplace; to quote Macaulay's *Essay on
History*, 'a perfect historian must possess an imagination
sufficiently powerful to make his narrative affecting and
picturesque'; but this is to underestimate the part played
by the historical imagination, which is properly not orna-
mental but structural. Without it the historian would have
no narrative to adorn. The imagination, that 'blind but indispensable faculty' without which, as Kant has shown, we
could never perceive the world around us, is indispensable

in the same way to history: it is this which, operating not capriciously as fancy but in its *a priori* form, does the entire work of historical construction.

Two misunderstandings may here be forestalled. First, it may be thought that by imagining we can present to ourselves only what is imaginary in the sense of being fictitious or unreal. This prejudice need only be mentioned in order to be dispelled. If I imagine the friend who lately left my house now entering his own, the fact that I imagine this event gives me no reason to believe it unreal. The imaginary, simply as such, is neither unreal nor real.

Secondly, to speak of *a priori* imagination may seem a paradox, for it may be thought that imagination is essentially capricious, arbitrary, merely fanciful. But in addition to its historical function there are two other functions of *a priori* imagination which are, or ought to be, familiar to all. One is the pure or free, but by no means arbitrary, imagination of the artist. A man writing a novel composes a story where parts are played by various characters. Characters and incidents are all alike imaginary; yet the whole aim of the novelist is to show the characters acting and the incidents developing in a manner determined by a necessity internal to themselves. The story, if it is a good story, cannot develop otherwise than as it does; the novelist in imagining it cannot imagine it developing except as it does develop. Here, and equally in all other kinds of art, the *a priori* imagination is at work. Its other familiar function is what may be called the perceptual imagination, supplementing and consolidating the data of perception in the way so well analysed by Kant, by presenting to us objects of possible perception which are not actually perceived: the under side of this table, the inside of an unopened egg, the back of the moon. Here again the imagination is *a priori*: we cannot but imagine what cannot but be there. The historical imagination differs from these not in being *a priori*, but in having as its special task to imagine the past: not an object of possible perception, since it does not now exist, but able through this activity to become an object of our thought.

The historian's picture of his subject, whether that sub-

ject be a sequence of events or a past state of things, thus
appears as a web of imaginative construction stretched between certain fixed points provided by the statements of his
authorities; and if these points are frequent enough and the
threads spun from each to the next are constructed with
due care, always by the *a priori* imagination and never by
merely arbitrary fancy, the whole picture is constantly verified by appeal to these data, and runs little risk of losing
touch with the reality which it represents.

Actually, this is very much how we do think of historical
work, when the common-sense theory has ceased to satisfy
us, and we have become aware of the part played in it by
the constructive imagination. But such a conception is in
one way seriously at fault: it overlooks the no less important part played by criticism. We think of our web of construction as pegged down, so to speak, to the facts by the
statements of authorities, which we regard as data or fixed
points for the work of construction. But in so thinking we
have slipped back into the theory, which we now know to
be false, that truth is given us ready made in these statements. We know that truth is to be had, not by swallowing
what our authorities tell us, but by criticizing it; and thus
the supposedly fixed points between which the historical
imagination spins its web are not given to us ready made,
they must be achieved by critical thinking.

There is nothing other than historical thought itself, by
appeal to which its conclusions may be verified. The hero
of a detective novel is thinking exactly like an historian
when, from indications of the most varied kinds, he constructs an imaginary picture of how a crime was committed,
and by whom. At first, this is a mere theory, awaiting verification, which must come to it from without. Happily for
the detective, the conventions of that literary form dictate
that when his construction is complete it shall be neatly
pegged down by a confession from the criminal, given in
such circumstances that its genuineness is beyond question.
The historian is less fortunate. If, after convincing himself
by a study of the evidence already available that Bacon
wrote the plays of Shakespeare or that Henry VII murdered
the Princes in the Tower, he were to find an autograph

document confessing the fact, he would by no means have verified his conclusions; the new document, so far from closing the inquiry, would only have complicated it by raising a new problem, the problem of its own authenticity.

I began by considering a theory according to which everything is given: according to which all truth, so far as any truth is accessible to the historian, is provided for him ready made in the ready-made statements of his authorities. I then saw that much of what he takes for true is not given in this way but constructed by his *a priori* imagination; but I still fancied that this imagination worked inferentially from fixed points given in the same sense. I am now driven to confess that there are for historical thought no fixed points thus given: in other words, that in history, just as there are properly speaking no authorities, so there are properly speaking no data.

Historians certainly think of themselves as working from data; where by data they mean historical facts possessed by them ready made at the beginning of a certain piece of historical research. Such a datum, if the research concerns the Peloponnesian War, would be, for example, a certain statement of Thucydides, accepted as substantially true. But when we ask what gives historical thought this datum, the answer is obvious: historical thought gives it to itself, and therefore in relation to historical thought at large it is not a datum but a result or achievement. It is only our historical knowledge which tells us that these curious marks on paper are Greek letters; that the words which they form have certain meanings in the Attic dialect; that the passage is authentic Thucydides, not an interpolation or corruption; and that on this occasion Thucydides knew what he was talking about and was trying to tell the truth. Apart from all this, the passage is merely a pattern of black marks on white paper: not any historical fact at all, but something existing here and now, and perceived by the historian. All that the historian means, when he describes certain historical facts as his data, is that for the purposes of a particular piece of work there are certain historical problems relevant to that work which for the present he proposes to treat as settled; though, if they are settled, it is

only because historical thinking has settled them in the
past, and they remain settled only until he or some one
else decides to reopen them.

His web of imaginative construction, therefore, cannot
derive its validity from being pegged down, as at first I described it, to certain given facts. That description represented an attempt to relieve him of the responsibility for
the nodal points of his fabric, while admitting his responsibility for what he constructs between them. In point of fact,
he is just as responsible for the one as for the other.
Whether he accepts or rejects or modifies or reinterprets
what his so-called authorities tell him, it is he that is responsible for the statement which, after duly criticizing
them, he makes. The criterion that justifies him in making
it can never be the fact that it has been given him by an
authority.

This brings me back to the question what this criterion
is. And at this point a partial and provisional answer can
be given. The web of imaginative construction is something
far more solid and powerful than we have hitherto realized.
So far from relying for its validity upon the support of given
facts, it actually serves as the touchstone by which we decide whether alleged facts are genuine. Suetonius tells me
that Nero at one time intended to evacuate Britain. I reject his statement, not because any better authority flatly
contradicts it, for of course none does; but because my reconstruction of Nero's policy based on Tacitus will not allow me to think that Suetonius is right. And if I am told
that this is merely to say I prefer Tacitus to Suetonius, I
confess that I do: but I do so just because I find myself
able to incorporate what Tacitus tells me into a coherent
and continuous picture of my own, and cannot do this for
Suetonius.

It is thus the historian's picture of the past, the product
of his own *a priori* imagination, that has to justify the
sources used in its construction. These sources are sources,
that is to say, credence is given to them, only because they
are in this way justified. For any source may be tainted:
this writer prejudiced, that misinformed; this inscription
misread by a bad epigraphist, that blundered by a careless

stonemason; this potsherd placed out of its context by an incompetent excavator, that by a blameless rabbit. The critical historian has to discover and correct all these and many other kinds of falsification. He does it, and can only do it, by considering whether the picture of the past to which the evidence leads him is a coherent and continuous picture, one which makes sense. The *a priori* imagination which does the work of historical construction supplies the means of historical criticism as well.

Freed from its dependence on fixed points supplied from without, the historian's picture of the past is thus in every detail an imaginary picture, and its necessity is at every point the necessity of the *a priori* imagination. Whatever goes into it, goes into it not because his imagination passively accepts it, but because it actively demands it.

The resemblance between the historian and the novelist, to which I have already referred, here reaches its culmination. Each of them makes it his business to construct a picture which is partly a narrative of events, partly a description of situations, exhibition of motives, analysis of characters. Each aims at making his picture a coherent whole, where every character and every situation is so bound up with the rest that this character in this situation cannot but act in this way, and we cannot imagine him as acting otherwise. The novel and the history must both of them make sense; nothing is admissible in either except what is necessary, and the judge of this necessity is in both cases the imagination. Both the novel and the history are self-explanatory, self-justifying, the product of an autonomous or self-authorizing activity; and in both cases this activity is the *a priori* imagination.

As works of imagination, the historian's work and the novelist's do not differ. Where they do differ is that the historian's picture is meant to be true. The novelist has a single task only: to construct a coherent picture, one that makes sense. The historian has a double task: he has both to do this, and to construct a picture of things as they really were and of events as they really happened. This further necessity imposes upon him obedience to three rules of method, from which the novelist or artist in general is free.

First, his picture must be localized in space and time. The artist's need not; essentially, the things that he imagines are imagined as happening at no place and at no date. Of *Wuthering Heights* it has been well said that the scene is laid in Hell, though the place-names are English; and it was a sure instinct that led another great novelist to replace Oxford by Christminster, Wantage by Alfredston, and Fawley by Marychurch, recoiling against the discord of topographical fact in what should be a purely imaginary world.

Secondly, all history must be consistent with itself. Purely imaginary worlds cannot clash and need not agree; each is a world to itself. But there is only one historical world, and everything in it must stand in some relation to everything else, even if that relation is only topographical and chronological.

Thirdly, and most important, the historian's picture stands in a peculiar relation to something called evidence. The only way in which the historian or any one else can judge, even tentatively, of its truth is by considering this relation; and, in practice, what we mean by asking whether an historical statement is true is whether it can be justified by an appeal to the evidence: for a truth unable to be so justified is to the historian a thing of no interest. What is this thing called evidence, and what is its relation to the finished historical work?

We already know what evidence is not. It is not ready-made historical knowledge, to be swallowed and regurgitated by the historian's mind. Everything is evidence which the historian can use as evidence. But what can he so use? It must be something here and now perceptible to him: this written page, this spoken utterance, this building, this finger-print. And of all the things perceptible to him there is not one which he might not conceivably use as evidence on some question, if he came to it with the right question in mind. The enlargement of historical knowledge comes about mainly through finding how to use as evidence this or that kind of perceived fact which historians have hitherto thought useless to them.

The whole perceptible world, then, is potentially and in principle evidence to the historian. It becomes actual evidence in so far as he can use it. And he cannot use it unless he comes to it with the right kind of historical knowledge. The more historical knowledge we have, the more we can learn from any given piece of evidence; if we had none, we could learn nothing. Evidence is evidence only when some one contemplates it historically. Otherwise it is merely perceived fact, historically dumb. It follows that historical knowledge can only grow out of historical knowledge; in other words, that historical thinking is an original and fundamental activity of the human mind, or, as Descartes might have said, that the idea of the past is an 'innate' idea.

Historical thinking is that activity of the imagination by which we endeavour to provide this innate idea with detailed content. And this we do by using the present as evidence for its own past. Every present has a past of its own, and any imaginative reconstruction of the past aims at reconstructing the past of this present, the present in which the act of imagination is going on, as here and now perceived. In principle the aim of any such act is to use the entire perceptible here-and-now as evidence for the entire past through whose process it has come into being. In practice, this aim can never be achieved. The perceptible here-and-now can never be perceived, still less interpreted, in its entirety; and the infinite process of past time can never be envisaged as a whole. But this separation between what is attempted in principle and what is achieved in practice is the lot of mankind, not a peculiarity of historical thinking. The fact that it is found there only shows that herein history is like art, science, philosophy, the pursuit of virtue, and the search for happiness.

It is for the same reason that in history, as in all serious matters, no achievement is final. The evidence available for solving any given problem changes with every change of historical method and with every variation in the competence of historians. The principles by which this evidence is interpreted change too; since the interpreting of evidence is a task to which a man must bring everything he knows: historical knowledge, knowledge of nature and man, mathematical knowledge, philosophical knowledge; and not knowledge only, but mental habits and possessions of

every kind: and none of these is unchanging. Because of
these changes, which never cease, however slow they may
appear to observers who take a short view, every new generation must rewrite history in its own way; every new
historian, not content with giving new answers to old questions, must revise the questions themselves; and—since historical thought is a river into which none can step twice—
even a single historian, working at a single subject for a
certain length of time, finds when he tries to reopen an old
question that the question has changed.

This is not an argument for historical scepticism. It is
only the discovery of a second dimension of historical
thought, the history of history: the discovery that the historian himself, together with the here-and-now which forms
the total body of evidence available to him, is a part of
the process he is studying, has his own place in that process,
and can see it only from the point of view which at this
present moment he occupies within it.

But neither the raw material of historical knowledge, the
detail of the here-and-now as given him in perception, nor
the various endowments that serve him as aids to interpreting this evidence, can give the historian his criterion of historical truth. That criterion is the idea of history itself: the
idea of an imaginary picture of the past. That idea is, in
Cartesian language, innate; in Kantian language, *a priori*.
It is not a chance product of psychological causes; it is an
idea which every man possesses as part of the furniture of
his mind, and discovers himself to possess in so far as he
becomes conscious of what it is to have a mind. Like other
ideas of the same sort, it is one to which no fact of experience exactly corresponds. The historian, however long
and faithfully he works, can never say that his work, even
in crudest outline or in this or that smallest detail, is done
once for all. He can never say that his picture of the past
is at any point adequate to his idea of what it ought to be.
But, however fragmentary and faulty the results of his work
may be, the idea which governed its course is clear, rational, and universal. It is the idea of the historical imagination as a self-dependent, self-determining, and self-justifying form of thought.

# PART II

# Clio—Science or Muse?

*This is the longest section of this volume; yet it is also the most incomplete, for the question, what is historical knowledge, has been more widely discussed than any other in recent literature.*

*In the last essay of Part I, Collingwood asked, "What is historical thinking?" and weighed the general problem whether history was a form of knowledge like science—or a form of art. Here Henri Pirenne (1862–1935), the great Belgian historian, asks more simply, "What are historians trying to do?" This innocent question conceals a host of puzzles and difficulties which beset history in its quest for knowledge. I have tried to give a brief survey of these epistemological problems in the general introduction. To deal with them adequately would require a systematic work.*

*No such ambitious inquiry emerges from the essays reprinted below. Instead, they are grouped around a subsidiary problem: the scope and limits of objectivity in historical works. Two of the selections are entitled: "Can history be objective?" This is a recurrent theme in the thinking about history. For one answer to the question of what historians are trying to do is, obviously, that they are trying to tell the truth, that they are claiming to write an impartial and objective history. How valid is this claim? How far does the historian achieve a degree of objectivity compara-*

ble to that in other "scientific" disciplines; where and why
does he fall short of this goal? Why is history called a
science? Where does it reveal an affinity with the arts,
painting a portrait of the past which, for all its faithfulness
to facts and logic, is suffused with subjective tones and
colors?

In general, the following selections divide in such a way
that the practicing historians tend to emphasize the limits
of objectivity in history, and its essential differences from
scientific discourse, whereas the professional philosophers
tend to emphasize the possibility of an objective knowledge
in history analogous to that in other scientific disciplines.
In this respect, they are of an entirely different breed from
their European colleagues whom we encountered in Part I.
They are, with one exception, American philosophers who
bring an empirical, pragmatic, or analytic approach to history; and this approach sets them off sharply from the kind
of historicism, idealism, or existentialism as expounded by
Dilthey, Croce, Ortega y Gasset, and Collingwood. On the
other hand, the professional historians reveal the profound
impact which this continental tradition has had upon their
thinking. The philosophers in this section, therefore, are at
odds both with the philosophical heritage of historicism and
with its repercussions among practicing historians.

1.

Pirenne's essay sets the stage for the debate that follows.
On the one hand, it is a plea for the status of history as a
science, a summary of the critical apparatus which modern
history, in conjunction with its "auxiliary sciences," has developed during the last hundred years. On the other hand,
it repeats the historicist insight that "to construct history
is to narrate it," not to formulate general laws, that each
narrative is a kind of hypothesis or partial explanation, that
the search for "the real meaning" of one's narrative may set
limits to the employment of the scientific apparatus, and
that the historian cannot but call upon the exercise of the
"creative imagination," which, in turn, introduces ineradicable subjective differences of personality and milieu.

*Hence, the scientific apparatus is a necessary but not a
sufficient condition for the writing of history.*

## HENRI PIRENNE

## WHAT ARE HISTORIANS TRYING TO DO?*

### I

The subject of historians' study is the development of human societies in space and time. This development is the
result of billions of individual actions. But in so far as they
are purely individual, these actions do not belong to the
domain of history, which has to take account of them only
as they are related to collective movements, or in the measure to which they have influenced the collectivity. History
is thus allied to sociology and psychology and at the same
time it differs from them.

Like sociology, it is interested in the phenomena of the
masses which arise from physiological necessities or from
moral tendencies which force themselves upon men, such,
for example, as nourishment and family solidarity. Like psychology, it is concerned with discovering the internal forces
which explain and determine the conduct of an individual.
But the comparison stops there. While the sociologist seeks
to formulate the laws inherent in its very nature which
regulate social existence—or, if one wishes, *in abstracto*—the
historian devotes himself to acquiring concrete knowledge
of this existence during its span. What he desires is to understand it thoroughly: trace in it all vicissitudes, describe
its particular characteristics, bring out all that has happened in the course of the ages to make of it what it has
in reality been. For him, chance and the deeds of prominent personalities, of which the sociologist cannot take account, constitute the essential data of his subject. In other
words, the sociologist seeks to separate the typical and the
general, while for the historian the typical and the general

* In *Methods in Social Science,* ed. by Stuart A. Rice (Chicago
1931), pp. 435–45; reprinted by kind permission of Mr. Rice.

are only the canvas upon which life has painted perpetually changing scenes. The former uses facts only with a view to the elaboration of a theory; the latter considers them as the episodes of a great adventure about which he must tell.

The sociologist is not concerned with the perturbing rôles of those who have taken prominent parts in affairs and must therefore be considered by the historian. For the latter, Alexander the Great, Caesar, Cromwell, Washington, or Napoleon I are subjects for study of the same value as a system of institutions or an economic organism. Here his task is allied to that of the psychologist, for in order to explain the feats of these "heroes" a knowledge of their minds is imperative. But here also the same difference is perceived between the psychologist and the historian as between the historian and the sociologist. For the psychologist the study of a great man's soul is merely a contribution to the general knowledge of the human soul, while this study is necessary for the historian only by virtue of the influence exerted by this man upon his contemporaries. Great as the genius of an individual may be, the historian concerns himself with him only if he has influenced other men.

Although sociology and psychology are sciences allied to history, it is no less true that they are clearly distinguished from it as much by their fields as by their methods.

In the same way that sociology takes for its subject *all* social phenomena, and psychology *all* psychological phenomena, history has for its subject *all* historical phenomena. In its chosen sphere, it presents the same character of universality as do the other sciences, whether they be human or natural sciences. It is universal in the same way as is chemistry or physics—in the sense that, like physics and chemistry, it lays claim to a knowledge of the ensemble of phenomena which constitute its subject. The historical concept necessarily implies the universal historical concept. It does not matter that in the present state of our knowledge enormous portions of history are still totally unknown, just as innumerable natural phenomena take place of which we are ignorant. It matters still less that no historian consecrates himself to the study of universal history, just as no chemist or physicist devotes himself to the study of the entire field of chemistry or physics. What is important is to have for an ideal the unity of science; similarly, to bear clearly in mind that all historical work is only a contribution to the history of human societies conceived as a whole, and that the value of historical work consists in the degree to which it promotes the advancement of history as a whole. Specialization is here only a necessity resulting from the inferiority of man's capacities. Although no man can know everything, everyone ought nevertheless to work with a view to enriching the common treasury of knowledge, and in the degree to which he is conscious of this collaboration, the result of his effort will endure and be useful.

In pursuance of the goal he has chosen, the historian finds himself confronted with a double task. He must first of all establish the facts which constitute the materials of his study, then make use of them. His method consists essentially in these two processes; in following them out he answers the question which serves as title for this article. Both result from the nature of history. Since history has been written, both have been applied consciously or unconsciously. Fundamentally, history presents itself to us as it did to our predecessors. Our present progress is only the effect which general scientific progress has had upon the work of historians. We possess processes and methods of research of which Herodotus or chroniclers of the Middle Ages were ignorant, and in the explanation of events we use a quantity of ideas and a skill in criticism of which they had no idea. We find in history an amplitude and a depth which they did not suspect. But our method of working is only an improvement on theirs.

## II

Historical facts are perceptible only by the vestiges which they have left. In this respect, the position of the historian vis-à-vis his subject is quite comparable to that of the geologist. The revolutions of men, like those of the earth, would be unknown if vestiges of their existence did not remain. But it is much easier to restore the picture of the latter than that of the former. The texture of the earth's surface is directly visible to the geologist; he can measure and analyze the material in it, and he knows that the elements of which it is composed act in conformity with the laws of mechanics, physics, and chemistry. The historian, on the contrary, only rarely finds himself face to face with an authentic fragment of the past. Almost always the monuments which have survived have been seriously altered either by the effect of time or by the hand of man which sought to demolish or restore. Nor can restoration reproduce an original state; too many factors due to individual genius, to need, to the circumstances of the moment—in short, to that imponderable which is human personality—have contributed to their construction for their genesis to be describable with the same accuracy as if they were the result of forces of nature. And how many difficulties are not raised in another way by the date, the origin, the nationality of an artifact which archaeologists' excavations or chance have revealed.

Thus even in the most favorable case the historian cannot deceive himself into thinking that he is observing the past directly. But the difficulties of his task are much greater when he works with written documents. Of all the sources of history, they are at once the most valuable and the most fallacious. The very way in which they have come down to us has almost always changed them more or less seriously. When we have the rare good fortune to possess the original text, its state of preservation generally makes its deciphering more or less difficult—torn, or disfigured as it usually is by words left out, smudges, or words written over others. But in most cases the original has disappeared. To reconstitute the text we have at our disposal mere copies, and often only copies of copies, all in some measure spoiled by negligence, ignorance, or the untrustworthiness of the copyist. But let us assume that this task is accomplished; other problems present themselves. It is important to know the origin of the document, to establish the exact date, to determine its degree of authenticity. Mistakes abound in all epochs, and individuals or governments have invented or modified texts to suit their interests.

Thus the materials to which the historian is reduced require singularly difficult and delicate treatment before they are ready for use. They are merely the vestiges of events and not even authentic vestiges. One might compare them with footprints in the sand which wind and rain have half-effaced. To reproduce even an approximation of the picture, arduous and minute work is indispensable.

This work involves different processes according to the special nature of the sources to which it is applied. These are the processes which, constantly being improved by use, have given rise to what are called the "auxiliary sciences of history." From the criticism of inscriptions is born epigraphy; from that of writings, paleography; from that of charters and deeds, diplomatics, or the art of deciphering documents; from that of monuments, archaeology; from that of money, numismatics; from that of seals, sigillography; from that of armorial bearings, heraldry. Each of these constitutes a particular application of historical criticism. And to each of these also are devoted, to the common advantage of science, specialized scholars. Of all historians, these specialists are the most favorably situated from the point of view of the results of their work. Thanks to the homogeneous character of the objects which they study, it is possible for them to establish methods of observation of such precision that conclusions often result in a probability so great as to border on certainty. But after all, perfected as the methods may be, it would be quite erroneous to believe that they do not leave a very large rôle to the tact, finesse, and intuition of the user. The most exact among them—epigraphy and diplomatics—are based in fact only upon empirical observations, and the regularity of the facts which they establish has nothing in common with the rigor of the laws which result from the natural sciences.

The complicated processes of source criticism which have been briefly indicated constitute only the prelude to the work of historians. After they furnish the evidence it must be evaluated. In other words, the criticism of authenticity must be followed by that of credibility. One sees at a glance that the second is infinitely more delicate and subjective than the first. In fact, it depends no longer upon the external character of the proofs but upon the personalities of their

authors. It is no longer a question of identifying the document but of judging its value. And this judgment depends
necessarily upon the training, the intelligence, and the
honor of the witness, as well as upon the circumstances
which surrounded the gathering of his evidence. Not only
is it indispensable to understand thoroughly what he
wanted to say but to extract from his words whatever of
truth lies in them.

Let us admit at once that it is impossible to be entirely
successful. Most often one cannot flatter himself that he has
even understood perfectly what the author of the document
wanted to say. For even when very familiar with the language used, one can never determine with sufficient exactitude the particular nuance which it has taken on under the
author's pen. To discover the real meaning which lies behind his words, one would have to identify one's self completely with him and to relive his life. That is, his personality
intervenes between us and the facts. And this interposition
transforms them. They suffer a distortion analogous to that
of the reflection of an object plunged in water. But easy as
it is to reconstitute the real appearance of the submerged
object, thanks to the laws of refraction of light, one can
only guess very roughly at the changes which historical narratives have inflicted upon reality. One has to be content
with examining the incomplete information at his disposal
as to the author's biography, his individual or national prejudices, his environment, and the conditions under which he
wrote. It goes without saying that all this can be obtained
only very approximately and insufficiently.

For the majority of events we fortunately possess more
than one proof. Although our evaluation of each proof is
necessarily defective, from the comparison of these judgments it is possible to deduce some true semblance of the
reality which otherwise disappears as each gives his own
account of it. Historical criticism can thus arrive at an approximate representation of past facts. It perceives them in
the wavering outline of objects which appear to us in mist.

Even of these inexact pictures of historical realities, we
possess relatively few. Whatever in the way of monuments
and writings has come down to us from preceding ages is

almost nothing in comparison with what has disappeared. Historians are only too happy today to glean in the sands of the Fayum some miserable débris from the libraries and archives of the hellenized cities of Egypt. Of millions of documents drawn up by the bureaucracies of the Roman and the Byzantine empires only a few remain. What will be left to our successors from our books made of wood-pulp and our stenographic copies? Moreover, even if we had conserved all that had been written about an event, we could not pretend to complete information. No account, detailed as it may be, ever exhausts its subject. The fulness of reality can never be expressed either by speech or by pen.

In spite of all his efforts, therefore, the historian cannot gain an adequate knowledge of what has been. Realizing this limitation, he resigns himself to it. He accepts the limits which the very conditions of the knowledge of real history impose upon written history. To perceive the facts in the measure in which this is possible must suffice. Although in relation to the absolute this is not much, it is still a great deal from the viewpoint of man.

The account of perceivable historical facts is still infinitely far from being complete. Enormous gaps appear in it at first glance. Of many peoples and nations—China, for example—we are almost entirely ignorant. We are certain also that innumerable products of human art and industry remain buried in the ground and that in spite of archaeological expeditions actively and successfully conducted today it is impossible to exhume all. As for written documents, besides a large part of these which are contained in the archives and public libraries—not yet studied—how many are concealed by unknown possessors of which we do not even suspect the existence? It is also necessary to take into account all the evidence surrounding us that we cannot perceive. The vocabulary of dead or living languages, names of places, customs, popular traditions, costumes, superstitions, and religious beliefs contain treasures which philology, topical nomenclature, and folk lore are far from having exhausted. Let us note finally that the development of historical work has resulted in the establishment of facts, knowledge of which came only from reasoning. To take a very

simple example—the historian can determine the unknown
date of the birth of a person if he knows that it was contemporary with an event of whose chronology he is certain.
Thus by hypothesis he adds a new fact to those already
known and enriches by one simple intellectual process our
knowledge of the past. This procedure is so frequent that
its application can be noted on almost every page of historical works. One would not be mistaken in saying that a
considerable portion of historical data has no other foundation than conjecture and is certified by no source; thus the
mass of the materials of science increases in proportion to
the progress of criticism.

It would be an error to conclude that it is necessary to
postpone writing history until all the materials are assembled. They will never all be assembled insomuch as they
will never all be known. Naturalists do not insist upon knowing *all* the phenomena of nature before formulating conclusions. No more can the historian abstain from making a
synthesis on the pretext that he does not possess all the
elements of his synthesis. We require nothing more or less
of him than that he utilize all the data at his disposal at
the moment.

### III

Historical construction, the utilization of facts, is the inevitable result of all the processes of criticism that we have
rapidly reviewed. They have meaning and value only
through it; they are only the means to the end.

To construct history is to narrate it. From its first existence it has consisted in narratives, that is, the telling of a
succession of related episodes. Indeed, the essential work
of the historian is to bring these episodes to light, to show
the relations existing between events, and in relating to explain them. Thus it appears that history is the expository
narration of the course of human societies in the past.

All historical narrative is at once a synthesis and a hypothesis. It is a synthesis insomuch as it combines the mass
of known facts in an account of the whole; it is a hypothesis
insomuch as the relations that it establishes between these

facts are neither evident nor verifiable by themselves. To unite the facts into an ensemble and relate them is in practice one and the same process. For it goes without saying that the grouping of facts will differ according to the idea one wants to give of their relation. Everything then depends upon this—as we are about to see—and upon the degree of creative imagination of the historian and upon his general conception of human affairs. This amounts to saying that in its highest and most essential expression history is a conjectural science, or, in other words, a subjective science.

This does not mean that it is at the mercy of fantasy and arbitrary procedures. It proceeds according to a method, but according to a method which its very subject obliges it to renew constantly. The historian is no less critical in making use of facts than in the study of sources, but the complexity of his task forces him here to have recourse in a much larger measure to conjecture.

All historical construction—which amounts to saying all historical narrative—rests upon a postulate: that of the eternal identity of human nature. One cannot comprehend men's actions at all unless one assumes in the beginning that their physical and moral beings have been at all periods what they are today. Past societies would remain unintelligible to us if the natural needs which they experienced and the psychical forces which stimulated them were qualitatively different from ours. How are the innumerable differences that humanity presents in time and space to be explained if one does not consider them as changing nuances of a reality which is in its essence always and everywhere the same?

The historian assumes, therefore, that he can treat the actions of the dead as he does those of the living who surround him. And this comparison suffices to make comprehensible the subjective element in his accounts. For to reason about men's actions is to trace them back to their motives and to attribute consequences to them. But where are these motives and consequences to be found if not in the mind of him who does the reasoning? Observers differ not only according to variations in intelligence but also in

the depth and the variety of their knowledge. It is by intelligence that Thucydides is a greater historian than Xeno-
phon, and Machiavelli than Froissart. But it is by the extent
of knowledge that modern historians have the advantage
over those of antiquity and the Middle Ages. They doubtless do not surpass their predecessors in point of vigor and
penetration of mind; but by the variety of their knowledge
they discover relationships between men's acts which have
escaped the former.

For long centuries the destinies of societies were explained only by the intervention of some deity and the influence of great men. History appeared essentially as drama.
Farsighted minds, Polybius, for example, perceived the importance of institutions in the activity of the state. But
taken all in all, history, even in the case of the most eminent
authors, was only the narration and the explanation of political events. The advance of the moral and social sciences
has made the narrowness and insufficiency of this conception apparent. What these sciences teach us about all sorts
of factors—religious, ethnic, geographic, economic—which
have determined the development of societies at various
epochs, has necessarily contributed to the understanding of
a mass of phenomena which formerly passed unnoticed.
The knowledge of social relations being inordinately aug-
mented, historians are in a position to discover between the
facts of the past a multitude of relations which were never
before taken into account. They consider the history of
much more remote periods than were formerly included,
and from their vantage point they discover infinitely more
variation, fulness, and life. One can say with strict accuracy
that with much less material at our disposal than Roman
and Greek historians had, we know Greek and Roman history better than they did. We know it better and yet we
are not in agreement about it at all, any more than we are
about any other part of history.

To achieve certainty about a subject as flowing, diverse,
and complex as social behavior is impossible. Each kind of
activity reacts upon all others. How, then, distinguish in the
ensemble the part taken by each? How evaluate exactly the
rôle which, for example, the economic or the religious factor

has played in a given evolution? The conditions indispensable to all really scientific knowledge—calculation and measurement—are completely lacking in this field. And the interference of chance and individuals increases still more the difficulty of the historian's task by constantly confronting him with the unforeseen, by changing at every moment the direction which events seemed to take.

Not to historical method but to the subjects with which history is concerned must be imputed the historians' want of precision and the fact that their results seem uncertain and contradictory. The human actions which they study cannot appear the same to different historians. It needs only a moment of reflection to understand that two historians using the same material will not treat it in an identical fashion, primarily because the creative imagination which permits them to single the factors of movements out of chaos varies, but also because they do not have the same ideas as to the relative importance of the motives which determine men's conduct. They will inevitably write accounts which will contrast as do their personalities, depending upon the relative value they place on individual action or on the influence of collective phenomena; and, among these, on the emphasis they place on the economic, the religious, the ethnic, or the political factor. To this first cause of divergence we must add others. Historians are not conditioned in various ways solely by inherited qualities; their milieu is also important. Their religion, nationality, and social class influence them more or less profoundly. And the same is true of the period in which they work. Each epoch has its needs and tendencies which demand the attention of students and lead them to concentrate on this or that problem.

Thus, historical syntheses depend to a very large degree not only upon the personality of their authors but upon all the social, religious, or national environments which surround them. It follows, therefore, that each historian will establish between the facts relationships determined by the convictions, the movements, and the prejudices that have molded his point of view. All historical narrative is, as we have said, a hypothesis. It is an attempt at explanation, a conjectural reconstitution of the past. Each author throws light on some part, brings certain features into relief, considers certain aspects. The more these accounts multiply, the more the infinite reality is freed from its veils. All these accounts are incomplete, all imperfect, but all contribute to the advancement of knowledge. Those whose results have passed out of date have served to elaborate others which are in their turn replaced. For, in order that history may progress, the parallel development of synthesis and source criticism is indispensable. Without criticism synthesis would be only a sterile play of the imagination, and criticism would be merely dead erudition if it did not continually enlarge the field of its investigation and open new roads by the problems which it raises and the conjectures to which it gives birth.

We must believe, moreover, that in the measure in which the field is enlarged the work of historians will be accomplished under more satisfactory conditions. Up to the present time it has touched only a very restricted part of the immense subject which concerns it. In the field of ancient history, Greece and Rome; and in more modern times, the various national histories have attracted the efforts of investigators almost exclusively. Only today have we begun to discover the Orient, and we know what a transformation has consequently taken place in our comprehension of ancient history. Hellenic and Roman genius, in the dim light of records coming from Crete, Syria, Babylon, and Egypt, appear today as results of contact and interpenetration among different civilizations.

The comparative method alone can diminish racial, political, and national prejudices among historians. These prejudices inevitably ensnare him who, confined within the narrow limits of national history, is condemned to understand it badly because he is incapable of comprehending the bonds attaching it to the histories of other nations. It is not due to *parti pris* but because of insufficient information that so many historians lack impartiality. One who is lost in admiration of his own people will inevitably exaggerate their originality and give them the honor for discoveries which are in reality only borrowed. He is unjust to others because he fails to understand them, and the exclusiveness of his knowledge lays him open to the deceptions of the idols set up by sentiment. The comparative method permits history to appear in its true perspective. What was believed to be a mountain is razed to the size of a molehill, and the thing for which national genius was honored is often revealed as a simple manifestation of the imitative spirit. But the point of view of comparative history is none other than that of universal history. Therefore to the degree in which history is viewed in the totality of its development, and in which one accustoms himself to study particular or national histories in the functioning of general evolution, will the weaknesses inherent in historical method be diminished. It will attain the maximum precision which its subject permits when the final goal is clearly perceived by its adepts to be the scientific elaboration of universal history.

### 2.

*Pirenne concludes with an appeal to "the comparative method," extended to a universal history of mankind, as the only means for diminishing "racial, political, and national prejudices among historians." Though different in detail,[1] this is, in principle, similar to the comparative method employed by Professor Toynbee in* A Study of History. *Toynbee has written a universal history by collecting and comparing twenty-one "societies" of his own choosing which differ sharply from the ordinary national, cultural, or periodic divisions employed in other historical works. These societies, according to Toynbee, are the only "intelligible fields" of historical study. In their totality, they comprise the history of mankind.*

*I have included the first chapter of Toynbee's well-known work as an interesting statement of this question—*

[1] For another statement of the "comparative method" advanced by French historians, cf. the article "History" by Henri Berr and Lucien Febvre in *The Encyclopedia of the Social Sciences* (IV), pp. 357–68.

*not otherwise discussed in these pages: what are the basic
units or divisions, in world history, and why?*[2] *This question
has more than professional interest. It raises the general issue of what is the subject matter of history, or of what
does it mean to assign historical "reality" to such vast, collective units as Professor Toynbee has chosen. It also has
a direct bearing upon the problem of historical explanation;
for it obviously makes a great deal of difference which
"units" we choose, and why, in order to explain historical
processes.*

*I have added a brief section called "History, Science and
Fiction" as Professor Toynbee's contribution to the general
topic discussed in this part. According to him, there are two
factors which limit the "application of the scientific technique to history": (1) The comparable units of history are
too few for valid generalizations. (2) Popular opinion is
right in holding that "no historian can be 'great' if he is
not also a great artist." History, I think, does differ in this
respect from other scientific disciplines: the excellence of
historical works is measured not only in terms of the "truth"
of its statements, but also in terms of the aesthetic quality
of its writing. To put it more precisely, the "truth" of a
historical work is more directly and intimately linked with
the "art" of its writing than in the generalizing sciences.*[3]
*This point throws another light upon the role played by
what Collingwood called the historical imagination as
against ordinary inductive inferences.*

[2] For a reference to Toynbee's work, see Professor Niebuhr's
article, Part IV, p. 313 ff. below. For the most careful, critical
analysis of *A Study of History,* cf. Pieter Geyl, *Debates with
Historians* (London 1955).

[3] For a similar sentiment, see G. M. Trevelyan, "Clio, a Muse,"
reprinted in F. Stern, *The Varieties of History* (pp. 227–45);
cf. also the comments by Professor Bullock, p. 298 below.

## *ARNOLD J. TOYNBEE*

## A. THE UNIT OF HISTORICAL STUDY*

Historians generally illustrate rather than correct the ideas of the communities within which they live and work, and the development in the last few centuries, and more particularly in the last few generations, of the would-be self-sufficient national sovereign state has led historians to choose nations as the normal fields of historical study. But no single nation or national state of Europe can show a history which is in itself self-explanatory. If any state could do so it would be Great Britain. In fact, if Great Britain (or, in the earlier periods, England) is not found to constitute in herself an intelligible field of historical study, we may confidently infer that no other modern European national state will pass the test.

Is English history, then, intelligible when taken by itself? Can we abstract an internal history of England from her external relations? If we can, shall we find that these residual external relations are of secondary importance? And in analysing these, again, shall we find that the foreign influences upon England are slight in comparison with the English influences upon other parts of the world? If all these questions receive affirmative answers we may be justified in concluding that, while it may not be possible to understand other histories without reference to England, it is possible, more or less, to understand English history without reference to other parts of the world. The best way to approach these questions is to direct our thought backwards over the course of English history and recall the principal chapters. In inverse order we may take these chapters to be:

* In *A Study of History;* abridgment of Vols. I–VI by D. C. Somervell (New York & London: Oxford University Press, 1947), pp. 1–11; reprinted by permission of the Oxford University Press. For the following selection, ibid., pp. 43–47. I have deleted the last sentence in both sections. H.M.

(a) the establishment of the Industrial System of economy (since the last quarter of the eighteenth century);

(b) the establishment of Responsible Parliamentary Government (since the last quarter of the seventeenth century);

(c) the expansion overseas (beginning in the third quarter of the sixteenth century with piracy and developing gradually into a world-wide foreign trade, the acquisition of tropical dependencies, and the establishment of new English-speaking communities in overseas countries with temperate climates);

(d) the Reformation (since the second quarter of the sixteenth century);

(e) the Renaissance, including the political and economic as well as the artistic and intellectual aspects of the movement (since the last quarter of the fifteenth century);

(f) the establishment of the Feudal System (since the eleventh century);

(g) the conversion of the English from the religion of the so-called Heroic Age to Western Christianity (since the last years of the sixth century).

This glance backwards from the present day over the general course of English history would appear to show that the farther back we look the less evidence do we find of self-sufficiency or isolation. The conversion, which was really the beginning of all things in English history, was the direct antithesis of that; it was an act which merged half a dozen isolated communities of barbarians in the common weal of a nascent Western Society. As for the Feudal System, Vinogradoff has brilliantly demonstrated that the seeds of it had already sprouted on English soil before the Norman Conquest. Yet, even so, the sprouting was stimulated by an external factor, the Danish invasions; these invasions were part of the Scandinavian *Völkerwanderung* which was stimulating simultaneously a similar growth in France, and the Norman Conquest undoubtedly brought the harvest to rapid maturity. As for the Renaissance, in both its cultural and its political aspect it is universally admitted to have been a breath of life from Northern Italy. If in Northern Italy Humanism, Absolutism and the Bal-

ance of Power had not been cultivated in miniature, like
seedlings in a sheltered nursery garden, during two centuries that fall approximately between 1275 and 1475, they
could never have been bedded out north of the Alps from
about 1475 onwards. The Reformation, again, was not a
specifically English phenomenon, but a general movement
of North-Western Europe for emancipation from the South,
where the Western Mediterranean held the eye fixed upon
worlds that were dead and gone. In the Reformation, England did not take the initiative, nor did she take it in the
competition between the European nations of the Atlantic
seaboard for the prize of the new worlds overseas. She won
that prize as a comparatively late comer, in a series of struggles with Powers that were before her in the field.

It remains to consider the two latest chapters: the geneses
of the Parliamentary System and the Industrial System—
institutions which are commonly regarded as having been
evolved locally on English soil and afterwards propagated
from England into other parts of the world. But the authorities do not entirely support this view. With reference to
the parliamentary system Lord Acton says: 'General history
naturally depends on the action of forces which are not
national but proceed from wider causes. The rise of modern
kingship in France is part of a similar movement in England. Bourbons and Stuarts obeyed the same law though
with different results.' In other words the Parliamentary
System, which was the local result in England, was the
product of a force which was not peculiar to England but
was operating simultaneously in England and France.

On the genesis of the Industrial Revolution in England
no higher authorities could be cited than Mr. and Mrs.
Hammond. In the preface to their book *The Rise of Modern
Industry* they take the view that the factor which goes farthest towards accounting for the genesis of the Industrial
Revolution in England rather than elsewhere is England's
general position in the eighteenth-century world—her geographical position in relation to the Atlantic and her political position in respect of the European balance of power.
It seems, then, that British national history never has been,
and almost certainly never will be, an 'intelligible field of

historical study' in isolation; and if that is true of Great
Britain it surely must be true of any other national state
*a fortiori.*

Our brief examination of English history, though its result has been negative, has given us a clue. The chapters
which caught our eye in our glance backward over the
course of English history were real chapters in some story
or other, but that story was the history of some society of
which Great Britain was only a part, and the experiences
were experiences in which other nations besides Great Britain were participants. The 'intelligible field of study', in
fact, appears to be a society containing a number of communities of the species represented by Great Britain—not
only Great Britain herself but also France and Spain, the
Netherlands, the Scandinavian countries and so on—and the
passage quoted from Acton indicates the relation between
these parts and that whole.

The forces in action are not national but proceed from
wider causes, which operate upon each of the parts and
are not intelligible in their partial operation unless a comprehensive view is taken of their operation throughout the
society. Different parts are differently affected by an identical general cause, because they each react, and each contribute, in a different way to the forces which that same
cause sets in motion. A society, we may say, is confronted
in the course of its life by a succession of problems which
each member has to solve for itself as best it may. The
presentation of each problem is a challenge to undergo an
ordeal, and through this series of ordeals the members of
the society progressively differentiate themselves from one
another. Throughout, it is impossible to grasp the significance of any particular member's behaviour under a particular ordeal without taking some account of the similar
or dissimilar behaviour of its fellows and without viewing
the successive ordeals as a series of events in the life of the
whole society.

This method of interpreting historical facts may, perhaps, be made clearer by a concrete example, which may
be taken from the history of the city states of Ancient

Greece during the four centuries falling between 725 and 325 B.C.

Soon after the beginning of that period the society of which these numerous states were all members was confronted with the problem of the pressure of population upon the means of subsistence—means which the Hellenic peoples at that time were apparently obtaining almost entirely by raising in their territories a varied agricultural produce for home consumption. When the crisis came, different states contended with it in different ways.

Some, like Corinth and Chalcis, disposed of their surplus population by seizing and colonizing agricultural territories overseas—in Sicily, Southern Italy, Thrace and elsewhere. The Greek colonies thus founded simply extended the geographical area of the Hellenic Society without altering its character. On the other hand certain states sought solutions which entailed a variation of their way of life.

Sparta, for instance, satisfied the land-hunger of her citizens by attacking and conquering her nearest Greek neighbours. The consequence was that Sparta only obtained her additional lands at the cost of obstinate and repeated wars with neighbouring peoples of her own calibre. In order to meet this situation Spartan statesmen were compelled to militarize Spartan life from top to bottom, which they did by re-invigorating and adapting certain primitive social institutions, common to a number of Greek communities, at a moment when, at Sparta as elsewhere, these institutions were on the point of disappearance.

Athens reacted to the population problem in a different way again. She specialized her agricultural production for export, started manufactures also for export and then developed her political institutions so as to give a fair share of political power to the new classes which had been called into being by these economic innovations. In other words, Athenian statesmen averted a social revolution by successfully carrying through an economic and political revolution; and, discovering this solution of the common problem in so far as it affected themselves, they incidentally opened up a new avenue of advance for the whole of the Hellenic Society. This is what Pericles meant when, in the crisis of his own city's material fortunes, he claimed that she was 'the education of Hellas'.

From this angle of vision, which takes not Athens or Sparta or Corinth or Chalcis but the whole of the Hellenic Society as its field, we are able to understand both the significance of the histories of the several communities during the period 725–325 B.C. and the significance of the transition from this period to that which followed. Questions are answered to which no intelligible answer could be found so long as we looked for an intelligible field of study in Chalcidian, Corinthian, Spartan or Athenian history examined in isolation. From this point of view it was merely possible to observe that Chalcidian and Corinthian history was in some sense normal whereas Spartan and Athenian history departed from the norm in different directions. It was not possible to explain the way in which this departure took place, and historians were reduced to suggesting that the Spartans and Athenians were already differentiated from the other Greeks by the possession of special innate qualities at the dawn of Hellenic history. This was equivalent to explaining Spartan and Athenian development by postulating that there had been no development at all and that these two Greek peoples were as peculiar at the beginning of the story as at the end of it. That hypothesis, however, is in contradiction with established facts. In regard to Sparta, for example, the excavations conducted by the British Archaeological School at Athens have produced striking evidence that down to about the middle of the sixth century B.C. Spartan life was not markedly different from that of other Greek communities. The special characteristics of Athens also, which she communicated to the whole Hellenic World in the so-called Hellenistic Age (in contrast to Sparta, whose peculiar turning proved to be a blind alley), were likewise acquired characteristics, the genesis of which can only be apprehended from a general standpoint. It is the same with the differentiation between Venice, Milan, Genoa and other cities of Northern Italy in the so-called Middle Ages and with the differentiation between France, Spain, the Netherlands, Great Britain and other national states of the West in more recent times. In order to understand the parts we must first focus our attention upon the whole, because this whole is the field of study that is intelligible in itself.

But what are these 'wholes', which form intelligible fields of study, and how shall we discover their spatial and temporal boundaries? Let us turn again to our summary of the principal chapters of English history, and see what larger whole is found to constitute the intelligible field of which English history is a part.

If we start with our latest chapter—the establishment of the Industrial System—we find that the geographical extension of the intelligible field of study which it presupposes is world-wide. In order to explain the Industrial Revolution in England we have to take account of economic conditions not only in Western Europe but in Tropical Africa, America, Russia, India and the Far East. When, however, we go back to the Parliamentary System and pass, in so doing, from the economic to the political plane, our horizon contracts. 'The law' which (in Lord Acton's phrase) 'Bourbons and Stuarts obeyed' in France and England was not in force for Romanovs in Russia or 'Osmanlis in Turkey or Timurids in Hindustan or Manchus in China or Tokugawas in Japan. The political histories of these other countries cannot be explained in the same terms. We here come up against a frontier. The operation of 'the law' which 'Bourbons and Stuarts obeyed' extended to the other countries of Western Europe and to the new communities planted overseas by West-European colonists, but its writ did not run beyond the western frontiers of Russia and Turkey. East of that line other political laws were being obeyed at that time with other consequences.

If we pass back to the earlier chapters of English history on our list, we find that the expansion overseas was confined not merely to Western Europe but almost entirely to the countries with seaboards on the Atlantic. In studying the history of the Reformation and the Renaissance we may ignore without loss the religious and cultural developments in Russia and Turkey. The feudal system of Western Europe was not causally connected with such feudal phenom-

ena as were to be found in contemporary Byzantine and
Islamic communities.

Finally, the conversion of the English to Western Christianity admitted us to one society at the cost of excluding
us from the possibility of membership in others. Down to
the Synod of Whitby in 664 the English might have become converts to the 'Far Western Christianity' of 'the
Celtic Fringe'; and, had Augustine's mission ultimately
proved a failure, the English might have joined the Welsh
and Irish in founding a new Christian church out of com-
munion with Rome—as veritable an *alter orbis* as the world
of the Nestorians on the Far Eastern fringe of Christendom.
Later on, when the Muslim Arabs appeared on the Atlantic
seaboard, these Far Western Christians of the British Isles
might have lost touch as completely as the Christians of
Abyssinia or Central Asia with their co-religionists on the
European Continent. They might conceivably have become
converts to Islam, as so many Monophysites and Nestorians
actually did when the Middle East passed under Arab rule.
These suggested alternatives might be dismissed as fantastic, but the contemplation of them serves to remind us that
while the conversion of 597 has made us one with Western
Christendom it has not made us one with all mankind, but
has simultaneously made a sharp line of division between
ourselves as Western Christians and the adherents of other
religious communions.

This second review of our chapters of English history has
given us a means for taking spatial cross-sections, at several
different dates, of that society which includes Great Britain
and which is 'the intelligible field of historical study' as far
as Great Britain is concerned. In taking these cross-sections
we shall have to distinguish between certain different planes
of social life—the economic, the political and the cultural
—because it is already evident that the spatial extension of
this society differs perceptibly according to the plane on
which we focus our attention. At the present day and on
the economic plane the society which includes Great Britain is undoubtedly co-extensive with the whole inhabitable
and navigable surface of the Earth. On the political plane,
again, the world-wide character of this society at the

present day is almost equally apparent. When, however, we pass to the cultural plane the present geographical extension of the society to which Great Britain belongs appears to be very much smaller. Substantially, it is confined to the countries occupied by Catholic and Protestant peoples in Western Europe, America and the South Seas. In spite of certain exotic influences exercised on this society by such cultural elements as Russian literature, Chinese painting and Indian religion, and in spite of the much stronger cultural influences exercised by our own society on other societies, such as those of the Orthodox and Oriental Christians, the Muslims, the Hindus and the peoples of the Far East, it remains true that all of these are outside the cultural world to which we belong.

As we take further cross-sections at earlier dates we find that, on all three planes, the geographical limits of the society which we are examining progressively contract. In a cross-section taken about the year 1675, while the contraction is not perhaps very great on the economic plane (at least if we confine ourselves to the extension of trade and ignore its volume and content), the boundaries on the political plane shrink until they coincide approximately with those on the cultural plane at the present day. In a cross-section taken about 1475 the overseas portions of the area disappear on all three planes alike, and even on the economic plane the boundaries contract until they, too, coincide approximately with those on the cultural plane, now confined to Western and Central Europe—except for a fast dissolving chain of outposts on the eastern shores of the Mediterranean. In a primitive cross-section, taken about the year 775, the boundaries shrink still further on all three planes. At that date the area of our society is almost restricted to what were then the dominions of Charlemagne together with the English 'successor states' of the Roman Empire in Britain. Outside these limits, almost all the Iberian Peninsula belongs at this date to the domain of the Muslim Arab Caliphate; Northern and North-Eastern Europe is in the hands of unconverted barbarians; the northwestern fringes of the British Isles are held by the 'Far

Western' Christians; and Southern Italy is under the rule of the Byzantines.

Let us call this society, whose spatial limits we have been studying, Western Christendom; and, as soon as we bring our mental image of it into focus by finding a name for it, the images and names of its counterparts in the contemporary world come into focus side by side with it, especially if we keep our attention fixed upon the cultural plane. On this plane we can distinguish unmistakably the presence in the world to-day of at least four other living societies of the same species as ours:

(i) an Orthodox Christian Society in South-Eastern Europe and Russia;

(ii) an Islamic Society with its focus in the arid zone which stretches diagonally across North Africa and the Middle East from the Atlantic to the outer face of the Great Wall of China;

(iii) a Hindu Society in the tropical sub-continent of India;

(iv) a Far-Eastern Society in the sub-tropical and temperate regions between the arid zone and the Pacific.

On closer inspection we can also discern two sets of what appear to be fossilized relics of similar societies now extinct, namely: one set including the Monophysite Christians of Armenia, Mesopotamia, Egypt and Abyssinia and the Nestorian Christians of Kurdistan and ex-Nestorians in Malabar, as well as the Jews and the Parsees; and a second set including the Lamaistic Mahayanian Buddhists of Tibet and Mongolia and the Hinayanian Buddhists of Ceylon, Burma, Siam and Cambodia, as well as the Jains of India.

It is interesting to notice that when we turn back to the cross-section at A.D. 775 we find that the number and identity of the societies on the world map are nearly the same as at the present time. Substantially the world map of societies of this species has remained constant since the first emergence of our Western Society. In the struggle for existence the West has driven its contemporaries to the wall and entangled them in the meshes of its economic and political ascendancy, but it has not yet disarmed them of their distinctive cultures. Hard pressed though they are, they can still call their souls their own.

The conclusion of the argument, as far as we have carried it at present, is that we should draw a sharp distinction between relations of two kinds: those between communities within the same society and those of different societies with one another.

And now, having explored the extension of our Western Society in space, we have to consider its extension in time; and we are at once confronted with the fact that we cannot know its future—a limitation which greatly restricts the amount of light that the study of this particular society, or of any of the still extant societies, can throw on the nature of the species to which these societies belong. We must content ourselves with the exploration of our Western Society's beginnings.

When Charlemagne's dominions were partitioned between his three grandsons by the treaty of Verdun in A.D. 843, Lothaire, as the eldest, established his claim to possess his grandfather's two capitals of Aachen and Rome; and, in order that these might be connected by a continuous belt of territory, Lothaire was assigned a portion which straggled across the face of Western Europe from the mouths of the Tiber and Po to the mouth of the Rhine. Lothaire's portion is commonly regarded as one of the curiosities of historical geography; none the less the three Carolingian brothers were right in believing that it was a zone of particular importance in our Western World. Whatever its future might be, it had a great past behind it.

Both Lothaire and his grandfather ruled from Aachen to Rome under the title of Roman Emperor, and the line stretching from Rome across the Alps to Aachen (and onwards from Aachen across the Channel to the Roman Wall) had once been one of the principal bulwarks of the then extinct Roman Empire. By running a line of communications north-westwards from Rome across the Alps, establishing a military frontier on the left bank of the Rhine, and covering the left flank of that frontier by the annexation of Southern Britain, the Romans had cut off the western extremity of Transalpine Continental Europe and annexed

it to an empire which, except in this quarter, was substantially confined to the Mediterranean Basin. Thus the
line embedded in Lotharingia entered into the geographical
structure of the Roman Empire before Lothaire's time as
well as into that of the Western Society after it, but the
structural function of this line for the Roman Empire and
for the subsequent Western Society were not the same. In
the Roman Empire it had been a frontier; in our Western
Society it was to be a base-line for lateral expansion on
either side and in all directions. During the deep sleep of
the interval (*circa* A.D. 375–675) which intervened between the break-up of the Roman Empire and the gradual
emergence of our Western Society out of the chaos, a rib
was taken from the side of the older society and was
fashioned into the backbone of a new creature of the same
species.

It is now plain that in tracing the life of our Western
Society backwards behind 775 we begin to find it presented
to us in terms of something other than itself—in terms of
the Roman Empire and of the society to which that empire belonged. It can also be shown that any elements
which we can trace back from Western history into the
history of that earlier society may have quite different
functions in these two different associations.

Lothaire's portion became the base-line of the Western
Society because the Church, pushing up towards the Roman frontier, here encountered the Barbarians pressing
down upon the frontier from the no-man's-land outside, and
eventually gave birth to a new society. Accordingly, the
historian of the Western Society, in tracing its roots down
into the past from this point, will concentrate his attention
on the histories of the Church and the Barbarians, and he
will find it possible to follow both these histories backwards
as far as the economic, social and political revolutions of
the last two centuries B.C., into which the Graeco-Roman
Society was thrown by the vast shock of the Hannibalic
War. Why did Rome stretch out a long arm towards the
north-west and gather into her empire the western corner
of Transalpine Europe? Because she was drawn in that
direction by the life-and-death struggle with Carthage.

Why, having once crossed the Alps, did she stop at the Rhine? Because in the Augustan Age her vitality gave out after two centuries of exhausting wars and revolutions. Why did the Barbarians ultimately break through? Because, when a frontier between a more highly and a less highly civilized society ceases to advance, the balance does not settle down to a stable equilibrium but inclines, with the passage of time, in the more backward society's favour. Why, when the Barbarians broke through the frontier, did they encounter the Church on the other side? Materially, because the economic and social revolutions following the Hannibalic War had brought multitudes of slaves from the Oriental World to work on the devastated areas of the West, and this forced migration of Oriental labour had been followed by a peaceful penetration of Oriental religions into the Graeco-Roman Society. Spiritually, because these religions, with their promise of an 'other-worldly' personal salvation, found fallow fields to cultivate in the souls of a 'dominant minority' which had failed, in This World, to save the fortunes of the Graeco-Roman Society.

To the student of Graeco-Roman history, on the other hand, both the Christians and the Barbarians would present themselves as creatures of an alien underworld—the internal and the external proletariat,[1] as he might call them, of that Graeco-Roman (or, to use a better term, Hellenic) Society in its last phase. He would point out that the great masters of Hellenic culture, down to and including Marcus Aurelius, almost ignore their existence. He would diagnose both the Christian Church and the Barbarian warbands as morbid affections which only appeared in the body of the Hellenic Society after its physique had been permanently undermined by the Hannibalic War.

This investigation has enabled us to draw a positive conclusion regarding the backward extension in time of our Western Society. The life of that society, though somewhat longer than that of any single nation belonging to it, has not been so long as the span of time during which the

[1] The word 'proletariat' is here and hereafter used to mean any social element or group which in some way is *in* but not *of* any given society at any period of that society's history.

species of which it is a representative has been in existence. In tracing its history back to its origins we strike upon the last phase of another society, the origins of which obviously lie much farther back in the past. The continuity of history, to use an accepted phrase, is not a continuity such as is exemplified in the life of a single individual. It is rather a continuity made up of the lives of successive generations, our Western Society being related to the Hellenic Society in a manner comparable (to use a convenient though imperfect simile) with the relationship of a child to its parent.

If the argument of this chapter is accepted it will be agreed that the intelligible unit of historical study is neither a nation state nor (at the other end of the scale) mankind as a whole but a certain grouping of humanity which we have called a society. We have discovered five such societies in existence to-day, together with sundry fossilized evidences of societies dead and gone; and, while exploring the circumstances of the birth of one of these living societies, namely our own, we have stumbled upon the deathbed of another very notable society to which our own stands in something like the relation of offspring—to which, in a single word, our own society is 'affiliated'. . . .

## *ARNOLD J. TOYNBEE*

## B.  HISTORY, SCIENCE AND FICTION

There are three different methods of viewing and presenting the objects of our thought, and, among them, the phenomena of human life. The first is the ascertainment and recording of 'facts'; the second is the elucidation, through a comparative study of the facts ascertained, of general 'laws'; the third is the artistic re-creation of the facts in the form of 'fiction'. It is generally assumed that the ascertainment and recording of facts is the technique of history, and that the phenomena in the province of this technique are the social phenomena of civilizations; that the elucidation and formulation of general laws is the technique of science, and that, in the study of human life, the science is anthropology and the phenomena in the province of the scientific technique are the social phenomena of primitive societies; and, lastly, that fiction is the technique of the drama and the novel, and that the phenomena in the province of this technique are the personal relations of human beings. All this, in essentials, is to be found in the works of Aristotle.

The distribution of the three techniques between the three departments of study is, however, less watertight than might be supposed. History, for example, does not concern itself with the recording of all the facts of human life. It leaves alone the facts of social life in primitive societies, from which anthropology elucidates its 'laws'; and it hands over to biography the facts of individual lives—though nearly all individual lives that are of sufficient interest and importance to make them seem worth recording have been lived, not in primitive societies, but in one or other of those societies in process of civilization which are conventionally regarded as history's province. Thus history concerns itself with some but not all the facts of human life; and, on the other hand, besides recording facts, history also has recourse to fictions and makes use of laws.

History, like the drama and the novel, grew out of mythology, a primitive form of apprehension and expression in which—as in fairy tales listened to by children or in dreams dreamt by sophisticated adults—the line between fact and fiction is left undrawn. It has, for example, been said of the *Iliad* that anyone who starts reading it as history will find that it is full of fiction but, equally, anyone who starts reading it as fiction will find that it is full of history. All histories resemble the *Iliad* to this extent, that they cannot entirely dispense with the fictional element. The mere selection, arrangement and presentation of facts is a technique belonging to the field of fiction, and popular opinion is right in its insistence that no historian can be 'great' if he is not also a great artist; that the Gibbons and Macaulays are greater historians than the 'Dryasdusts' (a name coined by Sir Walter Scott—himself a greater historian in some of his novels than in any of his 'histories') who have avoided their more inspired confrères' factual inaccuracies. In any case, it is hardly possible to write two consecutive lines of historical narrative without introducing such fictitious personifications as 'England', 'France', 'the Conservative Party', 'the Church', 'the Press' or 'public opinion'. Thucydides[1] dramatized 'historical' personages by putting 'fictitious' speeches and dialogues into their mouths, but his *oratio recta,* while more vivid, is really no more fictional than the laboured *oratio obliqua* in which the moderns present their composite photographs of public opinion.

On the other hand history has taken into her service a number of ancillary sciences which formulate general laws not about primitive societies but about civilizations: e.g. economics, political science and sociology.

Though it is not necessary to our argument, we might demonstrate that, just as history is not innocent of using the techniques associated with science and fiction, so science and fiction by no means confine themselves to what are supposed to be their own techniques. All sciences pass through a stage in which the ascertainment and recording of facts is the only activity open to them, and the science of anthropology is only just emerging from that phase. Lastly, the drama and the novel do not present fictions, complete fictions and nothing but fictions regarding personal relationships. If they did, the product, instead of deserving Aristotle's commendation that it was 'truer and more philosophical than history', would consist of nonsensical and intolerable fantasies. When we call a piece of literature a work of fiction we mean no more than that the characters could not be identified with any persons who have lived in the flesh, nor the incidents with any particular events that have actually taken place. In fact, we mean that the work has a fictitious personal foreground; and, if we do not mention that the background is composed of authentic social facts, that is simply because this seems so

[1] Thucydides is generally accounted the first and one of the greatest of severely factual historians, but F. M. Cornford has demonstrated in *Thucydides Mythistoricus* that his whole presentation of his subject is governed by the conventions of contemporary Greek tragedy.

self-evident that we take it for granted. Indeed, we recognize that the highest praise we can give to a good work of fiction is to say that it is 'true to life', and that 'the author shows a profound understanding of human nature'. To be more particular: if the novel deals with a fictitious family of Yorkshire woollen-manufacturers, we might praise the author by saying that he evidently knows his West Riding mill-towns through and through.

None the less, the Aristotelian distinction between the techniques of history, science and fiction remains valid in a general way, and we shall perhaps see why this is so if we examine these techniques again, for we shall find that they differ from each other in their suitability for dealing with 'data' of different quantities. The ascertainment and record of particular facts is all that is possible in a field of study where the data happen to be few. The elucidation and formulation of laws is both possible and necessary where the data are too numerous to tabulate but not too numerous to survey. The form of artistic creation and expression called fiction is the only technique that can be employed or is worth employing where the data are innumerable. Here, as between the three techniques, we have an intrinsic difference of a quantitative order. The techniques differ in their utility for handling different quantities of data. Can we discern a corresponding difference in the quantities of the data that actually present themselves in the respective fields of our three studies?

To begin with the study of personal relations, which is the province of fiction, we can see at once that there are few individuals whose personal relations are of such interest and importance as to make them fit subjects for that record of particular personal facts which we call biography. With these rare exceptions students of human life in the field of personal relations are confronted with innumerable examples of universally familiar experiences. The very idea of an exhaustive recording of them is an absurdity. Any formulation of their 'laws' would be intolerably platitudinous or intolerably crude. In such circumstances the data cannot be significantly expressed except in some notation which gives an intuition of the infinite in finite terms; and such a notation is fiction.

Having now found, in quantitative terms, at least a partial explanation of the fact that, in the study of personal relations, the technique of fiction is normally employed, let us see if we can find similar explanations for the normal employment of the law-making technique in the study of primitive societies and the fact-finding technique in the study of civilizations.

The first point to observe is that both these other studies are concerned with human relations, but not with the relations of the familiar, personal kind which come within the direct experience of every man, woman and child. The social relations of human beings extend beyond the farthest possible range of personal contacts, and these impersonal relations are maintained through social mechanisms called institutions. Without institutions societies could not exist. Indeed, societies themselves are simply institutions of the highest kind. The study of societies and the study of institutional relations are one and the same thing.

We can see at once that the quantity of data confronting students of institutional relations between people is very much smaller than the quantity confronting students of people's personal relations. We can see further that the quantity of recorded institutional relations that are relevant to the study of primitive societies will be much greater than the quantity of those relevant to the study of 'civilized' societies, because the number of known primitive societies runs to over 650, whereas our survey of societies in process of civilization has enabled us to identify no more than, at the outside, twenty-one. Now 650 examples, while far from necessitating the employment of fiction, are just enough to enable the student to make a beginning with the formulation of laws. On the other hand, students of a phenomenon of which only a dozen or two dozen examples are known are discouraged from attempting more than a tabulation of facts; and this, as we have seen, is the stage in which 'history' has remained so far.

At first sight it may seem a paradox to assert that the quantity of data which students of civilizations have at their command is inconveniently small, when our modern historians are complaining that they are overwhelmed by the mass of their materials. But it remains true that the facts of the highest order, the 'intelligible fields of study', the *comparable units* of history, remain inconveniently few for the application of the scientific technique, the elucidation and formulation of laws. . . .

3.

*Historical relativism is the major issue discussed in the following articles by Becker, Beard, and Aron. Both Carl L. Becker (1873–1945) and Charles A. Beard (1876–1948) were eminent historians who were seriously concerned about what they were doing. Both had a considerable influence upon American historiography during the last generation; in recent years they have suffered a decline in status, which, in my opinion, is not altogether justified. For both transplanted, in simplified form, the legacy of modern historicism to the American scene and both kept hammering away at logical difficulties which a so-called scientific or positivistic historiography—"let the facts speak for themselves"—often solved only by disregarding them. The facts, unfortunately, do not speak for themselves—in history or any other area of life.*

*Thus Becker poses a genuine problem: the impurity of historical facts and the inevitable conditioning of "facts" by interests, theory, and interpretation. He is quite clear on the distinction between the simple fact, on the one hand, which can be "established and agreed upon," and, on the other hand, "the meaning and significance" assigned to this fact in an interpretative narrative, which is an altogether different matter, indeed. But there is no need to take the essay apart; it is perfectly lucid in its own terms. What it owes to Croce and Collingwood is obvious from phrases such as this: "The world of history is an intangible world, recreated imaginatively, and present in our minds."*

## CARL L. BECKER

## WHAT ARE HISTORICAL FACTS?*

History is a venerable branch of knowledge, and the
writing of history is an art of long standing. Everyone knows
what history is, that is, everyone is familiar with the word,
and has a confident notion of what it means. In general,
history has to do with the thought and action of men and
women who lived in past times. Everyone knows what the
past is too. We all have a comforting sense that it lies behind us, like a stretch of uneven country we have crossed;
and it is often difficult to avoid the notion that one could
easily, by turning round, walk back into this country of the
past. That, at all events, is what we commonly think of the
historian as doing: he works in the past, he explores the
past in order to find out what men did and thought in
the past. His business is to discover and set forth the "facts"
of history.

When anyone says "facts" we are all there. The word
gives us a sense of stability. We know where we are when,
as we say, we "get down to the facts"—as, for example, we
know where we are when we get down to the facts of the
structure of the atom, or the incredible movement of the
electron as it jumps from one orbit to another. It is the
same with history. Historians feel safe when dealing with
the facts. We talk much about the "hard facts" and the
"cold facts," about "not being able to get around the facts,"
and about the necessity of basing our narrative on a "solid
foundation of fact." By virtue of talking in this way, the
facts of history come in the end to seem something solid,
something substantial like physical matter (I mean matter
in the common sense, not matter defined as "a series of
events in the ether"), something possessing definite shape,
and clear persistent outline—like bricks or scantlings; so that
we can easily picture the historian as he stumbles about in

* In *The Western Political Quarterly*, VIII, 3 (September
1955), pp. 327–40; reprinted by permission of the editor.

the past, stubbing his toe on the hard facts if he doesn't watch out. That is his affair of course, a danger he runs; for his business is to dig out the facts and pile them up for someone to use. Perhaps he may use them himself; but at all events he must arrange them conveniently so that some-one—perhaps the sociologist or the economist—may easily carry them away for use in some structural enterprise.

Such (with no doubt a little, but not much, exaggeration to give point to the matter) are the common connotations of the words historical facts, as used by historians and other people. Now, when I meet a word with which I am entirely unfamiliar, I find it a good plan to look it up in the diction-ary and find out what someone thinks it means. But when I have frequently to use words with which everyone is perfectly familiar—words like "cause" and "liberty" and "progress" and "government"—when I have to use words of this sort which everyone knows perfectly well, the wise thing to do is to take a week off and think about them. The result is often astonishing; for as often as not I find that I have been talking about words instead of real things. Well, "historical fact" is such a word; and I suspect it would be worthwhile for us historians at least to think about this word more than we have done. For the moment therefore, leaving the historian moving about in the past piling up the cold facts, I wish to inquire whether the historical fact is really as hard and stable as it is often supposed to be.

And this inquiry I will throw into the form of three simple questions. I will ask the questions, I can't promise to answer them. The questions are: (1) What is the historical fact? (2) Where is the historical fact? (3) When is the historical fact? Mind I say *is* not *was*. I take it for granted that if we are interested in, let us say, the fact of the Magna Carta, we are interested in it for our own sake and not for its sake; and since we are living now and not in 1215 we must be interested in the Magna Carta, if at all, for what it is and not for what it was.

First then, What is the historical fact? Let us take a sim-ple fact, as simple as the historian often deals with, viz.: "In the year 49 B.C. Caesar crossed the Rubicon." A famil-iar fact this is, known to all, and obviously of some im-

portance since it is mentioned in every history of the great
Caesar. But is this fact as simple as it sounds? Has it the
clear, persistent outline which we commonly attribute to
simple historical facts? When we say that Caesar crossed
the Rubicon we do not of course mean that Caesar crossed
it alone, but with his army. The Rubicon is a small river,
and I don't know how long it took Caesar's army to cross it;
but the crossing must surely have been accompanied by
many acts and many words and many thoughts of many
men. That is to say, a thousand and one lesser "facts" went
to make up the one simple fact that Caesar crossed the
Rubicon; and if we had someone, say James Joyce, to know
and relate all these facts, it would no doubt require a book
of 794 pages to present this one fact that Caesar crossed the
Rubicon. Thus the simple fact turns out to be not a simple
fact at all. It is the statement that is simple—a simple
generalization of a thousand and one facts.

Well, anyhow Caesar crossed the Rubicon. But what of
it? Many other people at other times crossed the Rubicon.
Why charge it up to Caesar? Why for two thousand years
has the world treasured this simple fact that in the year
49 B.C. Caesar crossed the Rubicon? What of it indeed? If
I, as historian, have nothing to give you but this fact taken
by itself with its clear outline, with no fringes or strings tied
to it, I should have to say, if I were an honest man, why
nothing of it, nothing at all. It may be a fact but it is
nothing to us. The truth is, of course, that this simple fact
*has* strings tied to it, and that is why it has been treasured
for two thousand years. It is tied by these strings to innumerable other facts, so that it can't mean anything except by losing its clear outline. It can't mean anything except as it is absorbed into the complex web of circumstances
which brought it into being. This complex web of circumstances was the series of events growing out of the relation
of Caesar to Pompey, and the Roman Senate, and the Roman Republic, and all the people who had something to
do with these. Caesar had been ordered by the Roman
Senate to resign his command of the army in Gaul. He
decided to disobey the Roman Senate. Instead of resigning
his command, he marched on Rome, gained the mastery of

the Republic, and at last, as we are told, bestrode the narrow world like a colossus. Well, the Rubicon happened to be the boundary between Gaul and Italy, so that by the act of crossing the Rubicon with his army Caesar's treason became an accomplished fact and the subsequent great events followed in due course. Apart from these great events and complicated relations, the crossing of the Rubicon means nothing, is not an historical fact properly speaking at all. In itself it is nothing for us; it becomes something for us, not in itself, but as a symbol of something else, a symbol standing for a long series of events which have to do with the most intangible and immaterial realities, viz.: the relation between Caesar and the millions of people of the Roman world.

Thus the simple historical fact turns out to be not a hard, cold something with clear outline, and measurable pressure, like a brick. It is so far as we can know it, only a *symbol,* a simple statement which is a generalization of a thousand and one simpler facts which we do not for the moment care to use, and this generalization itself we cannot use apart from the wider facts and generalizations which it symbolizes. And generally speaking, the more simple an historical fact is, the more clear and definite and provable it is, the less use it is to us in and for itself.

Less simple facts illustrate all this equally well, even better perhaps. For example, the fact that "Indulgences were sold in Germany in 1517." This fact can be proved down to the ground. No one doubts it. But taken by itself the fact is nothing, means nothing. It also is a generalization of a thousand and one facts, a thousand and one actions of innumerable sellers and buyers of indulgences all over Germany at many different times; and this also acquires significance and meaning only as it is related to other facts and wider generalizations.

But there are even more indefinite and impalpable facts than these. In the middle of the nineteenth century German historians (and others), studying the customs of the primitive German tribes, discovered a communal institution which they called the German or Teutonic Mark. The German Mark was the product of the historian's fertile imagination working on a few sentences in Caesar's *Gallic Wars* and a few passages in a book called *Germania* written by Tacitus, a disgruntled Roman who tried to get rid of a complex by idealizing the primitive Germans. The German Mark of the historians was largely a myth, corresponding to no reality. The German Mark is nevertheless an historical fact. The idea of the German Mark in the minds of the German historians is a fact in the intellectual history of the nineteenth century—and an important one too. All the elaborate notes I took in college on the German Mark I have therefore long since transferred to those filing cases which contain my notes on the nineteenth century; and there they now repose, side by side with notes on the Russian Mir, on Hegel's Philosophy of History, on the Positivism of August Comte, on Bentham's greatest good to the greatest number, on the economic theory of the British classical economists, and other illusions of that time.

What then is the historical fact? Far be it from me to define so illusive and intangible a thing! But provisionally I will say this: the historian may be interested in anything that has to do with the life of man in the past—any act or event, any emotion which men have expressed, any idea, true or false, which they have entertained. Very well, the historian is interested in some event of this sort. Yet he cannot deal directly with this event itself, since the event itself has disappeared. What he can deal with directly is a *statement about the event*. He deals in short not with the event, but with a statement which affirms *the fact that the event occurred*. When we really get down to the hard facts, what the historian is always dealing with is an *affirmation*— an affirmation of the fact that something is true. There is thus a distinction of capital importance to be made: the distinction between the ephemeral event which disappears, and the affirmation about the event which persists. For all practical purposes it is this affirmation about the event that constitutes for us the historical fact. If so the historical fact is not the past event, but a symbol which enables us to recreate it imaginatively. Of a symbol it is hardly worthwhile to say that it is cold or hard. It is dangerous to say even that it is true or false. The safest thing to say about a symbol is that it is more or less appropriate.

This brings me to the second question—Where is the historical fact? I will say at once, however brash it sounds, that the historical fact is in someone's mind or it is nowhere. To illustrate this statement I will take an event familiar to all. "Abraham Lincoln was assassinated in Ford's Theater in Washington on the 14th of April, 1865." That *was* an actual event, occurrence, fact at the moment of happening. But speaking now, in the year 1926, we say it *is* an historical fact. We don't say that it *was* an historical fact, for that would imply that it no longer is one. We say that it *was* an actual event, but *is now* an historical fact. The actual occurrence and the historical fact, however closely connected, are two different things. Very well, if the assassination of Lincoln is an historical fact, where is this fact now? Lincoln is not being assassinated now in Ford's Theater, or anywhere else (except perhaps in propagandist literature!). The actual occurrence, the event, has passed, is gone forever, never to be repeated, never to be again experienced or witnessed by any living person. Yet this is precisely the sort of thing the historian is concerned with—events, acts, thoughts, emotions that have forever vanished as actual occurrences. How can the historian deal with vanished realities? He can deal with them because these vanished realities give place to pale reflections, impalpable images or ideas of themselves, and these pale reflections, and impalpable images which cannot be touched or handled are all that is left of the actual occurrence. These are therefore what the historian deals with. These are his "material." He has to be satisfied with these, for the very good reason that he has nothing else. Well then, where are they—these pale reflections and impalpable images of the actual? Where are these facts? They are, as I said before, in his mind, or in somebody's mind, or they are nowhere.

Ah, but they are in the records, in the sources, I hear someone say. Yes, in a sense, they are in the sources. The historical fact of Lincoln's assassination is in the records—in contemporary newspapers, letters, diaries, etc. In a sense the fact is there, but in what sense? The records are after

all only paper, over the surface of which ink has been
distributed in certain patterns. And even these patterns
were not made by the actual occurrence, the assassination
of Lincoln. The patterns are themselves only "histories" of
the event, made by someone who had in *his* mind an image
or idea of Lincoln's assassination. Of course we, you and I,
can, by looking at these inky patterns, form in *our* minds
images or ideas more or less like those in the mind of the
person who made the patterns. But if there were now no
one in the world who could make any meaning out of the
patterned records or sources, the fact of Lincoln's assassination would cease to be an historical fact. You might perhaps
call it a dead fact; but a fact which is not only dead, but
not known ever to have been alive, or even known to be
now dead, is surely not much of a fact. At all events, the
historical facts lying dead in the records can do nothing
good or evil in the world. They become historical facts,
capable of doing work, of making a difference, only when
someone, you or I, brings them alive in our minds by means
of pictures, images, or ideas of the actual occurrence. For
this reason I say that the historical fact is in someone's
mind, or it is nowhere, because when it is in no one's mind
it lies in the records inert, incapable of making a difference
in the world.

But perhaps you will say that the assassination of Lincoln has made a difference in the world, and that this difference is now effectively working, even if, for a moment,
or an hour or a week, no one in the world has the image
of the actual occurrence in mind. Quite obviously so, but
why? Quite obviously because after the actual event people remembered it, and because ever since they have continued to remember it, by repeatedly forming images of it
in their minds. If the people of the United States had been
incapable of enduring memory, for example, like dogs (as
I assume; not being a dog I can't be sure) would the assassination of Lincoln be now doing work in the world,
making a difference? If everyone had forgotten the occurrence after forty-eight hours, what difference would the occurrence have made, then or since? It is precisely because
people have long memories, and have constantly formed

images in their minds of the assassination of Lincoln, that the universe contains the historical fact which persists as well as the actual event which does not persist. It is the persisting historical fact, rather than the ephemeral actual event, which makes a difference to us now; and the historical fact makes a difference only because it is, and so far as it is, in human minds.

Now for the third question—When is the historical fact? If you agree with what has been said (which is extremely doubtful) the answer seems simple enough. If the historical fact is present, imaginatively, in someone's mind, then it is now, a part of the present. But the word present is a slippery word, and the thing itself is worse than the word. The present is an indefinable point in time, gone before you can think it; the image or idea which I have now present in mind slips instantly into the past. But images or ideas of past events are often, perhaps always, inseparable from images or ideas of the future. Take an illustration. I awake this morning, and among the things my memory drags in to enlighten or distress me is a vague notion that there was something I needed particularly to remember but cannot —a common experience surely. What is it that I needed to remember I cannot recall; but I can recall that I made a note of it in order to jog my memory. So I consult my little pocket memorandum book—a little Private Record Office which I carry about, filled with historical sources. I take out my memorandum book in order to do a little historical research; and there I find (Vol. I, p. 20) the dead historical fact—"Pay Smith's coal bill today: $1,016." The image of the memorandum book now drops out of mind, and is replaced by another image—an image of what? Why an image, an idea, a picture (call it what you will) made up of three things more or less inseparable. First the image of myself ordering coal from Smith last summer; second, the image of myself holding the idea in mind that I must pay the bill; third, the image of myself going down to Smith's office at four o'clock to pay it. The image is partly of things done in the past, and partly of things to be done in the future; but it is more or less all one image now present in mind.

Someone may ask, "Are you talking of history or of the ordinary ills of every day that men are heir to?" Well, perhaps Smith's coal bill is only my personal affair, of no concern to anyone else, except Smith to be sure. Take then another example. I am thinking of the Congress of Berlin, and that is without doubt history—the real thing. The historical facts of the Congress of Berlin I bring alive in memory, imaginatively. But I am making an image of the Congress of Berlin for a purpose; and indeed without a purpose no one would take the trouble to bring historical facts to mind. My purpose happens to be to convey this image of the Congress of Berlin to my class in History 42, in Room C, tomorrow afternoon at 3 o'clock. Now I find that inseparable from this image of the Congress of Berlin, which occurred in the past, are flitting images of myself conveying this image of the Congress of Berlin to my class tomorrow in Room C. I picture myself standing there monotonously talking, I hear the labored sentences painfully issuing forth, I picture the students' faces alert or bored as the case may be; so that images of this future event enter into the imagined picture of the Congress of Berlin, a past event; enter into it, coloring and shaping it too, to the end that the performance may do credit to me, or be intelligible to immature minds, or be compressed within the limits of fifty minutes, or to accomplish some other desired end. Well, this living historical fact, this mixed image of the coal bill or the Congress of Berlin—is it past, present, or future? I cannot say. Perhaps it moves with the velocity of light, and is timeless. At all events it is real history to me, which I hope to make convincing and real to Smith, or to the class in Room C.

I have now asked my three questions, and have made some remarks about them all. I don't know whether these remarks will strike you as quite beside the mark, or as merely obvious, or as novel. If there is any novelty in them, it arises, I think, from our inveterate habit of thinking of the world of history as part of the external world, and of historical facts as actual events. In truth the actual past is gone; and the world of history is an intangible world, recreated imaginatively, and present in our minds. If, as I think, this is true, then there are certain important implications growing out of it; and if you are not already exhausted I should like to touch upon a few of these implications. I will present them "firstly," "secondly," and so on, like the points of a sermon, without any attempt at coordination.

One implication is that by no possibility can the historian present in its entirety any actual event, even the simplest. You may think this a commonplace, and I do too; but still it needs to be often repeated because one of the fondest illusions of nineteenth century historians was that the historian, the "scientific" historian, would do just that: he would "present all the facts and let them speak for themselves." The historian would contribute nothing himself, except the sensitive plate of his mind, upon which the objective facts would register their own unimpeachable meaning. Nietzsche has described the nineteenth-century "objective man" with the acid precision of his inimitable phrases.

> The objective man is in truth a mirror. Accustomed to prostrating himself before something that wishes to be known, with such desires only as knowing implies, he waits until something comes and then expands himself sensitively, so that even the light footsteps and gliding past of spiritual beings may not be lost on his surface and film. Whatever personality he still possesses seems to him —disturbing; so much has he come to regard himself as the reflection of outward forms and events. Should one wish love and hatred from him, he will do what he can, and furnish what he can. But one must not be surprised if it should not be much. His mirroring and eternally self-polishing soul no longer knows how to affirm, no longer how to deny. . . . He is an instrument, but nothing in himself—*presque rien!*

The classical expression of this notion of the historian as instrument, is the famous statement attributed to Fustel de Coulanges. Half a century ago the French mind was reacting strongly against the romantic idea that political liberty was brought into Gaul by the primitive Germans; and Fustel was a leader in this reaction. One day he was lecturing to his students on early French institutions, and sud-

denly they broke into applause. "Gentlemen," said Fustel,
"do not applaud. It is not I who speak, but history that
speaks through me." And all the time this calm disinter-
ested historian was endeavoring, with concentrated purpose, to prove that the damned Germans had nothing to
do with French civilization. That of course was why the
students applauded—and why Fustel told them that it was
history that was speaking.

Well, for twenty years I have taken it for granted that
no one could longer believe so preposterous an idea. But
the notion continues to bob up regularly; and only the
other day, riding on the train to the meeting of the Historical Association, Mr. A. J. Beveridge, eminent and honored
historian, assured me dogmatically (it would be dogmatically) that the historian has nothing to do but "present all
the facts and let them speak for themselves." And so I repeat, what I have been teaching for twenty years, that this
notion is preposterous; first, because it is impossible to present all the facts; and second, because even if you could
present all the facts the miserable things wouldn't say anything, would say just nothing at all.

Let us return to the simple fact: "Lincoln was assassinated in Ford's Theater, in Washington, April 14, 1865."
This is not all the facts. It is, if you like, a *representation*
of all the facts, and a representation that perhaps satisfies
one historian. But another historian, for some reason, is not
satisfied. He says: "On April 14, 1865, in Washington, Lincoln, sitting in a private box in Ford's Theater watching a
play, was shot by John Wilkes Booth, who then jumped to
the stage crying out, '*Sic semper tyrannis!*'" That is a true
affirmation about the event also. It represents, if you like,
all the facts too. But its form and content (one and the
same thing in literary discourse) is different, because it contains more of the facts than the other. Well, the point is
that any number of affirmations (an infinite number if the
sources were sufficient) could be made about the actual
event, all true, all representing the event, but some containing more and some less of the factual aspects of the total
event. But by no possibility can the historian make affirmations describing all of the facts—all of the acts, thoughts,

emotions of all of the persons who contributed to the actual event in its entirety. One historian will therefore necessarily *choose* certain affirmations about the event, and relate them in a certain way, rejecting other affirmations and other ways of relating them. Another historian will necessarily make a different choice. Why? What is it that leads one historian to make, out of all the possible true affirmations about the given event, certain affirmations and not others? Why, the purpose he has in his mind will determine that. And so the purpose he has in mind will determine the precise meaning which he derives from the event. The event itself, the facts, do not say anything, do not impose any meaning. It is the historian who speaks, who imposes a meaning.

A second implication follows from this. It is that the historian cannot eliminate the personal equation. Of course, no one can; not even, I think, the natural scientist. The universe speaks to us only in response to our purposes; and even the most objective constructions, those, let us say, of the theoretical physicist, are not the sole possible constructions, but only such as are found most convenient for some human need or purpose. Nevertheless, the physicist can eliminate the personal equation to a greater extent, or at least in a different way, than the historian, because he deals, as the historian does not, with an external world directly. The physicist presides at the living event, the historian presides only at the inquest of its remains. If I were alone in the universe and gashed my finger on a sharp rock, I could never be certain that there was anything there but my consciousness of the rock and gashed finger. But if ten other men in precisely the same way gash their fingers on the same sharp rock, we can, by comparing impressions, infer that there is something there besides consciousness. There is an external world there. The physicist can gash his finger on the rock as many times as he likes, and get others to do it, until they are all certain of the facts. He can, as Eddington says, make pointer-readings of the behavior of the physical world as many times as he likes for a given phenomenon, until he and his colleagues are satisfied. When their minds all rest satisfied they have an

explanation, what is called the truth. But suppose the physicist had to reach his conclusions from miscellaneous records, made by all sorts of people, of experiments that had
been made in the past, each experiment made only once,
and none of them capable of being repeated. The external
world he would then have to deal with would be the records. That is the case of the historian. The only external
world he has to deal with is the records. He can indeed
look at the records as often as he likes, and he can get
dozens of others to look at them: and some things, some
"facts," can in this way be established and agreed upon,
as, for example, the fact that the document known as the
Declaration of Independence was voted on July 4, 1776.
But the meaning and significance of this fact cannot be
thus agreed upon, because the series of events in which it
has a place cannot be enacted again and again, under varying conditions, in order to see what effect the variations
would have. The historian has to judge the significance of
the series of events from the one single performance, never
to be repeated, and never, since the records are incomplete
and imperfect, capable of being fully known or fully affirmed. Thus into the imagined facts and their meaning
there enters the personal equation. The history of any event
is never precisely the same thing to two different persons;
and it is well known that every generation writes the same
history in a new way, and puts upon it a new construction.

The reason why this is so—why the same series of vanished events is differently imagined in each succeeding generation—is that our imagined picture of the actual event is
always determined by two things: (1) by the actual event
itself insofar as we can know something about it; and (2)
by our own present purposes, desires, prepossessions, and
prejudices, all of which enter into the process of knowing
it. The actual event contributes something to the imagined
picture; but the mind that holds the imagined picture always contributes something too. This is why there is no
more fascinating or illuminating phase of history than historiography—the history of history: the history, that is, of
what successive generations have imagined the past to be
like. It is impossible to understand the history of certain

great events without knowing what the actors in those events themselves thought about history. For example, it helps immensely to understand why the leaders of the American and French Revolutions acted and thought as they did if we know what their idea of classical history was. They desired, to put it simply, to be virtuous republicans, and to act the part. Well, they were able to act the part of virtuous republicans much more effectively because they carried around in their heads an idea, or ideal if you prefer, of Greek republicanism and Roman virtue. But of course their own desire to be virtuous republicans had a great influence in making them think the Greek and Romans, whom they had been taught to admire by reading the classics in school, were virtuous republicans too. Their image of the present and future and their image of the classical past were inseparable, bound together—were really one and the same thing.

In this way the present influences our idea of the past, and our idea of the past influences the present. We are accustomed to say that "the present is the product of all the past"; and this is what is ordinarily meant by the historian's doctrine of "historical continuity." But it is only a half truth. It is equally true, and no mere paradox, to say that the past (our imagined picture of it) is the product of all the present. We build our conceptions of history partly out of our present needs and purposes. The past is a kind of screen upon which we project our vision of the future; and it is indeed a moving picture, borrowing much of its form and color from our fears and aspirations. The doctrine of historical continuity is badly in need of overhauling in the light of these suggestions; for that doctrine was itself one of those pictures which the early nineteenth century threw upon the screen of the past in order to quiet its deep-seated fears—fears occasioned by the French Revolution and the Napoleonic wars.

A third implication is that no one can profit by historical research, or not much, unless he does some for himself. Historical knowledge, however richly stored in books or in the minds of professors of history, is no good to me unless I have some of it. In this respect, historical research differs profoundly from research in the natural sciences, at least in some of them. For example, I know no physics, but I profit from physical researches every night by the simple act of pressing an electric light button. And everyone can profit in this way from researches in physics without knowing any physics, without knowing even that there is such a thing as physics. But with history it is different. Henry Ford, for example, can't profit from all the historical researches of two thousand years, because he knows so little history himself. By no pressing of any button can he flood the spare rooms of his mind with the light of human experience.

A fourth implication is more important than the others. It is that every normal person does know some history, a good deal in fact. Of course we often hear someone say: "I don't know any history; I wish I knew some history; I must improve my mind by learning some history." We know what is meant. This person means that he has never read any history books, or studied history in college; and so he thinks he knows no history. But it is precisely this conventional notion of history as something external to us, as a body of dull knowledge locked up in books, that obscures its real meaning. For, I repeat (it will bear repeating) every normal person—every man, woman, and child—does know some history, enough for his immediate purposes; otherwise he would be a lost soul indeed. I suppose myself, for example, to have awakened this morning with loss of memory. I am all right otherwise; but I can't remember anything that happened in the past. What is the result? The result is that I don't know who I am, where I am, where to go, or what to do. I can't attend to my duties at the university, I can't read this paper before the Research Club. In short, my present would be unintelligible and my future meaningless. Why? Why, because I had suddenly ceased to know any history. What happens when I wake up in the morning is that my memory reaches out into the past and gathers together those images of past events, of objects seen, of words spoken and of thoughts thought in the past, which are necessary to give me an ordered world to live in, necessary to orient me in my personal world. Well, this collection of images and ideas of things past is history, my command of living history, a series of images of the past which shifts and reforms at every moment of the day in response to the exigencies of my daily living. Every man has a knowledge of history in this sense, which is the only vital sense in which he can have a knowledge of history. Every man has some knowledge of past events, more or less accurate; knowledge enough, and accurate enough, for his purposes, or what he regards as such. How much and how accurate, will depend on the man and his purposes. Now, the point is that history in the formal sense, history as we commonly think of it, is only an extension of memory. Knowledge or history, insofar as it is living history and not dead knowledge locked up in note-books, is only an enrichment of our minds with the multiplied images of events, places, peoples, ideas, emotions outside our personal experience, an enrichment of our experience by bringing into our minds memories of the experience of the community, the nation, the race. Its chief value, for the individual, is doubtless that it enables a man to orient himself in a larger world than the merely personal, has the effect for him of placing the petty and intolerable present in a longer perspective, thus enabling him to judge the acts and thoughts of men, his own included, on the basis of an experience less immediate and restricted.

A fifth implication is that the kind of history that has most influence upon the life of the community and the course of events is the history that common men carry around in their heads. It won't do to say that history has no influence upon the course of events because people refuse to read history books. Whether the general run of people read history books or not, they inevitably picture the past in some fashion or other, and this picture, however little it corresponds to the real past, helps to determine their ideas about politics and society. This is especially true in times of excitement, in critical times, in time of war above all. It is precisely in such times that they form (with the efficient help of official propaganda!) an idealized picture of the past, born of their emotions and desires working on fragmentary scraps of knowledge gathered, or rather flowing in upon them, from every conceivable source, reliable or not matters nothing. Doubtless the proper function of erudite historical research is to be forever correcting the common image of the past by bringing it to the test of reliable information. But the professional historian will never get his own chastened and corrected image of the past into common minds if no one reads his books. His books may be as solid as you like, but their social influence will be nil if people do not read them and not merely read them, but read them willingly and with understanding.

It is, indeed, not wholly the historian's fault that the mass of men will not read good history willingly and with understanding; but I think we should not be too complacent about it. The recent World War leaves us with little ground indeed for being complacent about anything; but certainly it furnishes us with no reason for supposing that historical research has much influence on the course of events. The nineteenth century is often called the age of science, and it is often called the age of history. Both statements are correct enough. During the hundred years that passed between 1814 and 1914 an unprecedented and incredible amount of research was carried on, research into every field of history—minute, critical, exhaustive (and exhausting!) research. Our libraries are filled with this stored up knowledge of the past; and never before has there been at the disposal of society so much reliable knowledge of human experience. What influence has all this expert research had upon the social life of our time? Has it done anything to restrain the foolishness of politicians or to enhance the wisdom of statesmen? Has it done anything to enlighten the mass of the people, or to enable them to act with greater wisdom or in response to a more reasoned purpose? Very little surely, if anything. Certainly a hundred years of expert historical research did nothing to prevent the World War, the most futile exhibition of unreason, take it all in all, ever made by civilized society. Governments and peoples rushed into this war with undiminished stupidity, with unabated fanaticism, with unimpaired capacity for deceiving themselves and others. I do not say that historical research is to blame for the World War. I say that it had little or no influence upon it, one way or another.

It is interesting, although no necessary part of this paper, to contrast this negligible influence of historical research upon social life with the profound influence of scientific research. A hundred years of scientific research has transformed the conditions of life. How it has done this is known to all. By enabling men to control natural forces it has made life more comfortable and convenient, at least for the well-to-do. It has done much to prevent and cure disease, to alleviate pain and suffering. But its benefits are not unmixed. By accelerating the speed and pressure of life it has injected into it a nervous strain, a restlessness, a capacity for irritation and an impatience of restraint never before known. And this power which scientific research lays at the feet of society serves equally well all who can make use of it—the harbingers of death as well as of life. It was scientific research that made the war of 1914, which historical research did nothing to prevent, a world war. Because of scientific research it could be, and was, fought with more cruelty and ruthlessness, and on a grander scale, than any previous war; because of scientific research it became a systematic massed butchery such as no one had dreamed of, or supposed possible. I do not say that scientific research is to blame for the war; I say that it made it the ghastly thing it was, determined its extent and character. What I am pointing out is that scientific research has had a profound influence in changing the conditions of modern life, whereas historical research has had at best only a negligible influence. Whether the profound influence of the one has been of more or less benefit to humanity than the negligible influence of the other, I am unable to determine. Doubtless both the joys and frustrations of modern life, including those of the scholarly activities, may be all accommodated and reconciled within that wonderful idea of Progress which we all like to acclaim—none more so, surely, than historians and scientists.

### 4.

*The essay by Charles A. Beard, his presidential address to
the American Historical Association in 1933, makes a plea,
similar to Becker's (and Croce's) for "history as contemporary thought about the past." It alludes to a favorite distinction of Beard's between (a) history as actuality and
(b) written history (or history as thought)—which is analyzed critically in Professor White's essay reprinted below.[1]
But the most significant contribution of Beard's article is
perhaps the curious wavering, or ambivalence, which it reflects between a criticism of scientific conceptions in history, on the one hand, and the final endorsement of the
scientific method, on the other. Thus Beard first repudiates
"the intellectual formulas borrowed from natural science
(especially the models borrowed from physics and biology)
which have cramped and distorted the operations of history
as thought" and relegates Ranke's aspirations of writing history as it really happened to "the museum of antiquities."
In the end, however, the scientific method in history and
elsewhere is vigorously defended as "a precious and indispensable instrument of the human mind, the chief safeguard against the tyranny of authority, bureaucracy and
brute power," without which "society would sink down into
primitive animism and barbarism." Beard never reached a
satisfactory middle ground between his polemics against
the pretensions of the scientific method in history and his
awareness that some standards of truth and objectivity are
necessary in order to be a responsible historian. Since he is
often considered the foremost spokesman on behalf of what
is called "historical relativism," it is interesting to see that,
in this article, Beard calls "historical relativism" self-refut-
ing—an argument usually advanced by his critics.[2]*

*Beard's views have been the target of numerous criti-
cisms. Thus it may be appropriate to quote from a late re-*

[1] See p. 188 ff.
[2] Cf. the essays by Sir Isaiah Berlin and Professor Ernest Nagel
reprinted below.

*joinder of Beard's to his critics. In a review[3] of* The Problem of Historical Knowledge *(1938) by Maurice Mandelbaum, an early critic of Beard's relativism, Beard replied: "I have never meant to say that whatever 'truth' Ranke's works contain is 'limited' by psychological, sociological or other processes under which he wrote. What I have tried to say . . . is that no historian can describe the past as it actually was and that every historian's work—that is, his selection of facts, his emphasis, his omissions, his organization, his method of presentation—bears a relation to his own personality and the age and circumstances in which he lives." Professor Mandelbaum had suggested that explanation in history is analogous to that in any other empirical discipline. It is the task of the historian, as it is the task of the student of nature, to discover the network of causal relations which are relevant to a given historical situation. "Every historical statement," Mr. Mandelbaum wrote, "is given in some specific context in which it leads on to some other fact." Beard replied as follows: (1) Who supplies the context? (2) In whose historical work do we find one fact inexorably leading to another? (3) Would any historian maintain that he merely finds a fact in a context, and that this fact leads him to all other facts seriatim? "It would have been helpful," Beard concluded, "to have cited some work in history which tells the 'truth' of any brief time span . . . to say nothing of history in general. Does Rhodes or Channing or Bancroft?"*

This question, I think, is more than rhetorical. It points to the fact (a) that the factors chosen as "relevant" for a causal explanation in history may be loaded with tacit, inarticulate assumptions; (b) that philosophers may construct models of historical knowledge which have little to do with the actual practice of history; and (c) that, in addition to obvious distortions, falsehoods, and prejudices, which may be exposed in historical works, there may be other and more hidden limits to achieving a degree of objectivity in history which would compare with that in scientific works.

[3] See *The American Historical Review*, XLIV (1939), pp. 171–72.

## CHARLES A. BEARD

# WRITTEN HISTORY AS AN ACT OF FAITH*

History has been called a science, an art, an illustration of theology, a phase of philosophy, a branch of literature. It is none of these things, nor all of them combined. On the contrary, science, art, theology, and literature are themselves merely phases of history as past actuality and their particular forms at given periods and places are to be explained, if explained at all, by history as knowledge and thought. The philosopher, possessing little or no acquaintance with history, sometimes pretends to expound the inner secret of history,[1] but the historian turns upon him and expounds the secret of the philosopher, as far as it may be expounded at all, by placing him in relation to the movement of ideas and interests in which he stands or floats, by giving to his scheme of thought its appropriate relativity. So it is with systems of science, art, theology, and literature. All the light on these subjects that can be discovered by the human mind comes from history as past actuality.

What, then, is this manifestation of omniscience called history? It is, as Croce says, contemporary thought about the past. History as past actuality includes, to be sure, all that has been done, said, felt, and thought by human beings on this planet since humanity began its long career. History as record embraces the monuments, documents, and symbols which provide such knowledge as we have or can find respecting past actuality. But it is history as thought, not as actuality, record, or specific knowledge, that is really meant when the term history is used in its widest and most general significance. It is thought about past actuality, instructed and delimited by history as record and knowledge—record and knowledge authenticated by criti-

* In *The American Historical Review*, XXXIX, 2 (January 1934), pp. 219–29; reprinted by permission of the editors.

[1] For a beautiful example, see the passages on America in the introduction to Hegel's *Philosophy of History*.

cism and ordered with the help of the scientific method. This is the final, positive, inescapable definition. It contains all the exactness that is possible and all the bewildering problems inherent in the nature of thought and the relation of the thinker to the thing thought about.

Although this definition of history may appear, at first glance, distressing to those who have been writing lightly about "the science of history" and "the scientific method" in historical research and construction, it is in fact in accordance with the most profound contemporary thought about history, represented by Croce, Riezler, Karl Mannheim, Mueller-Armack, and Heussi, for example. It is in keeping also with the obvious and commonplace. Has it not been said for a century or more that each historian who writes history is a product of his age, and that his work reflects the spirit of the times, of a nation, race, group, class, or section? No contemporary student of history really believes that Bossuet, Gibbon, Mommsen, or Bancroft could be duplicated to-day. Every student of history knows that his colleagues have been influenced in their selection and ordering of materials by their biases, prejudices, beliefs, affections, general upbringing, and experience, particularly social and economic; and if he has a sense of propriety, to say nothing of humor, he applies the canon to himself, leaving no exceptions to the rule. The pallor of waning time, if not of death, rests upon the latest volume of history, fresh from the roaring press.

Why do we believe this to be true? The answer is that every written history—of a village, town, county, state, nation, race, group, class, idea, or the wide world—is a selection and arrangement of facts, of recorded fragments of past actuality. And the selection and arrangement of facts —a combined and complex intellectual operation—is an act of choice, conviction, and interpretation respecting values, is an act of thought. Facts, multitudinous and beyond calculation, are known, but they do not select themselves or force themselves automatically into any fixed scheme of arrangement in the mind of the historian. They are selected and ordered by him as he thinks. True enough, where the records pertaining to a small segment of history are few and

presumably all known, the historian may produce a fragment having an aspect of completeness, as, for example,
some pieces by Fustel de Coulanges; but the completeness
is one of documentation, not of history. True enough also,
many historians are pleased to say of their writings that
their facts are selected and ordered only with reference to
inner necessities, but none who takes this position will allow the same exactitude and certainty to the works of others, except when the predilections of the latter conform to
his own pattern.

Contemporary thought about history, therefore, repudiates the conception dominant among the schoolmen during
the latter part of the nineteenth century and the opening
years of the twentieth century—the conception that it is
possible to describe the past as it actually was, somewhat
as the engineer describes a single machine. The formula
itself was a passing phase of thought about the past. Its
author, Ranke, a German conservative, writing after the
storm and stress of the French Revolution, was weary of
history written for, or permeated by, the purposes of revolutionary propaganda. He wanted peace. The ruling
classes in Germany, with which he was affiliated, having
secured a breathing spell in the settlement of 1815, wanted
peace to consolidate their position. Written history that was
cold, factual, and apparently undisturbed by the passions
of the time served best the cause of those who did not
want to be disturbed. Later the formula was fitted into the
great conception of natural science—cold neutrality over
against the materials and forces of the physical world.
Truths of nature, ran the theory, are to be discovered by
maintaining the most severe objectivity; therefore the truth
of history may be revealed by the same spirit and method.
The reasoning seemed perfect to those for whom it was
satisfactory. But the movement of ideas and interests continued, and bondage to conservative and scientific thought
was broken by criticism and events. As Croce and Heussi
have demonstrated, so-called neutral or scientific history
reached a crisis in its thought before the twentieth century
had advanced far on the way.

This crisis in historical thought sprang from internal criticism—from conflicts of thought within historiography itself —and from the movement of history as actuality; for historians are always engaged, more or less, in thinking about their own work and are disturbed, like their fellow citizens, by crises and revolutions occurring in the world about them. As an outcome of this crisis in historiography, the assumption that the actuality of history is identical with or closely akin to that of the physical world, and the assumption that any historian can be a disembodied spirit as coldly neutral to human affairs as the engineer to an automobile have both been challenged and rejected. Thus, owing to internal criticism and the movement of external events, the Ranke formula of history has been discarded and laid away in the museum of antiquities. It has ceased to satisfy the human spirit in its historical needs. Once more, historians recognize formally the obvious, long known informally, namely, that any written history inevitably reflects the thought of the author in his time and cultural setting.

That this crisis in thought presents a distressing dilemma to many historians is beyond question. It is almost a confession of inexpiable sin to admit in academic circles that one is not a man of science working in a scientific manner with things open to deterministic and inexorable treatment, to admit that one is more or less a guesser in this vale of tears. But the only escape from the dust and storm of the present conflict, and from the hazards of taking thought, now before the historian, is silence or refuge in some minute particularity of history as actuality. He may edit documents, although there are perils in the choice of documents to be edited, and in any case the choice of documents will bear some reference to an interpretation of values and importance—subjective considerations. To avoid this difficulty, the historian may confine his attention to some very remote and microscopic area of time and place, such as the price of cotton in Alabama between 1850 and 1860, or the length of wigs in the reign of Charles II, on the pleasing but false assumption that he is really describing an isolated particularity as it actually was, an isolated area having no wide-reaching ramifications of relations. But even then the historian would be a strange creature if he never asked himself

why he regarded these matters as worthy of his labor and
love, or why society provides a living for him during his
excursions and explorations.

The other alternative before the student of history as
immense actuality is to face boldly, in the spirit of Cato's
soliloquy, the wreck of matter and the crush of worlds—
the dissolution of that solid assurance which rested on the
formula bequeathed by Ranke and embroidered by a thousand hands during the intervening years. And when he
confronts without avoidance contemporary thought about
the nature of written history, what commands does he hear?

The supreme command is that he must cast off his servitude to the assumptions of natural science and return to his
own subject matter—to history as actuality. The hour for
this final declaration of independence has arrived: the con-
tingency is here and thought resolves it. Natural science is
only one small subdivision of history as actuality with
which history as thought is concerned. Its dominance in
the thought of the Western World for a brief period can be
explained, if at all, by history; perhaps in part by reference
to the great conflict that raged between the theologians
and scientists after the dawn of the sixteenth century—an
intellectual conflict associated with the economic conflict
between landed aristocracies, lay and clerical, on the one
side, and the rising bourgeois on the other.

The intellectual formulas borrowed from natural science,
which have cramped and distorted the operations of history
as thought, have taken two forms: physical and biological.
The first of these rests upon what may be called, for con-
venience, the assumption of causation: everything that
happens in the world of human affairs is determined by
antecedent occurrences, and events of history are the illus-
trations or data of laws to be discovered, laws such as are
found in hydraulics. It is true that no historian has ever
been able to array the fullness of history as actuality in
any such deterministic order; Karl Marx has gone further
than any other. But under the hypothesis that it is possible,
historians have been arranging events in neat little chains
of causation which explain, to their satisfaction, why succeeding events happen; and they have attributed any short-

comings in result to the inadequacy of their known data, not to the falsity of the assumption on which they have been operating. Undiscouraged by their inability to bring all history within a single law, such as the law of gravitation, they have gone on working in the belief that the Newtonian trick will be turned some time, if the scientific method is applied long and rigorously enough and facts are heaped up high enough, as the succeeding grists of doctors of philosophy are ground out by the universities, turned loose on "research projects", and amply supplied by funds.

Growing rightly suspicious of this procedure in physico-historiography, a number of historians, still bent on servitude to natural science, turned from physics to biology. The difficulties and failures involved in all efforts to arrange the occurrences of history in a neat system of historical mechanics were evident to them. But on the other side, the achievements of the Darwinians were impressive. If the totality of history could not be brought into a deterministic system without doing violence to historical knowledge; perhaps the biological analogy of the organism could be applied. And this was done, apparently without any realization of the fact that thinking by analogy is a form of primitive animism. So under the biological analogy, history was conceived as a succession of cultural organisms rising, growing, competing, and declining. To this fantastic morphological assumption Spengler chained his powerful mind. Thus freed from self-imposed slavery to physics, the historian passed to self-imposed subservience to biology. Painfully aware of the perplexities encountered as long as he stuck to his own business, the historian sought escape by employing the method and thought of others whose operations he did not understand and could not control, on the simple, almost childlike, faith that the biologist, if not the physicist, really knew what he was about and could furnish the clue to the mystery.

But the shadow of the organismic conception of history had scarcely fallen on the turbulent actuality of history when it was scrutinized by historians who were thinking in terms of their own subject as distinguished from the terms of a mere subdivision of history. By an inescapable demonstration Kurt Riezler has made it clear that the organismic theory of history is really the old determinism of physics covered with murky words. The rise, growth, competition, and decline of cultural organisms is meaningless unless fitted into some overarching hypothesis—either the hypothesis of the divine drama or the hypothesis of causation in the deterministic sense. Is each cultural organism in history, each national or racial culture, an isolated particularity governed by its own mystical or physical laws? Knowledge of history as actuality forbids any such conclusion. If, in sheer desperation, the historian clings to the biological analogy, which school is he to follow—the mechanistic or the vitalistic? In either case he is caught in the deterministic sequence, if he thinks long enough and hard enough.

Hence the fate of the scientific school of historiography turns finally upon the applicability of the deterministic sequence to the totality of history as actuality. Natural science in a strict sense, as distinguished from mere knowledge of facts, can discover system and law only where occurrences are in reality arranged objectively in deterministic sequences. It can describe these sequences and draw from them laws, so-called. From a given number of the occurrences in any such sequence, science can predict what will happen when the remainder appear.

With respect to certain areas of human occurrences, something akin to deterministic sequences is found by the historian, but the perdurance of any sequence depends upon the perdurance in time of surrounding circumstances which cannot be brought within any scheme of deterministic relevancies. Certainly all the occurrences of history as actuality cannot be so ordered; most of them are unknown and owing to the paucity of records must forever remain unknown.

If a science of history were achieved, it would, like the science of celestial mechanics, make possible the calculable prediction of the future in history. It would bring the totality of historical occurrences within a single field and reveal the unfolding future to its last end, including all the apparent choices made and to be made. It would be omniscience. The creator of it would possess the attributes ascribed by the theologians to God. The future once re-vealed, humanity would have nothing to do except to await its doom.

To state the case is to dispose of it. The occurrences of history—the unfolding of ideas and interests in time-motion—are not identical in nature with the data of physics, and hence in their totality they are beyond the reach of that necessary instrument of natural science—mathematics—which cannot assign meaningful values to the impon-derables, immeasurables, and contingencies of history as actuality.

Having broken the tyranny of physics and biology, con-temporary thought in historiography turns its engines of verification upon the formula of historical relativity—the formula that makes all written history merely relative to time and circumstance, a passing shadow, an illusion. Con-temporary criticism shows that the apostle of relativity is destined to be destroyed by the child of his own brain. If all historical conceptions are merely relative to passing events, to transitory phases of ideas and interests, then the conception of relativity is itself relative. When absolutes in history are rejected the absolutism of relativity is also re-jected. So we must inquire: To what spirit of the times, to the ideas and interests of what class, group, nation, race, or region does the conception of relativity correspond? As the actuality of history moves forward into the future, the con-ception of relativity will also pass, as previous conceptions and interpretations of events have passed. Hence, accord-ing to the very doctrine of relativity, the skeptic of relativity will disappear in due course, beneath the ever-tossing waves of changing relativities. If he does not suffer this fate soon, the apostle of relativity will surely be executed by his own logic. Every conception of history, he says, is rela-tive to time and circumstances. But by his own reasoning he is then compelled to ask: To what are these particular times and circumstances relative? And he must go on with receding sets of times and circumstances until he confronts an absolute: the totality of history as actuality which em-braces all times and circumstances and all relativities.

Contemporary historical thought is, accordingly, return-

ing upon itself and its subject matter. The historian is casting off his servitude to physics and biology, as he formerly
cast off the shackles of theology and its metaphysics. He
likewise sees the doctrine of relativity crumble in the cold
light of historical knowledge. When he accepts none of the
assumptions made by theology, physics, and biology, as
applied to history, when he passes out from under the fleeting shadow of relativity, he confronts the absolute in his
field—the absolute totality of all historical occurrences past,
present, and becoming to the end of all things. Then he
finds it necessary to bring the occurrences of history as
actuality under one or another of three broad conceptions.

The first is that history as total actuality is chaos, perhaps
with little islands of congruous relativities floating on the
surface, and that the human mind cannot bring them objectively into any all-embracing order or subjectively into
any consistent system. The second is that history as actuality is a part of some order of nature and revolves in cycles
eternally—spring, summer, autumn, and winter, democracy, aristocracy, and monarchy, or their variants, as imagined by Spengler. The third is that history as actuality
is moving in some direction away from the low level of
primitive beginnings, on an upward gradient toward a more
ideal order—as imagined by Condorcet, Adam Smith, Karl
Marx, or Herbert Spencer.

Abundant evidence can be marshaled, has been marshaled, in support of each of these conceptions of history
as actuality, but all the available evidence will not fit any
one of them. The hypothesis of chaos admits of no ordering
at all; hence those who operate under it cannot write history, although they may comment *on* history. The second
admits of an ordering of events only by arbitrarily leaving
out of account all the contradictions in the evidence. The
third admits of an ordering of events, also by leaving contradictions out of consideration. The historian who writes
history, therefore, consciously or unconsciously performs an
act of faith, as to order and movement, for certainty as to
order and movement is denied to him by knowledge of the
actuality with which he is concerned. He is thus in the
position of a statesman dealing with public affairs; in writ-

ing he acts and in acting he makes choices, large or small, timid or bold, with respect to some conception of the nature of things. And the degree of his influence and immortality will depend upon the length and correctness of his forecast —upon the verdict of history yet to come. His faith is at bottom a conviction that something true can be known about the movement of history and his conviction is a subjective decision, not a purely objective discovery.

But members of the passing generation will ask: Has our work done in the scientific spirit been useless? Must we abandon the scientific method? The answer is an emphatic negative. During the past fifty years historical scholarship, carried on with judicial calm, has wrought achievements of value beyond calculation. Particular phases of history once dark and confused have been illuminated by research, authentication, scrutiny, and the ordering of immediate relevancies. Nor is the empirical or scientific method to be abandoned. It is the only method that can be employed in obtaining accurate knowledge of historical facts, personalities, situations, and movements. It alone can disclose conditions that made possible what happened. It has a value in itself—a value high in the hierarchy of values indispensable to the life of a democracy. The inquiring spirit of science, using the scientific method, is the chief safeguard against the tyranny of authority, bureaucracy, and brute power. It can reveal by investigation necessities and possibilities in any social scene and also offerings with respect to desirabilities to be achieved within the limits of the possible.

The scientific method is, therefore, a precious and indispensable instrument of the human mind; without it society would sink down into primitive animism and barbarism. It is when this method, a child of the human brain, is exalted into a master and a tyrant that historical thought must enter a caveat. So the historian is bound by his craft to recognize the nature and limitations of the scientific method and to dispel the illusion that it can produce a science of history embracing the fullness of history, or of any large phase, as past actuality.

This means no abandonment of the tireless inquiry into

objective realities, especially economic realities and relations; not enough emphasis has been laid upon the conditioning and determining influences of biological and
economic necessities or upon researches designed to disclose
them in their deepest and widest ramifications. This means
no abandonment of the inquiry into the forms and development of ideas as conditioning and determining influences;
not enough emphasis has been laid on this phase of history
by American scholars.

But the upshot to which this argument is directed is
more fundamental than any aspect of historical method.

It is that any selection and arrangement of facts pertaining to any large area of history, either local or world, race
or class, is controlled inexorably by the frame of reference
in the mind of the selector and arranger. This frame of
reference includes things deemed necessary, things deemed
possible, and things deemed desirable. It may be large,
informed by deep knowledge, and illuminated by wide experience; or it may be small, uninformed, and unillumi-
nated. It may be a grand conception of history or a mere
aggregation of confusions. But it is there in the mind, inexorably. To borrow from Croce, when grand philosophy
is ostentatiously put out at the front door of the mind, then
narrow, class, provincial, and regional prejudices come in at
the back door and dominate, perhaps only half-consciously,
the thinking of the historian.

The supreme issue before the historian now is the determination of his attitude to the disclosures of contemporary
thought. He may deliberately evade them for reasons pertaining to personal, economic, and intellectual comfort,
thus joining the innumerable throng of those who might
have been but were not. Or he may proceed to examine
his own frame of reference, clarify it, enlarge it by acquiring knowledge of greater areas of thought and events, and
give it consistency of structure by a deliberate conjecture
respecting the nature or direction of the vast movements
of ideas and interests called world history.

This operation will cause discomfort to individual historians but all, according to the vows of their office, are
under obligation to perform it, as Henry Adams warned the

members of this Association in his letter of 1894. And as Adams then said, it will have to be carried out under the scrutiny of four great tribunals for the suppression of unwelcome knowledge and opinion: the church, the state, property, and labor. Does the world move and, if so, in what direction? If he believes that the world does not move, the historian must offer the pessimism of chaos to the inquiring spirit of mankind. If it does move, does it move backward toward some old arrangement, let us say, of 1928, 1896, 1815, 1789, or 1295? Or does it move forward to some other arrangement which can be only dimly divined—a capitalist dictatorship, a proletarian dictatorship, or a collectivist democracy? The last of these is my own guess, founded on a study of long trends and on a faith in the indomitable spirit of mankind. In any case, if the historian cannot know or explain history as actuality, he helps to make history, petty or grand.

To sum up contemporary thought in historiography, any written history involves the selection of a topic and an arbitrary delimitation of its borders—cutting off connections with the universal. Within the borders arbitrarily established, there is a selection and organization of facts by the processes of thought. This selection and organization—a single act—will be controlled by the historian's frame of reference composed of things deemed necessary and of things deemed desirable. The frame may be a narrow class, sectional, national, or group conception of history, clear and frank or confused and half conscious, or it may be a large, generous conception, clarified by association with the great spirits of all ages. Whatever its nature the frame is inexorably there, in the mind. And in the frame only three broad conceptions of all history as actuality are possible. History is chaos and every attempt to interpret it otherwise is an illusion. History moves around in a kind of cycle. History moves in a line, straight or spiral, and in some direction. The historian may seek to escape these issues by silence or by a confession of avoidance or he may face them boldly, aware of the intellectual and moral perils inherent in any decision—in his act of faith.

5.

*The brief contribution by M. Aron is perhaps the strongest case for "relativism in history," because it takes account of some technical philosophical issues. M. Aron is Professor of Sociology at the Sorbonne and, as an editorial writer in Figaro, an active participant in the political history of France. His statement is a careful weighing of the objective and subjective factors which may enter into the writing of history. It is not, as he says, a question "of throwing doubt on the merits of the scientific method" as a necessary prerequisite for knowledge, in history as elsewhere; it is a question of whether, having made this concession, we do not encounter additional problems on the "stage of critical reflexion."*

*The crucial issue is stated in terms of man's involvement in history. "Man is at the same time both subject and object of historical knowledge"; and this existential involvement seems to distinguish history, in significant respects, from inquiries into nature. It raises again the question of the relevance of "present interests"; and it poses the problem of values which impinge upon history in striking ways.*

*The problem of values, or judgments of history in terms of one's own moral concepts, is the subject of Part III below. Here it is worth noting (a) that, as for Max Weber, value becomes the principle of selection for M. Aron and (b) that he restates the relativistic implications of modern historicism: "The values and interests which are the concern of history have no universal validity; for they vary from age to age." He then discusses the view of some recent German philosophers of a neo-Kantian persuasion, especially Heinrich Rickert (also referred to in Mr. Nagel's article below), who thought it was possible to discover "a universal system of values" on a priori grounds. If there were such a system, over and above the clamor of conflicting values in history, this would provide an objective, transhistorical standpoint from which a universal history could be written. M. Aron rejects this dubious thesis, as well as "the vulgar idea of historical relativism," and reaffirms the consequences of a modified relativistic outlook. His final statement, incidentally, is clearly reminiscent of Dilthey: "One can comprehend different perspectives (in history) even when they seem contradictory and see in their multiplicity a sign not of defeat but of the richness of life."[1] Perspectivism—as an alternative to the traditional search for an objective, universal structure in history—is the more modest intellectual model of our age.*

## RAYMOND ARON

## RELATIVISM IN HISTORY*

English, French and German have the same word both for what has happened in the past and for our knowledge of it: 'history', 'histoire', 'Geschichte' mean both man's past and the knowledge which men strive to build up about their past. (This ambiguity is less in German, which has two words, 'Geschehen' and 'Historie', for these two concepts.)

This ambiguity seems to have a sound basis, because reality and knowledge of reality are inseparable, in a way that has nothing to do with the unity of object and subject. Physical science is not a part of those natural phenomena which it studies, even though it becomes such by changing the course of nature; but consciousness of the past is a constituent part of the historic process. Man has in fact no past unless he is conscious of having one, for only such consciousness makes dialogue and choice possible. Without it, individuals and societies merely embody a past of which they are ignorant and to which they are passively subject; they merely afford to the outside observer a series of transformations, comparable to those of animal species, which can be

---

[1] Cf. Mr. Barraclough's formulation, p. 30 above. For a systematic statement of M. Aron's views on history, cf. his *Introduction à la philosophie de l'histoire* (Paris 1938).

* Excerpt from the article on "The Philosophy of History" in *Chambers Encyclopedia*, Vol. 7, pp. 147–49; reprinted by permission of the editors.

set out in a temporal series. If men have no consciousness of what they are and have been, they do not attain to the dimensions proper to history.

Man, then, is at the same time both the subject and object of historical knowledge. It is only by starting with man that we shall understand the real nature of the science and philosophy of history. . . .

History is the reconstitution by and for those who are living of the life of those who are dead. It is born therefore of the present interest which thinking, feeling, acting men find in exploring the past. The endeavour to get to know an ancestor whose prestige and glory have survived to the present; the praise of the virtues which have made the city; the recital of the misfortunes decreed by the gods or incurred by human faults, which have ruined the city; in every case the memory, be it of the individual or the group, starts from fiction, myth or legend and clears a painful path towards the truth. We must not be deceived by the freshness of impressions: a good memory is not a prerogative of the young.

Historical science, then, begins (speaking of course of a logical and not a temporal succession) by reaction to the imagined happenings of the past. An effort is made to establish and reconstruct the facts in accordance with the most rigorous techniques and to fix the chronology; the myths and legends themselves are used in order to discover the tradition underlying them and thereby to reach the events that produced them; briefly, in Ranke's famous phrase, the highest aim of the historian is to discover and relate *'wie es Geschehen ist'*, how it happened. His ultimate and sole objective is pure reality.

The results achieved by several generations of historians broken in to the methods of historical criticism are well known. Thanks to the achievements of historical science, even though there are still vast gaps in our knowledge, our civilization, for the first time in history, has been able to form a picture of the majority of former civilizations. It stands as a living civilization among those that are dead, conscious of its uniqueness and its frailty. It is true, of course, that no modern historian is able to master the whole mass of material that has been accumulated. The victory of historical science has been a victory for the specialists. The unity of history is lost in the multiplicity of disciplines, each confined to a fragment of the ages or to one aspect of past societies. What does this dispersion of interest mean? It is the inevitable weakness but at the same time the triumph of science and in this history does not differ from the natural sciences. The age of the encyclopaedist has passed and everyone now has to reconcile himself to limitation. What has been achieved is that the past, forever gone yet still surviving in its monuments and documents, has been bit by bit reconstituted in its precise dimensions and infinitely varied perspectives by generations of patient inquiry.

There is no question here of throwing doubt on the merits of the scientific method or, by any cheap scepticism, of impeding the proper development of learned research and disciplined exposition. But it would be a fundamental misconception of the present position of history to forget that the second dialectical stage, that of scientific achievement, is necessarily followed by the third, namely, the stage of critical reflexion, which, while it does not reject scientific achievement as that rejects mythological credulity, yet determines its limits and value. This critical method appears in two forms: that of the *Unseasonable Reflexions* of Nietzsche and that of the application to historical knowledge of Kantian philosophy (Dilthey, Rickert, Simmel, Max Weber).

The *Unseasonable Reflexions* of Nietzsche have, it is true, been interpreted and exploited in a great variety of ways. But the essential idea behind them seems to be still valid. They amount to this simple proposition: the reconstruction of the past is not an end in itself. Just because it is inspired by a present interest, it has a present purpose. What the living seek from a knowledge of the past is not merely the satisfaction of a thirst for knowledge, but either an enrichment of the spirit or a lesson.

What has survived of Nietzsche's thesis is the conception of history as a 'monumental', directly opposed to the pure science of the positivists. Nothing is more obvious than that

all men and all events are not equally worth studying and
that certain persons and certain achievements have a value
and significance which makes them particularly deserving
of our attention. Science itself works on this assumption,
in spite of the fact that erudition for erudition's sake would
tend to consider any and every phenomenon interesting.
Above all, the application of concepts of value to reality
itself dispels the illusion of a reproduction pure and simple
of that which has been and makes clear the inevitable and
legitimate links between the present and the past, the historian and the historical person, the masterpiece and the
admirer.

Nietzsche indeed does not deny either the necessity or
the merit of erudition, the accumulation of materials, the
rigorous criticism of sources and the ascertainment of the
facts. He merely maintains that these preparatory steps are
justified by what follows, namely history proper, 'monumental', critical and archaeological. History is the hand-
maid of life as long as it provides examples, judges the
past and puts the present in its proper place in the historical process. History is a dialogue between the past
and the present in which the present takes and keeps the
initiative.

Whatever its faults or merits, Nietzsche's theory ran a
grave risk: it was easy for it to slip into a contempt for
learning and truth. It suggested an opposition between
types of historian and of history: between those who merely
collect materials and those who expound their significance.
Such opposition is both unreal and fatal, for the essence of
history, the science of the concrete, is to seek for significance
at the level of a unique event or unique society; because
an interpretation which is not disentangled from the facts
is arbitrary and because 'bare fact' is nonsense, or better,
unthinkable.

Historical analyses of the type inspired by Kant have had
the merit of re-establishing this unity and of bringing to
light a solidarity in practice, a logical necessity, where the
Nietzschean concept aroused a suspicion of a duality,
which was not inevitable but only desirable in the interests
of living society.

The Kantian type of critique of historical knowledge derives fairly simply from certain controlling ideas. Historical science is no more the mere reproduction of that which has been than natural science is the reproduction of nature. In both cases mind intervenes and, starting with the raw material, constructs an intelligible world. But though history, like natural science, is a reconstruction, it is a reconstruction of a very different type. The ultimate aim of natural science is a systematized complex of laws, of which each is capable of being deduced from the others. The ultimate subject of history is a unique series of events which will never be repeated, the procession of human societies and civilizations. Natural science seeks for law, history for the particular.

No science is concerned with total reality; each has its own principle of selection, seeking to isolate that which is worth examining or that which serves to explain what is worth examining. The scientist's principle of selection has, it is true, often varied during the centuries from Aristotle to Einstein. The scientist is not interested in the particular stone which fell and killed Archimedes but in the way in which bodies fall, for it is not concerned with space-time data, the precise where and when, but with the abstract and, so to speak, theoretical considerations which are deduced by the reduction of the complex to the simple, such as gravitation in a vacuum or in air. Such a reduction in the historical field is inconceivable. What then is the method of that selection without which research would go on for ever without exhausting the smallest fragment of reality or the least moment of time? The Kantian critique has answered this question by introducing the concept of value. The events which survive in historical consciousness are those which have some relation to the values in which either the actors or the spectators believe. There is not space here for any closer analysis of the concept of value. In the simple form given to it by Max Weber, it is nearly equivalent to the conception of a 'centre of interest.' We preserve from the past that which interests us. Historical selection is guided by the questions which the present asks of the past. The succession of pictures which we make of

past civilizations is determined by the constant changing of
the leading question we ask.

This succession is the more significant because by selection is not to be understood an initial step taken once and
for all, but a continuing orientation of historical work. Selection is not just the decision to study or ignore this or that
fact; it is a certain way of construing facts, of choosing concepts, arranging complexes and of putting events and periods into perspective. This also explains how it is that the
Kantians have succeeded in this case, not in establishing
the universal validity of knowledge, but in suggesting a
kind of relativity. Forms of sensibility and mental categories are the guarantee of universality in the same degree in
which, as conditions of knowledge, they are valid for all
men. But the values and interests which are the concern of
history have no universal validity, for they vary from age
to age. Thus it is that they justify a dictum that has already become classical: every society has its history and
rewrites it as often and as far as the society itself changes.
The past is never definitively fixed except when it has no
future.

Must we to-day envisage a fourth stage of historical approach, one which will integrate the two previous stages
on a higher level and be yet another dialectical development? It does not seem necessary to go beyond relativism
as relativism went beyond the antithesis of legend and
science; it will be enough to define the limits of that relativism at which we have arrived.

One of the Kantians, Rickert, has defined those limits by
using the concept of values. Historical selection is only valid
for those who accept the system of reference employed and
therefore in this sense it is not universally valid. Nevertheless, once such a decisive, if not arbitrary, selection has been
made, the subsequent steps of the historian may well be
rigorously scientific and claim to be universally valid. More
concretely and simply Max Weber said that each historian
asks his own questions and chooses them freely. Once the
questions have been asked the answers to them are given
solely by the facts. The causal relations between the facts,
even if the assemblage of the facts has been dictated by

some topical interest, are either true or false (however difficult the proof may be and whatever the resultant coefficient
of probability). Over and above this hypothetical universality, i.e. the universal validity of the deductions subsequent on a free choice of starting point, Rickert believes
that even the initial relativity due to selection can be overcome, either by studying each period in relation to the
values proper to it, or by elaborating a universal system of
values.

This latter conception would inevitably subordinate scientific truth to the truth of the system of values, that is to
say, to a philosophy. On the other hand the universal system of values is bound to be formal, but the questions which
the historian asks of reality are usually precise and concrete.
Finally, the simple fact of relating one epoch to the values
of a later epoch introduces a principle of constant reinter-
pretation of the past. It is not clear why an historian should
be made to rethink a society exclusively in the same way
in which it thought of itself (or, what comes to the same
thing, to relate each society to its own values and not to
later values). It is by no means certain that the historian
can achieve complete detachment from the present, nor
that he ought to do so: it is only by relating the past to the
unfinished present that it can be made to yield up the secrets which have remained hidden hitherto even from the
most careful research. In fine, the theory of hypothetical
objectivity which satisfied Max Weber, and which incon-
trovertibly applies to causal relations, rests on too simple a
conception of selection. If the totality of an historical reconstruction is orientated by the question asked or the values of reference, the total reconstruction will bear the mark
of the historian's chosen principles of selection, and will be
self-consistent from a single point of view, which at the best
can be recognized as legitimate and fruitful, but is not necessarily universally true.

Nevertheless this relativism, which the very history of
historical science evinces, does not seem to be destructive
of scientific history, as long as it is correctly interpreted.
The fact that we acknowledge the existence of such relativism is a sign, not of scepticism, but of philosophical prog-

ress. In the first place, the degree of relativity is limited by
the utmost rigour in establishing facts and by that impartiality which the scholar can and must have as long as he
is merely unravelling texts and assessing evidence. Next, it
is limited by the partial relationships which, starting from
certain data, can be discerned in reality itself. A certain
degree of uncertainty (but not of essential relativism) is
adduced by the causal relation between an event and its
antecedents and by calculating in accordance with probability the part played by each of the antecedents. The relation between an act or the motives for it, between a ritual
and a faith, between the problems bequeathed by a philosophical system and the solutions given by subsequent systems, is capable of being understood because the subjects
studied are themselves intelligible. What is more, relativism
is itself transcended as soon as the historian ceases to claim
a detachment which is impossible, recognizes what his point
of view is and consequently puts himself into a position to
be able to recognize the points of view of others: not that
it is strictly possible to move from one centre of perspective
to another; there is no numerical constant or calculable
equation which makes such a transition possible. Nevertheless one can comprehend different perspectives even when
they seem contradictory and see in their multiplicity a sign
not of defeat but of the richness of life.

That is what corrects the vulgar idea of historical relativism. When once we cease to interpret our knowledge of
the past by the criterion of a transcendental ego which
gives form to an inert mass of material, when once we put
the historian back into reality and take the structure of reality as the point of reference, then the whole sense of the
relativist formula is transformed. Past human existence is
rich in the same significances and the same fruitful ambiguities as historical knowledge itself. History cannot give a
final, universally valid account of societies, epochs and extinct civilizations, for the very reason that they never had
a unique and universally valid significance. The never-
ending discovery and rediscovery of the past is the expression of a dialectic which will last as long as the human race
and which is the very essence of history: individuals and

communities alike find contact with others enriching and self-revealing. . . .

### 6.

*Whereas the historians are conscious, to different degrees, of the ineluctably subjective factors—the creative imagination, the "art" of writing history, inarticulate philosophical assumptions, and the dubious status of value concepts—that seem to intrude upon the subject of history, the professional philosophers joining this debate are primarily concerned with defending the possibility of an* objective *history; i.e., the thesis that, at least in principle, there are no limits to approximating an ideal of truth in history which corresponds to that in other empirical disciplines. These philosophers, therefore, tend to assimilate the logic of history to the logic of the sciences in general.*

*There is much to be said for this empirical protest against the subjective and idealistic trends inherent in modern historicism. For if a historical work presumes, as it does, to convey some kind of knowledge about what happened, it must obviously conform, in some essential respects at least, to models and criteria of knowledge as we employ them in other scientific disciplines. In other words, it must be possible to say what knowledge in history has in common with other types of knowledge, and what the specific criteria are by which we decide whether a historical work qualifies as a* bona fide *piece of knowledge—or as a piece of propaganda and historical fiction.*

*I begin this philosophical rebuttal with a selection from John Dewey (1859–1952), the most impressive figure in American philosophy during the last generation. Dewey dealt with the problem of historical knowledge in a brief aside, as it were, of a massive, general treatise called* Logic: The Theory of Inquiry; *but the few pages reprinted below are packed with interesting ideas. Unfortunately, he did not write in a particularly felicitous style so that a special effort is needed to sustain one's interest.*

*The key to Dewey's analysis is the statement that "the*

*writing of history is an instance of judgment as a resolution through inquiry of a problematic situation."* This means that historical statements are like statements in any other discourse that claim to be true. They serve the same purpose—to solve a specific problem—and, despite their reference to the past, they are subject to the same kind of *"logic"* which we use in ordinary language or in science. Dewey then gives a brief account of how historical inquiry satisfies these general conditions.

For an understanding of his views, it is important to remember that, according to Dewey, there are no empirical statements, whether general or particular, whether scientific or historical, which are absolutely true or indubitably certain. Human knowledge consists of a body of beliefs, or assertions, which are more or less probable—or *"warranted,"* as Dewey chose to call it. Hence, his neat formulation of the specific problem confronting history: *"The question is not . . . whether history can be a science. It is: Upon what grounds are some judgments about a course of past events more entitled to credence than are certain other ones."*

In these respects, Dewey tended to assimilate historical knowledge to the problem of human knowledge in general. His view, however, is a highly qualified endorsement of *"objectivity and impartiality"* in history. For he also subscribed to the Crocean view (or Beard's) that annals are not history, that *"history is necessarily written from the standpoint of the present,"* and that the selection and arrangement of a historical work is *"controlled by the dominant problems and conceptions of the culture . . . in which it is written."* These are, obviously, sentiments, partly relativistic, partly pragmatic, which impair the status of objectivity in history.

*JOHN DEWEY*

## HISTORICAL JUDGMENTS*

We come to the theme of historical judgments in the
ordinary sense of history. In the latter case, there is no such
need to dwell upon the issue of temporal continuity of
subject-matter as there was in the topics that have been discussed. For history is admittedly history. The logical problem involved now takes a more restricted form: Given temporal continuity, what is the relation of propositions about
an extensive past durational sequence to propositions about
the present and future? Can the historical continuum involved in admittedly historical propositions of the past be
located in the past or does it reach out and include the
present and future? There are of course, many technical
methodological problems that have to be met by the historian. But the central logical problem involved in the existence of grounded judgment of historical subject-matter is, I
take it, that which has just been stated. What conditions
must be satisfied in order that there may be grounded propositions regarding a sequential course of past events? The
question is not even whether judgments about remote
events can be made with *complete* warrant much less is it
whether "History can be a science." It is: Upon what
grounds are some judgments about a course of past events
more entitled to credence than are certain other ones?

That evidential data for all historical propositions must
exist at the time the propositions are made and be contemporaneously observable is an evident fact. The data are
such things as records and documents; legends and stories
orally transmitted; graves and inscriptions; urns, coins,
medals, seals; implements and ornaments; charters, diplo-
mas, manuscripts; ruins, buildings and works of art; exist-

* In *Logic: The Theory of Inquiry* (New York: Henry Holt &
Co., Inc., 1938), pp. 230–39; reprinted by permission of Henry
Holt & Co. I have made a slight change in the title and deleted
part of the first sentence. H.M.

ing physiographical formations, and so on indefinitely. Where the past has left no trace or vestige of any sort that endures into the present its history is irrecoverable. Propositions about the things which can be contemporaneously observed are the ultimate data from which to infer the happenings of the past. This statement, in spite of its obviousness, needs to be made. Although it is taken for granted as a matter of course by those who work with source material, readers of the works which historians compose on the basis of available source-material are likely to suffer from an illusion of perspective. Readers have before them the ready-made products of inferential inquiry. If the historical writer has dramatic imagination, the past seems to be directly present to the reader. The scenes described and episodes narrated appear to be directly given instead of being inferred constructions. A reader takes conclusions as they are presented by the historian to be directly given almost as much as he does in reading a well constructed novel.

Logical theory is concerned with the relation existing between evidential data as grounds and inferences drawn as conclusions, and with the methods by which the latter may be grounded. With respect to logical theory, there is no existential proposition which does not operate either (1) as material for locating and delimiting a problem; or (2) as serving to point to an inference that may be drawn with some degree of probability; or (3) as aiding to weigh the evidential value of some data; or (4) as supporting and testing some conclusion hypothetically made. At every point, exactly as in conducting any inquiry into contemporary physical conditions, there has to be a search for relevant data; criteria for selection and rejection have to be formed as conceptual principles for estimating the weight and force of proposed data, and operations of ordering and arranging data which depend upon systematized conceptions have to be employed. It is because of these facts that the writing of history is an instance of judgment as a resolution through inquiry of a problematic situation.

The first task in historical inquiry, as in any inquiry, is that of controlled observations, both extensive and intensive —the collection of data and their confirmation as authentic.

Modern historiography is notable for the pains taken in these matters and in development of special techniques for securing and checking data as to their authenticity and relative weight. Such disciplines as epigraphy, paleography, numismatics, linguistics, bibliography, have reached an extraordinary development as auxiliary techniques for accomplishing the historiographic function. The results of the auxiliary operations are stated in existential propositions about facts established under conditions of maximum possible control. These propositions are as indispensable as are those resulting from controlled observation in physical inquiry. But they are not final historical propositions in themselves. Indeed, strictly speaking they are not in their isolation historical propositions at all. They are propositions about what now exists; they are historical in their *function* since they serve as material data for inferential constructions. Like all data they are selected and weighed with reference to their capacity to fulfill the demands that are imposed by the evidential function.

In consequence, they are relative to a problem. Apart from connection with some problem, they are like materials of brick, stone and wood that a man might gather together who is intending to build a house but before he has made a plan for building it. He ranges and collects in the hope that some of the materials, he does not yet know just what, will come in usefully later after he has made his plan. Again, because of connection with a problem, actual or potential, propositions about observed facts correspond strictly with conceptual subject-matter by means of which they are ordered and interpreted. Ideas, meanings, as hypotheses, are as necessary to the construction of historical determinations as they are in any physical inquiry that leads to a definite conclusion. The formation of historical judgments lags behind that of physical judgments not only because of greater complexity and scantiness of the data, but also because to a large extent historians have not developed the habit of stating to themselves and to the public the systematic conceptual structures which they employ in organizing their data to anything like the extent in which the physical inquirers expose their conceptual framework.

Too often the conceptual framework is left as an implicit presupposition.

The slightest reflection shows that the conceptual material employed in writing history is that of the period in which a history is written. There is no material available for leading principles and hypotheses save that of the historic present. As culture changes, the conceptions that are dominant in a culture change. Of necessity new standpoints for viewing, appraising and ordering data arise. History is then rewritten. Material that had formerly been passed by, offers itself as data because the new conceptions propose new problems for solution, requiring new factual material for statement and test. At a given time, certain conceptions are so uppermost in the culture of a particular period that their application in constructing the events of the past seems to be justified by "facts" found in a ready-made past. This view puts the cart before the horse. Justification if it is had proceeds from the verification which the conceptions employed receive in the present; just as, for example, the warrant for the conceptual structures that are employed to reconstruct what went on in geological ages before the appearance of man or indeed of life on the earth, is found in verified laws of existing physical-chemical processes. For example, the institution of paleolithic, neolithic and bronze ages of "prehistoric times," with their subdivisions, rests upon a knowledge of the relation between technological improvements and changes in culture which is obtained and verified on the ground of contemporaneous conditions. Since differences in, say, the refinement of quality of the edges of stone implements do not bring their relative dates engraved upon them, it is clear that their use as signs of successive levels of culture is an inference from conceptions that are warranted, if at all, by facts that *now* exist. An extensive doctrinal apparatus is required in order to correlate with one another such varied data as fossil survivals, artefacts, ashes, bones, tools, cave-drawings, geographical distributions, and the material that is drawn from study of existing "primitive" peoples. Yet without these extensive correlations the reconstruction of "prehistoric" times could not proceed.

Recognition of change in social states and institutions is a precondition of the existence of historical judgment. This recognition in all probability came about slowly. In early days it was confined, we may suppose, to emergencies so great that change could not escape notice: such as mass migrations, plagues, great victories in war, etc. As long as these changes were supposed to constitute isolated episodes, history cannot be said to have emerged. It came into existence when changes were related together to constitute courses, cycles or stories having their beginnings and closings. Annals are material for history but hardly history itself. Since the idea of history involves cumulative continuity of movement in a given direction toward stated outcomes, the fundamental conception that controls determination of subject-matter as historical is that of a *direction* of movement. History cannot be written *en masse*. Strains of change have to be selected and material sequentially ordered according to the direction of change defining the strain which is selected. History is of peoples, of dynasties; is political, ecclesiastical, economic; is of art, science, religion and philosophy. Even when these strains are woven together into an effort to construct a comprehensive strand that covers a movement taken to be relatively complete, the various strains must first be segregated and each followed through its course.

From acceptance of the idea that inferential determinations of history depend upon prior selection of some direction of movement, there follows directly a consideration of basic logical importance. *All historical construction is necessarily selective.* Since the past cannot be reproduced *in toto* and lived over again, this principle might seem too obvious to be worthy of being called important. But it is of importance because its acknowledgment compels attention to the fact that everything in the writing of history depends upon the principle used to control selection. This principle decides the weight which shall be assigned to past events, what shall be admitted and what omitted; it also decides how the facts selected shall be arranged and ordered. Furthermore, if the fact of selection is acknowledged to be primary and basic, we are committed to the conclusion that all history is necessarily written from the standpoint of the present, and is, in an inescapable sense, the history not only of the present but of that which is contemporaneously judged to be important in the present.

Selection operates in a three-fold way. The first selection in order of time is made by the people of the past whose history is now written, during the very time when they lived. Herodotus wrote, he said, "in order that the things which have been done might not in time be forgotten." But what determined his selection of the things which should not be forgotten? To some minor extent, doubtless, his personal preferences and tastes; such factors cannot be wholly excluded in any case. But if these factors had been the only or main agency, his history would itself have soon been forgotten. The decisive agency was what was prized by the Athenian people for whom he directly wrote; the things this people judged worthy of commemoration in their own lives and achievements. They themselves had their appraisals of worth which were operating selectively. The legends they transmitted and the things they forgot to retell, their monuments, temples and other public buildings, their coins and their grave-stones, their celebrations and rites, are some of the selective evaluations they passed upon themselves. Memory is selective. The memories that are public and enduring, not private and transitory, are the primary material within which conscious and deliberate historians do their work. In more primitive peoples, folklore, implements, enduring relics, serve, in spite of the accidental ravages of time, the same function of self-appraisal that is passed by living peoples upon their own activities and accomplishments.

The historiographer adds a further principle of selection. He elects to write the history of a dynasty, of an enduring struggle, of the formation and growth of a science, an art or a religion, or the technology of production. In so doing, he postulates a career, a course and cycle of change. The selection is as truly a logical postulate as are those recognized as such in mathematical propositions. From this selection there follow selective appraisals as to (1) the relative weight and relevancy of materials at his disposal and

(2) as to the way they are to be ordered in connection with one another. There is no event which ever happened that was *merely* dynastic, merely scientific or merely technological. As soon as the event takes its place as an incident in a particular history, an act of judgment has loosened it from the total complex of which it was a part, and has given it a place in a new context, the context and the place both being determinations made in inquiry, not native properties of original existence. Probably nowhere else is the work of judgment in discrimination and in creation of syntheses as marked as in historical evocations. Nowhere is it easier to find a more striking instance of the principle that new forms accrue to existential material when and because it is subjected to inquiry.

What has been said finds its conspicuous exemplification in the familiar commonplace of the double sense attached to the word *history*. History is that which happened in the past and it is the intellectual reconstruction of these happenings at a subsequent time. The notion that historical inquiry simply reinstates the events that once happened "as they actually happened" is incredibly naive. It is a valuable methodological canon when interpreted as a warning to avoid prejudice, to struggle for the greatest possible amount of objectivity and impartiality, and as an exhortation to exercise caution and scepticism in determining the authenticity of material proposed as potential data. Taken in any other sense, it is meaningless. For historical inquiry is an affair (1) of selection and arrangement, and (2) is controlled by the dominant problems and conceptions of the culture of the period in which it is written. It is certainly legitimate to say that a certain thing happened in a certain way at a certain time in the past, in case adequate data have been procured and critically handled. But the statement "It actually happened in this way" has its status and significance *within* the scope and perspective of historical writing. It does not determine the logical conditions of historical propositions, much less the identity of these propositions with events in their original occurrence. *Das geschichtliche Geschehen,* in the sense of original events in the existential occurrence, is called *"geschichtlich"* only proleptically; as that which is *subject* to selection and organization on the basis of existing problems and conceptions.

A further important principle is that the writing of history is itself an historical event. It is something which happens and which in its occurrence has existential consequences. Just as the legends, monuments, and transmitted records of, say, Athens, modified the subsequent course of Athenian life, so historical inquiry and construction are agencies in enacted history. The acute nationalism of the present era, for example, cannot be accounted for without reckoning with historical writing. The Marxian conception of the part played in the past by forces of production in determining property relations and of the role of class struggles in social life has itself, through the activities it set up, accelerated the power of forces of production to determine future social relations, and has increased the significance of class struggles. The fact that history as inquiry which issues in reconstruction of the past, is itself a part of what happens historically, is an important factor in giving "*history*" a double meaning. Finally, it is in connection with historical propositions that the logical significance of the emphasis placed upon temporal continuity of past-present-future in dealing with the first two themes of this chapter most fully comes to light.

Our entire discussion of historical determinations has disclosed the inadequacy and superficiality of the notion that since the *past* is its immediate and obvious object, therefore, the past is its exclusive and complete object. *Books* treat of the history of Israel, of Rome, of Medieval Europe, and so on and so on; of nations, institutions, social arrangements that existed in the past. If we derive our logical idea of history from what is contained within the covers of these books, we reach the conclusion that history is exclusively of the past. But the past is of logical necessity the past-of-the-present, and the present is the-past-of-a-future-living present. The idea of the continuity of history entails this conclusion necessarily. For, to repeat, changes become history, or acquire temporal significance, only when they are interpreted in terms of a direction *from* something *to* something. For the purposes of a particular inquiry, the *to* and *from* in question may be intelligently located at any chosen date and place. But it is evident that the limitation is relative to the purpose and problem of the inquiry; it is not inherent in the course of ongoing events. The *present* state of affairs is in some respect the *present* limit-*to*-which; but it is itself a moving limit. As historical, it is becoming something which a future historian may take as a limit *ab quo* in a temporal continuum.

That which is now past was once a living present, just as the now living present is already in course of becoming the past of another present. There is no history except in terms of movement toward some outcome, something taken as an issue, whether it be the Rise and Fall of the Roman Empire, Negro Slavery in the United States, the Polish Question, the Industrial Revolution or Land Tenure. The selection of outcome, of what is taken as the close, determines the selection and organization of subject-matter, due critical control being exercised, of course, with respect to the authenticity of evidential data. But the selection of the end or outcome marks an interest and the interest reaches into the future. It is a sign that the issue is not closed; that the close in question is not existentially final. The urgency of the social problems which are now developing out of the forces of industrial production and distribution is the source of a new interest in history from the economic point of view. When current problems seem dominantly political, the political aspect of history is uppermost. A person who becomes deeply interested in climatic changes readily finds occasion to write history from the standpoint of the effect of great changes that have taken place over large areas in, say, the distribution of rainfall.

There is accordingly, a double process. On the one hand, changes going on in the present, giving a new turn to social problems, throw the significance of what happened in the past into a new perspective. They set new issues from the standpoint of which to rewrite the story of the past. On the other hand, as judgment of the significance of past events is changed, we gain new instruments for estimating the force of present conditions as potentialities of the future.

Intelligent understanding of past history is to some extent
a lever for moving the present into a certain kind of future.
No historic present is a mere redistribution, by means of
permutations and combinations, of the elements of the past.
Men are engaged neither in mechanical transposition of the
conditions they have inherited, nor yet in simply preparing
for something to come after. They have their own problems
to solve; their own adaptations to make. They face the
future, but for the sake of the present, not of the future.
In using what has come to them as an inheritance from the
past they are compelled to modify it to meet their own
needs, and this process creates a new present in which the
process continues. History cannot escape its own process.
It will, therefore, always be rewritten. As the new present
arises, the past is the past of a different present. Judgment
in which emphasis falls upon the historic or temporal phase
of redetermination of unsettled situations is thus a culminating evidence that judgment is not a bare enunciation of
what already exists but is itself an existential requalifica-
tion. That the requalifications that are made from time to
time are subject to the conditions that all authentic inquiry
has to meet goes without saying.

### 7.

*The next three essays by Professors Lovejoy, White, and
Nagel are the most unequivocal assertions on behalf of
writing an objective history. Lovejoy's essay is a direct rejoinder to Dewey and deals with the passage from Dewey's
Logic just concluded. White's essay is a reply to Beard as
well as to the philosophical sources—"Croce, Mannheim,
and Meinecke from whom he [Beard] received . . . most
of his confusion about history." Both White and Nagel reflect Dewey's influence in their approach and language; but
they do not endorse the relativistic or pragmatic aspects of
Dewey's thought.*

*It is these aspects which called forth the article "Present
Standpoints and Past History" by Arthur O. Lovejoy, who
is Professor Emeritus at Johns Hopkins University and who*

*is perhaps best known for his influential work called* The Great Chain of Being, *to which he alludes in the essay reprinted below. His is a general critique, not unlike that of Professor Butterfield's* The Whig Interpretation of History, *of the fallacy that the function of history is to solve "problems of our present." By implication, Lovejoy makes out a strong case for the historian's interest in the past for its own sake, as against the interests of the Whig or "social reformer," and for an "effort of self-transcendence"[1] on the part of the historian as a necessary prerequisite for studying history as an end in itself. Thus the essay is a spirited defense of objectivity against any pragmatic distortions of history. It is interesting to note Professor Lovejoy's brief reference to the ultimate function of history in human life: "History is a branch of anthropology, and the historian is contributing to mankind's effort to fulfil the Delphian imperative." This view evokes Hegelian echoes and hints at the kind of "philosophical anthropology" which some recent philosophers have tried to extract from history.*

## ARTHUR O. LOVEJOY

## PRESENT STANDPOINTS AND PAST HISTORY*

A number of eminent writers, both historians and philosophers, have of late noted, with a certain air of discovery, that, though historiography at least ostensibly relates to the past, a historian writes in the present—that is, in some "present"; and they appear to draw from this observation conclusions to which they attach some importance concerning the epistemology or metaphysics of historical knowledge. With the various issues which have been raised about this branch of knowledge, it is, of course, impossible

[1] Professor Butterfield speaks of an "act of self-emptying"; cf. his essay reprinted in Part III, p. 229 below.

* In *The Journal of Philosophy*, XXXVI, 18 (August 31, 1939), pp. 477–89; reprinted by permission of the editors. I have deleted a few passages referring to other contributions at a symposium for which Professor Lovejoy's article was originally written. H.M.

to deal comprehensively in a brief paper. . . . I shall here limit myself to some comments on a now rather widely current combination of propositions about historiography which runs as follows:

1. Historiography is necessarily selective; it never deals with the "total welter of past happenings," but picks out some limited portion of these.

2. Selection necessarily presupposes some "principle" which is determined by the historian; he chooses to relate some *particular* history, and "everything in the writing of history depends upon the principle used to control selection."[1]

3. The selection "of an event to take its place in such a particular history," is both a subtraction from the facts and an addition to them; as Mr. Dewey has said, it "loosens the event from the total complex of which it was a part and gives it a place in a new context, the context and the place both being determinations made in the inquiry, not native properties of original existence."[2]

4. Historiography, again, if anything more than "bare chronicle," is not only selective but interpretative and "explanatory"; and interpretation and explanation mean seeing in the event relations and significances which were not themselves contained in the event.

5. Historiography, moreover, though it is (largely) about past events, is itself a present event, and both the selections and the interpretations are determined by present causes or motives operating in the mind of the historian, and of the historian as representative of a particular "period." Again in Mr. Dewey's words, "all history is necessarily written from the standpoint of the present, and is, in an inescapable sense, the history not only of the present but of that which is contemporaneously judged to be important in the present." "The conceptual material employed in writing history is that of the period in which the history is written."[3] . . .

To these five propositions are often added further speci-

[1] Dewey, *Logic*, p. 235.
[2] Ibid., p. 236.
[3] Ibid., pp. 235, 236.

fications concerning the nature of the present determinants which control the historian's selection, interpretation, and reconstruction; I shall here mention only two of these, viz.

6. These determinants are present judgments of value.

7. They are essentially "cultural"; again in Mr. Dewey's words, "historical inquiry is controlled by the dominant problems and conceptions of the culture of the period in which it was written."[4]

I am far from suggesting that there is not much truth to be found among these propositions, or that some of the truths are not deserving of emphasis. But, as often expressed in highly general terms, even the true propositions here are equivocal; unless their legitimate meanings are *précisés* and particularized, they lend themselves to, and, if I am not mistaken, sometimes receive, misinterpretation into propositions that are untrue and, if given any practical application, have pernicious consequences in historiography.

What is true, not to say truistic, is that the historian always and necessarily does *some* selecting and some interpreting, that it is he that does it, that his selection and interpretation are determined by *some* motivation now operative in him, that *some* kind or other of value-judgments enter into this motivation implicitly or explicitly, and that—if "the culture of his period" means *all* the modes of thought, feeling, and practice to be found existing in his time—it is a tautological proposition that *some* "cultural factor" affects his selection and interpretation. But these statements mean nothing definite until we inquire *what* he selects, what kind of interpretation he, *quâ* historian, engages in, what sort of motives necessarily and legitimately affect his procedure, which of these are value-judgments, and of what specific type, and what, out of the multitude of contemporary cultural factors, must or should influence him.

Now the only factual generalization which it is safe to make about the selection of subject-matter by historians is that it is always determined by the *interestingness*, for the historian or for somebody, of some question, to which data

4 Ibid., p. 236.

consisting of texts or other supposedly evidential material might conceivably yield a more or less probable answer. The initial selection of a question in turn, of course, determines the selection, from the mass of material, of the particular data which appear relevant to the question. "Interestingness" is, no doubt, a category of value, and an extremely important and rather neglected one; but it is also extremely general. None less general, however, will serve for describing the determinants of the actual choice of subjects in historiography; and no universal proposition on this matter less truistic than that histories are written to answer questions concerning the past which are of interest to somebody in the present, is true at all. To the range of possible interests in such questions no limit can be set: the questions may be vague or precise, enormously comprehensive or exceedingly minute, capable of answers of a high or a very low degree of probability. If a historian feels called upon to justify his particular interest—or if he hopes to induce others to read him—he is likely to say that an answer to his question is "important"; in doing so he is undoubtedly claiming a social, that is, a more than personal and idiosyncratic, value for the potential answer to his question. But the claim need not, and often does not, mean more than that other persons are also interested in knowing the answer. That they *are* interested is no doubt a fact about "the culture of the period"; but this statement is little more than another way of saying that in the period certain histories do in fact get written and read. The further factual question may be asked why, through what "causes," a certain number of persons of the time find the subject of a given history interesting; or the normative question, whether people in this age ought to be interested in it. To the former there are again many answers; but to both questions there is one answer which is erroneous. And that is an answer sometimes apparently deduced from the set of propositions earlier enumerated. It is that the practical or speculative problems of the present either must or should determine the selection of historical questions to be asked—of the subject-matter of historical inquiry. Either as a factual generalization or as a moral exhortation this is peculiarly inapplicable to intellectual historiography—the history of ideas. It results from a confusion of the interests and aims of the historian as such with those of the philosopher as such—or of the social reformer. For the philosopher, *quâ* philosopher, the mass of factual data—the record of other men's thoughts—is of value as a repository of "considerations" pertinent to some problem or problems to which he thinks it important to get, if possible, a solution—of hypotheses which may be worthy of examination, of distinctions to be borne in mind, of reasonings which may contribute to a valid conclusion (or to the support of his dogmas), or, at worst, of plausible fallacies or blind alleys to be avoided. *He,* therefore, necessarily selects from the data only those parts which seem logically apposite to the present philosophical or practical question to which he seeks a reasoned answer. But the historian's selection neither always nor usually is, nor ought to be, controlled and restricted by such philosophic or practical interests. It is not, or need not be, so restricted in fact, because it does not appear to be a true psychological generalization that no question about the past is ever interesting to anybody unless the answer to it is conceived to be instrumental to the settlement of a present philosophic problem or the determination of a present program of action. The inquiry of the historian, to be sure, is always, in intent, instrumental to the present—or more precisely, the future—satisfaction of having a verified probable answer to his *historical* question; and the knowledge of the answer, if attained, will presumably continue to afford some sort of satisfaction. But the answer need not, in any other sense, be assumed to be contributory to the solution of a problem which is *not* about the past. The historian's question may be—indeed, perhaps most frequently is—prompted by a desire to "understand" the present, or some present, by ascertaining its antecedents. An explorer finds in the midst of a flat plain an isolated, roughly quadrangular mound. No accepted geological hypothesis explains its presence there. He therefore tentatively adopts the hypothesis that it is of human construction, and was a burial-place or place of worship of some vanished race once resident in that area; to test the hypothesis, he excavates the mound, and dis-

covers, perhaps, skeletons and artifacts which not only
verify his hypothesis but give him much information which
anthropologists and historians find "interesting" about the
physical characters and the life of an otherwise unknown
people. The only "problem of our present" which his investigation has served to resolve is a problem about the past
events which explain some now observable fact. Nor need
the motive of the inquiry even be the desire to *explain* the
present fact; it may be, in the etymological sense of the
adjective, a purely archeological motive—a curiosity to
know more about the manner of life of the bygone men
who, from the outset, the investigator assumes must have
built the mound. And the motives prompting the student
of the history of ideas may be of the same sorts. He may
find, in some product of a "present" not ours—say in Pope's
*Essay on Man,* if I may be permitted to adduce a personal
experience which is not inapposite—a good deal of rather
obscure talk about something called "the great Chain of
Being." Reading other eighteenth-century writings he finds
copious other indications of the vogue, in that period, of
ideas associated with this term. He thereupon becomes
curious to know more precisely what these ideas were, how
they were conceived to be inter-related, and—partly as a
means to understanding their inter-relations—where they
came from and through what processes they developed;
and this inquiry will lead him back through early modern
and medieval philosophy to—as I think—Plato. In all of
this he may be—though, if he be also a philosopher, it may
by some be thought scandalous that he should be—quite
innocent of any preoccupation with any "problems of the
present" except the specifically historical problem from
which he started; and even though—if a philosopher—he
may in the end seem to himself to discover in the story as
a whole some intimations of an argument pertinent to contemporary metaphysics, this will be a pure by-product; and
it will be as philosopher and not as historian that he discovers it.

It is not, then, I suggest, factually true that historical
inquiries are necessarily or commonly motivated by present
non-historical problems; and I have added that they should

not be determined by or restricted to such problems, least of all in the case of intellectual history. For one, at least, of the functions of the historiography of ideas is to throw light upon the workings of the human mind and the range of its diversities. If there are problems which were of concern, or reasonings which seemed sound, or beliefs which seemed valuable, to men in the past, though they do not seem so to me or to most of my contemporaries, this is a fact of prime historical and psychological interest. If any normative criterion for the intellectual historian's selection is to be set up, it is that the selection should be determined, not by what seems important to him, but by what seemed important to other men; for it is precisely this that differentiates historical from any other type of relevance and significance. General histories of philosophy have sometimes been inadequate and misleading, as *histories*, through a disregard of this canon. Their authors, being usually philosophers, have tended to select for exposition those aspects of past philosophizing which are pertinent to the issues that interest their own age, or even to view the entire course of reflection as leading up (by a more or less devious route) to their own philosophies—and therefore to overlook or minimize ideas engrossing and potent in the thought of earlier generations, which can not be fitted into that pattern. The more a historian has his eye on "the problems which history has generated in the present," or has his inquiry shaped by the *philosophic* conceptual material of the period in which he writes, the worse historian he is likely to be—though he may be the better philosopher. For he may not assume *a priori* that the major problems of the present were the major problems of the past, or that the controlling categories and presuppositions of thinkers of all former ages were those now commonly accepted; he may, and often does, need to exercise his mind in thinking in concepts that —though not intrinsically alien to the potentialities of the human mind—are alien to his and his contemporaries' habitual modes and moods of thinking. M. Lévy-Bruhl has sought to show how different the mental processes of primitive peoples are from our own. I will not attempt to judge of the degree of his success in this undertaking; but the undertaking itself is inspired by properly historiographical, and not by historically irrelevant and potentially misleading philosophical, preconceptions and interests. For it is improbable that we shall find much in what is distinctive in the mental processes of primitive men that will aid in the solution of our problems. The contemporary astronomer or cosmographer can get no help whatever in his present inquiries from the reasonings upon which Aristotle based his theory of the heavens; but it would be a strange history of philosophy or of science which left them out.

To study history is always to seek in some degree to get beyond the limitations and preoccupations of the present; it demands for success an effort of self-transcendence. It is not impossible nor unprofitable for a rational animal—and it is imperative for the historian—to realize that his ancestors had ends of their own which were not solely instrumental to his ends, that the content and meaning of their existence are not exhaustively resolvable into those of the existence of their posterity. In these aspects of history lie not the least of its values; for it is they, especially, which make of it a mind-enlarging, liberalizing, sympathy-widening discipline, an enrichment of present experience. True, historical study, when thus initially freed from the engrossment of contemporary problems, may lead, and not infrequently has led, to the recognition of other genuine problems (and of considerations relevant to their solution) of which the historian or his readers were at the outset oblivious; thus intellectual history sometimes generates new, or regenerates old, philosophical interests, inquiries, or insights. But if history is thus to suggest to you *new* "present problems," it is upon condition that you first escape from obsession with the old.

This, however, it may be objected, is itself a present value-judgment, arising out of one feature of the "culture of our period"—namely, our interest in just knowing how other men have thought and felt, and what the diversities of operation of the human mind are—which is advanced as pertinent to the historian's selection. That is obvious. But the value-judgment in question is that it is of value to us to understand interests and valuations not our own; and the objection simply illustrates what I am suggesting—that the mere insistence upon the rôle in historiography of present and culturally determined value-judgments is, of itself, so all-comprehensive that it excludes no specific principles of selection whatever—not even its own apparent opposite— and is therefore of no practical service to the historiographer; while it at the same time tends to be interpreted in a way which would result in selections and exclusions contrary to the essence of the intellectual historian's enterprise, and adverse to some of the chief values of that enterprise. . . .

The historian's, and especially the intellectual historian's, general and perennial problem is, as I have already intimated, the problem of human nature and human behavior, including under the latter intellectual behavior—the processes by which individual and group interests, opinions, and tastes are formed and the sequences and laws, if any, of their changes—so far as a knowledge of the acts, thoughts, and feelings of men in the past may throw light upon these matters. History is a branch of anthropology, in the largest sense of the term, and the historian is contributing in his own fashion to mankind's effort to fulfil the Delphian imperative. But his contribution to *this* "present problem" will be sound and, within the limitations imposed by the nature of his evidential material, adequate, only if it is *not* restricted and biased by a fixation upon distinctive present problems. His task is to become acquainted, as thoroughly and as objectively as he can, with both the variables and the constants in human thought and feeling and action; and he is less likely to accomplish it if he limits his interest to that which bears only upon those variables which differentiate the present from the past. And it is especially difficult to see why relevance to our specifically "present problems" should render either the questions which a historian asks about past events—including past philosophies— or his answers to those questions, more "objective." It would seem rather that a concern with problems or with conceptions which are, in any exclusive sense, "present," would tend to render his inquiries and conclusions less "objective." It is, indeed, true that, in so far as the historiographer attempts to "explain" past events, and especially past ideas or beliefs, he will naturally employ for that purpose present explanatory hypotheses—e.g., psychological or psychopathological hypotheses—which he regards as having objective validity. . . . But this proposition seems to me to be expressed in too general and therefore potentially misleading terms when it is said that the "ultimate focus" of his historical inquiries either is or should be "our present problems" . . .

I have thus far been discussing the propositions mentioned at the outset, and especially propositions 1, 2, 5, 6, and 7, as either universal assertions of fact about the determinants of the historiographer's selections or as normative judgments professing to tell us to what sort of questions his inquiries ought to be restricted. But the same set of propositions, especially numbers 3 to 7, may be and sometimes are construed as theses in logic or epistemology, applied to the special case of historical knowledge; and, so construed, their general upshot is that the conditions and nature of the historian's inquiry necessarily shape or transform the objects of that inquiry—that something analogous to Heisenberg's principle holds good of historiography. Thus it is urged (Prop. 3) that any selection is, if not a falsification, at least an alteration, of the events selected out of the totality of past events, since it detaches them from their original context and places them in a new context. This contention, I can't but think, is mainly a vestigial survival of the dogma of the internality of all relations—which obviously can not be discussed at length here. I can only say that I find no difficulty in the supposition that any entity, or subject of discourse, may actually have one set of properties which are relevant to one context, and others which are relevant to other contexts, and that, in attending to one of these sets, you do not thereby alter either it or the others. One aspect of the life of George Washington is relevant to the history of American foreign policy, another to the history of dentistry and to that of early American portrait-painting. In selecting for separate inquiry his rôle in the formation of our foreign policy, the political historian does not appear to me to imply any transformation of the event that in later life Washington wore a bulky set of artificial ivory teeth, a fact, it seems, of some interest to the historians of dentistry and to students of his portraits. Both the ideas of the Farewell Address and the teeth I should suppose to have been, not, indeed, native, but actual—and probably not interdependent—properties of the "original existence"; and their relevance to two different histories is not "made" but discovered in the process of historical inquiry.

But the theorem that the characters of the historian's object are made what they are by him—i.e., by the purpose and procedure of his inquiry—is not wholly a deduction from the postulate of the internality of relations. Its logic does not appear to rest merely upon the simple, gratuitous, and, indeed, contradictory assumption that diversity of contexts means diversity of that which is in those contexts. It is sometimes an application to the case of history of a familiar general type of epistemological argument which rests upon the duality of the cognitive event and its *cognoscendum*. Retrospective judgments seem the clearest instances of such duality. The historian, at least, never *possesses* the object to which he ostensibly refers; what he apprehends is never the past event *an-und-für-sich*, but only its perspective appearance from his "present standpoint"; and that appearance, it is sometimes added, is essentially a function of the standpoint and of his present subjective state—*his* "conceptual material," concrete practical situation, valuations, purposes, and the like. The historiographer is involved in what may be called—if the barbarism may for the nonce be permitted—a presenticentric predicament, which is a particular form, and an especially acute form, of the egocentric predicament. "It is idle," observes Mead in his *Philosophy of the Present,* "to have recourse to a 'real' past within which we are making constant discoveries; for that past must be set over against a present within which the emergent appears, and the past, which must then be looked at from the standpoint of the emergent, becomes a different past"—just as "from every new rise the landscape becomes a different landscape." "If we are referring to any . . . in itself correctness," in our historical judgments, "it must be to that of a reality which by

definition could never get within our experience, or to that
of a goal in which the type of experience in which we find
ourselves ceases. . . . The metaphysical demand for a set
of events which is irrevocably there in the past, to which
[our] histories seek a constantly approaching agreement,
comes back to motives other than those at work in the most
exact scientific research."[5] Thus Proposition 5 tends to pass
over into a generalized historical impressionism or relativism. "History" consists simply in the present "emergents,"
the reactions or states of mind evoked in historians when
acted upon by those present stimuli which are euphemis-
tically called "records of the past." That this is by no means
what most historians are trying to get, and think they are
getting, from their researches, no one, I suppose, would
deny; what the argument implies is that, do what they
will, it is all that they *can* get.

If this argument were accepted, epistemology would be
qualified to issue a general and definitive injunction against
the historian's usual ambition or pretension. The initial
premise of the argument is, I think, true, and obvious: that
intertemporal cognition is inevitably dualistic, that the historian's act of knowing and its referent are existentially external to one another. And from any such dualism you may
always conclude to the impossibility of knowledge of the
object "in itself," if you mean by "knowing" the immediate
possession of the referent within the cognitive event. But
the only experience that is in this sense cognitive consists
in the momentary awareness of transient and private data,
the blank glare of the content of any specious present, devoid of external relations or continuants, of all reference to
"others" or "beyonds." The "kind of experience in which we
find ourselves" as actual knowers, or claimants of knowledge, is utterly different from this experience of bare pre-
sentedness. It always consists of *judgments* about that
which is not merely here, not merely now, and not merely
mine; in short, about that which by definition can never
get "within my experience" when this, or any, particular
event of judging is occurring. All knowing is involved in

[5] *Philosophy of the Present*, pp. 2, 9, 8, 28.

the presenticentric predicament—which, if there be any knowledge, can not be a hopeless predicament. For all knowledge, except in the spurious sense mentioned—all science and all practical intelligence—rest upon history; that is to say, they rest upon the postulate of the reality of past events and of the possibility of now knowing something of what they were—be they only the operations performed at an earlier moment of an experiment which a physicist is now conducting, or the results of the experiments of his predecessors. It *is* a pure postulate; for it can never be empirically verified in any strict sense. Unfortunately, the expression "empirical verification" is commonly used, even by philosophers, in a singularly loose and uncritical manner. All so-called "verification in actual experience" is at this or that or the other particular moment of experience; but what is verified is not at that particular moment experienced. It is, however, possible to recognize—without ever "empirically verifying"—the basic general postulates which are implicit in and indispensable for the belief in the possibility of any factual knowledge, or of action guided by a knowledge of the past uniformities of events; and, accepting these postulates, we are enabled, in any given present, to frame more specific hypotheses about these uniformities, and then move on into future presents, testing our hypotheses by collating and comparing new experiences with remembered ones—the remembered ones being then, in turn, *un*experienced, and actually, though not necessarily consciously, postulational. We have in this way built up a system of concrete working generalizations based upon remembered or recorded experience, by which we judge of the probability of any particular alleged experience—of testimony offered in a law-court, for example, such testimony always consisting of statements concerning events which by definition are not a part of the experience of the court. But the testimony, true or false, is about those events "in themselves"; and the necessary assumption that it *is* either true or false is equivalent to the assumption that it refers to events which either did or did not occur, and if they occurred, had characters of their own which do not become "different" by the subsequent prosecution of an

inquiry concerning them. Courts do not recognize the presenticentric predicament. And though the inquiries of the
historiographer, especially if they relate to events remote in
time, are often more difficult, and sometimes at a lower
level of probability, than the inquiries of courts, they have
the same implicit logical structure, which is simply the
structure of all inquiry about the not-now-presented; and,
if they *are* historical inquiries, and not criticism or evaluation, their objective is the same—to know whether, by the
canons of empirical probability, certain events, or sequences of events, happened at certain past times, and
what, within the existential limits of those times, the characters of those events were.[6] The more specific canons
themselves, indeed, are sometimes subject to revision, as
the result of further experience or fuller analysis of past
experience; and in their application there are often difficulties. But the difficulties are technical difficulties of detail;
and even the revision of particular canons rests upon the
same fundamental postulates of the reality and knowability
of the not-presented, and is itself an inference based upon
the acceptance of other and more general canons.

I conclude, therefore, that the consequences sometimes
drawn with respect to historiography from the presenticentric predicament are inadmissible. The predicament, indeed, is a fact; but it is the predicament of *all* knowing at
every instant at which a knowing can occur; the only consequence which could be drawn from it would be a universal scepticism, in which all science would disappear and all
exercise of intelligence be interdicted; and even in drawing
this sceptical consequence you would contradict it. If you
are willing to accept the fundamental postulates of science
and common sense, you can no longer deduce solely from
the *general* fact of the presenticentric predicament any
special conclusions with regard to historical inquiry and
knowledge. So far as that predicament is concerned, it is in
the same position as any other knowledge. There *are* certain special predicaments of the historian, which in many

---

[6] The question of "causal explanation" in history is another
issue, which, in order to keep this paper within due limits of
length, I refrain from discussing.

cases are serious—those arising, e.g., from the fact that his evidential material is usually purely documentary—which amounts to saying that the often truth-eliciting process of cross-examination is not available to him—from the scarcity of such material, especially in the case of remote events, from conflicts of evidence, changes in the meanings of words, and the like. But these are all familiar to all critical historians; and the very recognition of them as constituting difficulties not only presupposes definite empirical criteria of the adequacy and trustworthiness of evidence, but also presupposes that the primary objects of the historian's inquiry are "a set of events irrevocably there in the past," having their own properties and relations in their own times, which it is his first business to endeavor to ascertain. In so far as philosophers say things which seem to suggest that this is not his first business, they merely tend to undermine his morals as a historian. And this should be especially insisted upon by those who hold that the historiographer's function is to contribute to the solution of our present practical problems. For it is obvious that the only way in which he can do so is by making us better acquainted with events as they were in their several times and places, and their actual past antecedents and consequences and uniformities. Light is thrown upon such problems only by the extrapolation of the past—but an *analyzed* past—into the future; planning is retrospection in reverse. It is not, perhaps, "pragmatically" important whether a man believe or disbelieve in metempirical physical realities; but it is of manifest pragmatic importance that he be a straightforward realist about history—since "history" is another name for the mass of experience which, in the interest of practice, he needs to know, and yet can never directly make his own. Doubtless we can not wholly escape from the effects of perspective, in retrospection or in vision. But "perspective effects" are, precisely, forms of illusion; and it is characteristic of intelligence that it can recognize them as such and endeavor, not wholly without success, to correct them. And this is not less true of that exercise of intelligence which is historical inquiry than of any other.

## 8.

*Mr. Morton White, Professor of Philosophy at Harvard University, defends an objective view of history by exposing a fallacy which he believes is "typical of the philosophy of history, the confusion between the psychology of historical interpretation and its logic." The point is that there is a fundamental difference between (a) the process of discovering a historical truth and (b) the process of justifying a historical interpretation, i.e., of giving empirical and rational arguments in support of one's findings. A number of psychological and social factors may influence the process of discovery; but in the process of justifying his work, the historian, according to Mr. White, as much as the scientist, must submit to objective tests and methods of confirmation which have nothing to do with his personality, milieu, or general world view.*

*Whether this distinction disposes of the challenge of historical relativism is a difficult matter; for it should be evident from the previous readings that the central issue in history is precisely (a) whether the historian is not more deeply involved as a person in his subject matter than a scientist and (b) whether this involvement does not also enter into the "logic" of history to an extent to which it does not enter into the logic of bacteriology—to use the case of Pasteur cited by Professor Sidney Hook (see below, p. 199).*

### MORTON WHITE

### CAN HISTORY BE OBJECTIVE?*

. . . Robinson** and Beard were more interested in questions about the nature and function of history than

* In *Social Thought in America* (New York: Viking Press, 1949), pp. 220–35; reprinted by permission of the Viking Press. A revised and expanded edition was published in 1957 as a Beacon Press paperback. I have deleted a few passages referring to earlier parts of the book.

** James Harvey Robinson, author of *The New History* (New York: Macmillan, 1912) H.M.

most American historians. They were amateurs in philosophy who assumed a job which their philosophical colleagues had neglected. Few major philosophers of their generation apart from Dewey dealt seriously with the procedures and aims of history; there were at best a couple of essays by James, a chapter by Santayana, and almost nothing by Peirce or the realists (whether critical or naive). This lack of interest may be explained in many ways. First of all, the philosophy of history has been associated in America with Spengler, Toynbee, Hegel, and Marx, and hence regarded with a certain coolness by anti-metaphysical pragmatists, naturalists, and realists. When history was approached epistemologically it raised no special problems for American philosophers, since they saw no peculiarities in historical knowledge. They worried so much about knowledge in general that they hardly had time to treat a mere special case. This was one of the reasons, I suspect, why Beard sought help from the Continent—why his later writings are dotted with references to Croce, Mannheim, and Meinecke, from whom he received stimulation and, if he reported them accurately, most of his confusion about history. Beard's ideas about the method of history and social sciences as expressed in later books like *The Nature of the Social Sciences* (1934) and *The Discussion of Human Affairs* (1936) were quite different from those defended by Robinson in *The New History* (1912) and also different from Beard's own early views.

There is one thread of continuity between Robinson's new history of 1912 and Beard's later conception of history —they both opposed the views of Ranke. . . . The earliest attacks on Ranke were made from a relatively simple point of view. Robinson attacked Ranke because the latter conceived the "facts" in a narrow way. Ranke seemed to eliminate the dynamic aspect of history, the aspect that corresponded to Darwin's theory of evolution, and hence conceived of history as the counterpart of Darwin's duller and more "Baconian" efforts. Ranke also seemed to eliminate a number of important facts when he limited himself to political history. In conformity with historicism and organicism Robinson urged that history be construed as the

study of all kinds of social facts, whereas Ranke had nar-
rowed the task of the historian first by eliminating what
might be called interpretative facts and then by restricting
the remainder to those which were political.

At no point did Robinson doubt that the procedure of
the historian in establishing either detailed singular statements or interpretations were "objective." At no point did
he suggest that the method of confirming them is radically
different from that used in confirming empirical statements
of common sense or science. He emphasized the similarities
between history and natural sciences rather than their differences. Historical knowledge, whether it was interpretative or merely "descriptive," was to be established according to the canons of all reliable knowledge. There might
be differences between the method of verifying the bank
balance of a member of the Constitutional Convention and
the method of verifying Beard's economic interpretation of
the Constitution, but these differences were quite analogous
to the different methods of verifying the observation reports
of a chemist in a laboratory and verifying the theory which
explained them. In his *Economic Interpretation of the Constitution* Beard said he was seeking proximate and remote
causes, but he certainly thought that the fundamental
thesis of that book was objective and factual. The trouble
with non-interpretative history from the point of view of
Beard's early writings was its narrow conception of a factual statement. According to that conception, the statement
"Booth shot Lincoln in 1865" was factual, but the statement
"Because Lincoln was assassinated in 1865 the Reconstruction turned out as it did" no longer expressed a fact. Therefore the new historians urged a broader conception of factual statement. They wanted the historian to admit that he
could and should give explanations of how and why things
came to pass without ceasing to be objective. When Beard
enlarged his conception of the historian's duties he found
himself defending causal statements like "The Constitution
was created *because* certain men wished to protect their
economic interests," but causal statements, on his early
view, were just as susceptible of objective test as the singular statements which made up his economic biographies of

the framers of the Constitution. This is plainly implied in his writing at that time. The interpretative thesis, "Our fundamental law was not the product of the whole people but rather of a group of economic interests which must have expected beneficial results from its adoption," was supported in an objective way. Without raising the question as to whether he proved the thesis conclusively, we must admit that Beard marshaled evidence in its behalf just as zealously as he marshaled evidence in behalf of a statement about the number of slaves owned by Charles Cotesworth Pinckney.

In approaching Beard's later philosophical views it must be remembered that in 1913 he presented an economic interpretation of the Constitution; and interpretations, according to Beard's *later* views, are not subject to the same kind of tests as "Booth shot Lincoln." But originally Beard saw no profound epistemological implications in the process of historical interpretation. In embarking on the new history Beard and Robinson did not believe that they were entering a realm in which the usual canons of scientific procedure no longer applied and in which the values of the historian precluded scientific objectivity. . . . I stress this so much because of the change which came over Beard in later years on precisely these questions. While he continued to argue for interpretation and broad syntheses, and connecting the past with the present, a new note emerged in his philosophical writings. He came to feel that precisely this need for synthesis and interpretation leads to a more relativistic position. He came to worry about whether objectivity is possible once we leave the "solid historical knowledge" that Washington crossed the Delaware, and ascend to the value-charged "historical thought" involved in a history of American civilization.

In his later writings Beard came to distinguish between *history as actuality*, that is, the actual historical process "out there," and *historical record, knowledge, and thought*, which are discursive in character and which communicate things *about* history as actuality. Beginning with the records the historian tries to create *history as knowledge*, a "collection of facts verified, authenticated, and generally

agreed upon," like "George Washington was the first president of the United States under the Constitution; John
Adams succeeded him; and Thomas Jefferson was inaugurated in 1801."[1] But historical *thought,* according to Beard
is different from all of this. It involves selection, arrangement, and interpretation of facts based on the records and
historical knowledge, and selection takes place only with
reference to ideas and purposes in the mind of the historian.

The distinction between historical knowledge and historical thought is most crucial. On it Beard builds his most
serious philosophical conclusion. Historical knowledge, it
would appear, is a set of propositions which are formally
singular, like "Caesar crossed the Rubicon" and "Washington crossed the Delaware," in contradistinction to general
propositions like "All bodies attract each other" and "All
gases expand when heated." Beard seems to believe that
the propositions which make up history as knowledge are
relatively easy to discover. History as thought, on the other
hand, brings us into the realm of synthesis, interpretation,
and selection; and here a new kind of process takes place,
a process which is so tinged with the value preconceptions
of the historian that we can no longer have the agreement
and objectivity possible on the "George Washington slept
here" level. The problem for the philosopher is to investigate the comparative objectivity of these two kinds of
history: (1) the compendium or conjunction of known
historical propositions which constitute Beard's *history
as knowledge* and (2) that entity, however describable,
which issues as the result of *history as thought.*

Let us forget the Platonic notion of proposition and the
vaguer notion of fact for the moment, and let us simply
distinguish two kinds of language. One is a chronicle or an
almanac; it contains sentences about the dates of office of
presidents, about the dates of battles, and other sentences
deemed to be true by the historian before he begins to
"think" (in Beard's sense), before he begins to select and
interpret. A chronicle is a vast logical conjunction of the
sentences which compose it. "George Washington was the

[1] Charles A. Beard, *The Nature of the Social Sciences* (New
York: Scribner's 1934), p. 50.

first president *and* John Adams was the second *and . . .*"
and so on. Each one of these component statements is presumably true, and known to be true by the historian. Hence
the problem of defining the truth or adequacy of the whole
almanac is a relatively simple matter—the almanac will be
true just in case every one of its conjuncts is true. One supposes that Beard would have agreed with this since he
makes no fuss about our not *knowing* the truth of such
elementary statements. But now let us turn to the profound
historical synthesis, the product of history as thought, and
ask, What is its relation to the elementary statements composing the almanac or chronicle? This is an extremely important question, and so far as one can tell it is the one
that bothers most philosophers of history who agree with
Beard, although they never formulate it in quite this way.
Considering it will give us some idea of the manner in
which "thought" is supposed to enter the procedures of the
historian.

If selection simply means paring down the original list
(known to be true), the result of selection will also be true.
Any part of a true conjunction remains true. And surely
any reordering of the true statements on the original list
will also be true by virtue of well-known properties of conjunction. It makes no difference whether you say "John
Adams was the second president of the United States and
George Washington was the first" or whether you reverse
the order in the sentence (so long as you keep Washington
the first president and Adams the second). Surely no problem is created by this kind of selection and ordering, and
yet one is sure that followers of Beard will be annoyed and
charge that we are missing the point. So let us reformulate
the problem in a way that brings us closer to their worries.

Their problem starts on the assumption that we can
never have a complete history. The list which would exhaustively formulate all the true singular statements that
we want to make is beyond our reach. But if history be
construed as the result of selecting and ordering those
statements which we *can* lay our hands on, and if we have
a limited amount of space in which to write that history
down, we are faced with a choice. There are many different

alternative sets of statements about the object whose history we are writing which compete with each other, and they are produced with different principles of selection in mind. The situation may best be understood by imagining that two historians decide to write the history of the United States independently in a certain number of sentences of prescribed length. We want to know which is the better history. We check each statement in them and find they are all true. How, then, shall we choose between the two histories? They contain different statements, but as conjunctions they are both true. Obviously the factual truth of the account is not enough of a basis for decision, but what is the extra factor? How shall we decide? I suggest that the answer may be found if we reflect on the purpose of history. The ideal purpose of history, admitted even by some relativists, is to tell the *whole* truth. But we can't tell the whole truth, and so we are reduced to lists of statements which formulate only certain parts of it. The issue then arises as to whether a choice among true parts of the same size can be made in some objective way, a choice which will allow us to say that one history is objectively better than another.

From some of the things Beard said, one may gather that he despaired of ever being able to do this. His point was that relativism is inescapable because selection is made in terms of values, schemes of reference, and purposes which vary from historian to historian. There can be no doubt, of course, that historians are in fact dominated by their values in the course of their investigations. But even Beard speaks of historical thought being "large, generous, universal in range" as opposed to that which is "small, provincial, and personal in nature,"[2] so that he had some conviction that some selections are better than others. But can we formulate a neutral standpoint from which one particular judgment of the worth of principles of selection can be made? The mere fact that historians are biased is no argument against the existence of impersonal standards, and it seems absurd to argue from their limitations to standards which would justify their limitations. It has been argued falla-

[2] Ibid., p. 51.

ciously that because of the admitted existence of value-dominated selection we must recognize that it is part of the accredited procedure of history. However, it is important to remember that this hurried flight to relativism starts with recognizing that the whole truth is the aim of the historian. And since he cannot attain his ideal, since he cannot record all the true statements, he is advised by relativists to pick out those which accord with his scheme of reference, his interests, and his problems. In short, he is advised to pay no attention to his unattainable ideal; he is advised to forget about it. But this is a non sequitur. Since we cannot present the whole truth we are fallaciously advised to select those truths which interest us. But the net effect of this is not to help the historian approximate his admitted ideal. How can he approximate it if he forswears the task of approximating it and turns to selection guided by his values and prejudices? We cannot deny his right to study what he pleases, but we may point out that he abandons for poor reasons a task which is usually associated with the study of history. Although the historian cannot present the enormous list which would constitute history in the ideal sense, his task remains that of presenting a briefer one which is *representative* of the enormous list. His selection, in other words, is to be justified on the basis of a connection with the ideal history, analogous to (though not identical with) the way in which a good statistical sample is said to represent an infinite population. It may be said that we have pushed the argument one step further back and that we shall now conduct disputes as to which lists are in fact more representative. This is true, but at least it presupposes agreement on a standard. And once standards are agreed on, debates as to which histories satisfy the standard will undoubtedly take place. But here the situation is quite analogous to what goes on in mathematics. The fact that we can formulate laws of logical deduction does not prevent some people from erroneously supposing that their reasoning is logical. It is not maintained that any conception of a representative list is one which is understood perfectly and which has been clarified or defined. On the contrary, its clarification is a great problem for the philosophy of history. But it is maintained that some such standard is implicitly used by historians who try to give objective arguments back and forth in favor of the credibility of different historical works on a given problem. We may conclude that the fact of selection need not of itself drive us into the kind of relativism espoused by Beard. But we must now turn to interpretation. Does interpretation involve value commitments which destroy historical objectivity?

The process of thought which the historian applies to the records and to historical knowledge in Beard's sense is not limited to selecting and ordering. It also involves what is called "interpretation." And if Beard's own work is taken as an example, historical interpretation amounts to adding a kind of statement not present in "historical knowledge." The historian does not merely select and order singular propositions like "George Washington was the first president of the United States," but advances claims like "Our fundamental law was not the product of the whole people but rather of a group of economic interests which must have expected beneficial results from its adoption." But if the latter is typical of what interpretation adds, we must ask whether it is tested in an objective spirit quite like that which dominates (or ought to dominate) the natural sciences. Oddly enough Beard in 1935, just when he came to hold extremely relativistic views, said something that did not fit in with his new philosophy: "An economic analysis may be coldly neutral, and in the pages of this volume no words of condemnation are pronounced upon the men enlisted on either side of the great controversy which accompanied the formation and adoption of the Constitution. Are the security holders who sought to collect principal and interest through the formation of a stronger government to be treated as guilty of impropriety or praised? That is a question to which the . . . inquiry is not addressed. An answer to that question belongs to moralists and philosophers, not to students of history as such."[3] But in 1934, while arguing for his new relativism, he had said: "The assumption that any historian can be a disembodied spirit

[3] Introduction to the 1935 edition of *An Economic Interpretation of the Constitution* (New York: Macmillan), pp. ix–x.

as coldly neutral to human affairs as the engineer to an automobile . . . [has] been challenged and rejected."[4] He went even further and speculated in a disparaging tone on the social roots of such an attitude. "Written history that was cold, factual, and apparently undisturbed by the passions of the time served best the cause of those who did not want to be disturbed."[5]

This contradiction is typical of Beard's later writings on this subject. But we are easily confused even if we stay with one half of the contradiction—the relativistic half—and ask: Did Beard think that interpretations like his own could be checked by objective methods? Sometimes his answer is "yes." But sometimes he speaks as though scientific method is applicable only in connection with historical *knowledge*. Scientific method is acceptable within limits. "It is when this method, a child of the human brain, is exalted into a master and a tyrant that historical *thought* [my italics] must enter a caveat. So the historian is bound by his craft to recognize the nature and limitations of the scientific method and to dispel the illusion that it can produce a science of history embracing the fullness of history."[6] But this still does not help us. It may be that we can never achieve a science of history in the nineteenth-century sense, but the question remains whether there is any possibility of formulating criteria for deciding about the scientific adequacy of different histories. Beard never gave any evidence of being able to comprehend this problem. He moved around it but never came to grips with it. He suggested that the historian's values prevent him from objectively weighing the evidence for his contentions, and yet did not want to abandon "inquiry into objective realities, especially economic realities."[7] He kept insisting in vaguer and vaguer language that the historian needed frames of reference which included "things deemed necessary," and "things deemed desirable."[8] Such frames could be large, informed

[4] Charles A. Beard, "Written History as an Act of Faith," see above, p. 143.

[5] See above, p. 142.

[6] See above, p. 149.

[7] See above, pp. 149–50.

[8] See above, p. 150.

by deep knowledge, and illuminated by wide experience. But if they were large, wouldn't they coincide with what has been called the objective attitude? What does "largeness" imply here if not a desire to approximate the whole truth? In the end Beard spoke of the historian's need for faith in a theory of the nature and direction of the movements of world history. Having rejected the scientific attitude of the nineteenth century, Beard was incapable of substantiating his theories on this subject, and so he fell back on an act of faith in one of the most incoherent of all his reflections on the subject. "Does the world move and, if so, in what direction? If he believes that the world does not move, the historian must offer the pessimism of chaos to the inquiring spirit of mankind. If it does move, does it move backward . . . or . . . forward to some other arrangement which can be only dimly divined—a capitalist dictatorship, a proletarian dictatorship, or a collectivist democracy? The last of these is my own guess, *founded on a study of long trends* [my italics] and on a faith in the indomitable spirit of mankind."[9]

Faced with this we must continue to ask calmly whether Beard thought that historical synthesis couldn't possibly be carried out without commitment on these subjects. If he did, of course, we can only be amazed. Certainly his own work on the Constitution did not logically presuppose such a commitment, and he himself has told us how little interested he was in the politics of the Progressive era. Furthermore, it is important to distinguish between a belief that one of these kinds of society will dominate the world and a hope that one will. Apparently Beard thought a choice on both levels was necessary. Historians must say what they deem desirable as well as likely and then trust in faith. But it would seem that a commitment on neither subject is necessary for the successful prosecution of historical inquiry, much less one based on faith. And even if the historian needed such faith in order to get worked up psychologically, there is absolutely no reason to suppose that a fair test of the adequacy of his historical interpretation would depend on the examiner's sharing his faith.

[9] See above, p. 151.

Beard was guilty of a confusion which is typical in the philosophy of history, the confusion between the psychology of historical interpretation and its logic. It may very well be true that a historian has to ally himself with some speculative theory or some morality before he can get interested in historical synthesis. But the fact that he is attached to it does not bear on the truth or credibility or adequacy of his history. As Sidney Hook says: "The possession of bias or passion on the part of the historian does not preclude the possibility of his achieving objectivity in testing his hypothesis any more than a physician's passion to relieve men from the ravages of a disease . . . precludes the possibility of a discovery of a medical . . . truth. The prepossession of Pasteur's work on antitoxins was that God in his infinite goodness could not have created a scourge for mankind without at the same time creating a remedy. And this did not prevent Pasteur from rigorously testing his hypothesis."[10] At best Beard's "faith" may function in the same way. What is most dangerous about such a faith, however, is the way in which it can justify historical distortion. The views of relativists cease to be obscure when they lead to a surrender of the distinction between fact and fable. An historian attached to the present Soviet regime might well erase certain names from the history of the Russian revolution, but one can hardly sympathize with a relativist logician willing to conclude that this was valid or justified in any sense of those words.

In more concrete moments Beard gave a clearer version of historical thought in operation. Medieval history, he said,[11] had two great tasks: the narration of the struggle in which Christianity triumphed over paganism and the task of reconciling the events of the world with the Catholic faith. But consider an attempt to study the way in which Christianity struggled with paganism. This would be a typical developmental account but certainly not above being

[10] Charles A. Beard and Sidney Hook, "Problems of Terminology in Historical Writing," in *Theory and Practise in Historical Study* (New York: Social Science Research Council, 1946), p. 126.

[11] Charles A. Beard, *The Nature of the Social Sciences*, p. 53.

compared with the evidence. One might still ask whether
the account was true or well confirmed, and one would
check this by reference to evidence. And when medieval
historians "explained the events of the world," when they
said that history was a dream revealing the plan of God,
couldn't they be criticized in the light of evidence if the
hypothesis could be shown testable? The fact that medieval
historians had certain theological and moral purposes in no
way freed them from being subject to the canons of validity, evidence, and historical truth. The fact that they had
their own purposes in writing these accounts no more
makes judgment of their work a matter of taste than does
the allegedly high purpose of medieval astronomy free it
from condemnation by modern science. Beard gives the
impression that the peculiar purposes of medieval historians render them free from the critical judgment of those
who do not share their purposes. But this, I think, is simply
wrong and a plain result of the confusion I have mentioned—the confusion between the psychology and logic of
historical interpretation.

Beard's later views on the philosophy of history were
more developed than those of almost any other American
historian. But they fall short of the intellectual standards
set by his work in history and political science. In one respect they represent a different strain from that which I
have been examining throughout this book. The later philosophical writings of Beard, in spite of being frequently
associated with Dewey's theory of knowledge, are really
part of another tradition. It is sounder to say that the new
history of Robinson and of Beard in his early years was the
expression in the philosophy of history of the movement
we have been considering in this book. Beard's later views
had more in common with those of Croce and Mannheim,
and he absorbed the amount of obscurity from them which
one might expect. Of all the philosophical positions examined in this book, Beard's later philosophy of history seems
most implausible. It is obscure and contradictory, and it
reveals the worst defect of the tradition on which his later
philosophical work depended—a lack of respect for logical
rigor and clear thinking which is paralleled only by other

writings in the philosophy of history. One must be thankful for the fact that Beard's philosophy did not adequately describe his own scientific work, which, at its best, exhibited none of the features he came to regard as the essence of history.

It is misleading to associate Beard's later philosophy of history with the modern theory of scientific method, as so many historians do. The criticism of history conceived as a statement of the facts "as they really happened" was at first merely a protest against narrow conceptions which excluded historical explanation and everything but political facts. And in the later writings of Beard there was another reasonable point which was added—the sound methodological reminder that there are no " 'raw facts' lying around in the world awaiting collection by the historian" and that there is something absurd about "the idea that facts duly assembled, in a library or laboratory, automatically and inexorably suggest or dictate their own conclusions in all cases."[12] Beard had read, with profit, some of the sounder texts on scientific method which emphasized the need for hypothesis and which criticized the limitations of the extreme Baconian aversion to anticipating nature. But his conclusions would have shocked the authors of the texts from which he imbibed this sound advice, for he went on to suggest that the need for hypothesis in history somehow ushered in an initial *value* commitment. But obviously, if hypotheses are necessary for physical research as well as for historical research, physics too has to begin with some kind of alleged value commitment. Yet Beard thought there was a radical difference between physics and history. Physics, he seemed to think, was cold and neutral, while history needed value hypotheses. The attack on Bacon in the nineteenth century on the subject of hypothesis came to an ironic end in Beard. When Bacon was first attacked for refusing to anticipate nature, he was not attacked for the one good point he made, namely, that we ought not to expect nature to behave as we *want* her to behave. What he was attacked for was his alleged failure to see that re-

[12] Ibid., p. 58.

search cannot get on without hypotheses to guide it. But these hypotheses were not moral or ethical in character. Beard, I think, simply made the one error which Bacon was right in criticizing, and proceeded to justify himself by citing the standard assaults on Bacon.

It should be said in Beard's behalf that he was the only member of the group I have examined who has given a full account of the methods and aims of the social sciences. It is not surprising, therefore, that his ideas should be subject to detailed criticism. He raced around fields where most of the others stepped lightly and infrequently. And very often he says what they really thought, while they merely mumbled it incoherently or kept it to themselves. For all his mistakes and his philosophical confusions, Beard's later work in the methodology of the social sciences remains stimulating. It goes without saying that his errors in philosophy cast no reflection on his work in social science itself. In this respect he takes his position in a long and worthy line of scientists—physical and social—who have worked with standards in philosophy which they dared not use in science.

9.

*The following essay by Ernest Nagel, Professor of Philosophy at Columbia University, is written from the same logical perspective as Mr. White's; but it pursues the defense of the case for objectivity beyond the specific issues raised by Beard.*

*The few pages are closely reasoned and introduce a number of extremely important arguments and issues. It would be gratuitous to restate them here. Mr. Nagel analyzes the alleged obstacles to objectivity: (a) that the primary aim of history is to assert particular statements rather than general laws; (b) that the choice of a particular subject matter in history or the possibility of alternate solutions for a historical problem introduces subjective factors; (c) that the value-charged nature of history or the undeniable influence of personal bias and social conditioning, i.e., the existential*

*and sociological roots of human knowledge, impose logical
limitations upon writing an objective history. He goes over
each argument with a fine-tooth comb and comes to the
conclusion that "none of these facts precludes the possibility of warranted explanation" in history.*

*Which side—the advocates of the limits, or the advocates
of the possibility of objectivity in history—wins the day
should be left to the reader to decide.*

## ERNEST NAGEL

## THE LOGIC OF HISTORICAL ANALYSIS*

According to Aristotle, poetry, like theoretical science, is
"more philosophic and of graver import" than history, for
the former is concerned with the pervasive and universal,
and the latter is addressed to the special and the singular.
Aristotle's remark is a possible historical source of a widely
held current distinction between two allegedly different
types of sciences: the nomothetic, which seek to establish
abstract general laws for indefinitely repeatable processes;
and the idiographic, which aim to understand the unique
and nonrecurrent. It is often maintained that the natural
sciences are nomothetic, whereas history (in the sense of an
account of events) is idiographic; and it is claimed in consequence that the logic and conceptual structure of historical explanations are fundamentally different from those
of the natural sciences. It is my aim here to examine this
and related issues in the logic of historical analysis.

## I

Even a cursory examination of treatises in theoretical
natural science and of books on history reveals the prima
facie difference between them, that by and large the statements of the former are general in form, and contain few if
any references to specific objects, places, and times, whereas

* In *The Scientific Monthly,* Vol. 74 (1952), pp. 162–69. I
have omitted Section III of the original essay. H.M.

the statements of the latter are almost without exception singular and replete with proper names, dates, and geographic specifications. To this extent, at least, the alleged contrast between the natural sciences as nomothetic and history as idiographic appears to be well founded.

It would, however, be a gross error to conclude that singular statements play no role in the theoretical sciences or that historical inquiry makes no use of universal ones. No conclusions concerning the actual character of specific things and processes can be derived from general statements alone; and theories and laws must be supplemented by initial or boundary conditions when the natural sciences attempt to explain any particular occurrence. Nor does the familiar and often useful distinction between "pure" and "applied" natural science impair the relevance of this point. For, clearly, even the pure natural sciences can assert their general statements as empirically warranted only on the basis of concrete factual evidence, and therefore only by establishing and using a variety of singular statements. And there are branches of natural science, such as geophysics and animal ecology, that are concerned with the spatio-temporal distribution and development of individual systems. It follows, in short, that neither the natural sciences taken as a whole nor their purely theoretical subdivisions can be regarded as being exclusively nomothetic.

Neither can historical study dispense with at least a tacit acceptance of universal statements of the kind occurring in the natural sciences. Thus, although the historian may be concerned with the nonrecurrent and the unique, he selects and abstracts from the concrete occurrences he studies, and his discourse about what is individual and singular requires the use of common names and general descriptive terms. Such characterizations are associated with the recognition of various kinds or types of things and occurrences, and therefore with the implicit acknowledgment of numerous empirical regularities. Again, one phase of a historian's task is to establish the authenticity of documents and other remains from the past, the precise meaning of recorded assertions, and the reliability of testimony concerning past events. For the effective execution of this task of external and internal criticism, the historian must be armed with a wide assortment of general laws, borrowed from one or the other of the natural and social sciences. And, since historians usually aim to be more than mere chroniclers of the past, and attempt to understand and explain recorded actions in terms of their causes and consequences, they must obviously assume supposedly well-established laws of causal dependence. In brief, history is not a purely idiographic discipline.

Nonetheless, there is an important asymmetry between theoretical and historical sciences. A theoretical science like physics seeks to establish both general and singular statements, and in the process of doing so physicists will employ previously established statements of both types. Historians, on the other hand, aim to assert warranted singular statements about the occurrence and interrelations of specific actions; and though this task can be achieved only by assuming and using general laws, historians do not regard it as part of their task to *establish* such laws. The distinction between history and theoretical science is thus somewhat analogous to the difference between medical diagnosis and physiology, or between geology and physics. A geologist seeks to ascertain, for example, the sequential order of geologic formations, and he is able to do so by applying various physical laws to the materials he encounters; it is not the geologist's task, qua geologist, to establish the laws of mechanics or of radioactive disintegration that he may employ.

The fact that historical research is concerned with the singular, and seeks to ascertain the causal dependencies between specific occurrences, does not warrant the widespread contention that there is a radical difference between the logical structure of explanations in the historical and the generalizing sciences. I shall consider only one specific argument to support the claim that there is such a difference. It has been said that there is a demonstrable *formal* difference between the "general concepts" of the theoretical sciences and the "individual concepts" assumed to be the goals of historical inquiry. Concepts of the first kind are alleged to conform to the familiar logical principle of the inverse variation of the extension and intension of terms:

when a set of general terms is arranged in order of their increasing extensions, their intensions decrease. But quite the reverse is said to be the case for the individual concepts of historical explanations, since the more inclusive the "scope" of such a concept, the richer and fuller is its "meaning." Thus, the term "French Enlightenment" is claimed to have not only a more inclusive scope than the term "the life of Voltaire," but also to possess a fuller intension.[1]

But this is simply a confusion, derived in part from a failure to distinguish the relation of *inclusion* between the extensions of terms, from some form of *whole-part* relation between an instance of a term and a component of that instance. Thus, the French Enlightenment may be said to "contain" as one of its "components" the life of Voltaire; and it is doubtless correct to maintain that the term "French Enlightenment" is "richer in meaning or content" than the term "the life of Voltaire." But the *extension* of the term "French Enlightenment" does *not* include the *extension* of the term "the life of Voltaire," so that the logical principle under discussion cannot be significantly applied to these terms.

More generally, there appears to be no good reason for claiming that the general pattern of explanations in historical inquiry, or the logical structure of the conceptual tools employed in it, differs from those encountered in the generalizing and the natural sciences. The explanatory premises in history, as in the natural sciences, include a number of implicitly assumed laws, as well as many explicitly (though usually incompletely) formulated singular statements of initial conditions. The tacitly assumed laws may be of various kinds. They may be statements of regularities well attested in some special science, or they may be uncodified assumptions taken from common experience; they may be universal statements of invariable concomitance, or they may be statistical in form; they may assert a uniformity in temporal sequence, or they may assert some relation of co-existent dependence. The singular statements of initial conditions are of comparable variety, and although the

[1] Rickert, H. *Die Grenzen der naturwissenschaftlichen Begriffsbildung*. Tübingen: J. C. B. Mohr, 281 (1921).

truth of many of them is often incontrovertible it is frequently highly conjectural. Indeed, the relevance of such singular statements to the specific problems under investigation, as well as their truth, are questions upon which historians are often undecided or unable to achieve unanimity. There are, in fact, several problems in this connection that are of much concern to historical research, although they are not without relevance to other branches of social science as well. I therefore turn to consider briefly some of the real and alleged difficulties that plague the pursuit of historical knowledge.

## II

It is a platitude that research in history as in other areas of science selects and abstracts from the concrete occurrences studied, and that however detailed a historical discourse may be it is never an exhaustive account of what actually happened. Curiously enough, it is the very selectivity of history that generates many of the broader questions relating to the nature of historical inquiry and is sometimes made the occasion for wholesale skepticism concerning the possibility of "objective" explanations in historical matters. Since a historian exercises selection in choosing problems for study, and also in his proposed solutions to them, it will be convenient to examine some of the relevant issues under these two heads.

1) Historians do not all concern themselves with the same things, and there are undoubtedly many past events that have received attention from no historian. Why does one historian occupy himself with ancient Greece, another with modern Germany, still another with the development of legal institutions in the American colonies, a fourth with the evolution of mathematical notation, and so on? Is there some general feature which differentiates those occurrences that are of concern to historians from those that are not? And, above all, is a historian prevented from giving a warranted or objective account of things because of his initial choice of a limited problem?

It is clear that there is no uniform answer to the first of

these queries, for in historical inquiry as in other branches of science a variety of circumstances may determine what problems are to be investigated. It may be individual preference and endowment, controlled by education and the influence of teachers; it may be professional obligation or the desire for financial gain; it may be national pride, social pressure, or a sense of political mission. Historians of ideas have given some attention to this matter, and have uncovered interesting data concerning stimuli to specific investigations. But there is no prima facie reason to believe that, because a historical inquiry begins with a specific problem, or because there are causal determinants for his choice, a historian is in principle precluded—any more than is a natural scientist—from rendering an adequate account to the subjects he is investigating.

Many writers maintain, however, that the selectivity of history is peculiar in that the historian is inescapably concerned with "value-impregnated" subject matter. Thus, according to one influential view, an individual or process can be properly labeled as "historical" only if it is "irreplaceable," either because it uniquely embodies some universally accepted cultural value or because it is instrumental to the actualization of such a value. In consequence, the supposition that historical inquiry can ignore theoretical value relations is said by some writers to involve a self-deception,[2] whereas other commentators have concluded that unlike the physical sciences "history is violently personal," since "stars and molecules have no loves and hates, while men do."[3] There is, however, no basis for the claim that historical study is addressed exclusively to value-impregnated occurrences, unless indeed the word "history" is arbitrarily redefined so as to conform with the claim. For, although undoubtedly much historical inquiry is concerned with events that may be so characterized, there are also many investigations commonly called "historical" that are not of this nature—for example, inquiries into the development of the stars, biological species, and much else. More generally,

[2] Ibid., 254.
[3] Nevins, A. The Gateway to History. New York: Appleton-Century, 29 (1938).

there appears to be no warrant for any of the various claims that the occurrences studied by historians are distinguished by some inherent differentiating feature from those that are not. Moreover, even when a historian is concerned with admittedly value-impregnated subject matter or with occurrences manifesting various passions, it by no means follows that he must himself share or judge those values or passions. It is an obvious blunder to suppose that only a fat cowherd can drive fat kine. It is an equally crude error to maintain that one cannot inquire into the conditions and consequences of values and evaluations without necessarily engaging in moral or aesthetic value judgments.

There is also the broad question whether historical inquiry is inevitably guilty of distorting the facts because it is addressed to limited problems and is concerned only with certain selected materials of the past. The supposition that it is entails the view that one cannot have competent knowledge of anything unless one knows everything, and is a corollary to the philosophic doctrine of the "internality" of all relations. It will suffice here to note that, were the doctrine sound, not only would every historical account ever written be condemned as a necessarily mutilated and distorted version of what has happened, but a similar valuation would have to be placed on all science, and indeed on all analytical discourse. In short, the fact that inquiry is selective because it originates in a specific and limited problem places the historian in no worse position than it does other scientists with respect to the possibility of achieving what is commonly characterized as objectively warranted knowledge.

2) Historical inquiry is selective not only in its starting point; it is also selective in proposing solutions to its problems. A variety of skeptical doubts about the possibility of an objective history has been expressed in consequence.

One such expression takes the form that, in view of the inexhaustibly numerous relations in which a given event stands to other events, no account can ever render the "full reality" of what has occurred. Accordingly, since every historical account covers only a few aspects of an occurrence and stops at some point in the past in tracing back its antecedents, every proposed explanation of that occurrence is said to bear the mark of arbitrariness and subjectivity. Part of this objection can be summarily dismissed with the reminder that it is never the task of any inquiry initiated by a specific problem to *reproduce* its subject matter, and that it would be a gratuitous performance were a historian in the pursuit of such a problem to formulate "all that has been said, done, and thought by human beings on the planet since humanity began its long career." Not only is the bare fact that inquiry is selective no valid ground for doubting the objectively warranted character of its conclusions; on the contrary, unless an inquiry were selective it would never come near to resolving the specific question by which it is generated.

However, the objection under discussion also rests on another misconception: it in effect assumes that since every causal condition for an event has its own causal conditions, the event is never properly explained unless the entire regressive series of the latter conditions are also explained. It has been maintained, for example, that

> A Baptist sermon in Atlanta, if we seek to explain it, takes us back through the Protestant Reformation to Galilee— and far beyond in the dim origins of civilization. We can, if we choose, stop at any point along the line of relations, but that is an arbitrary act of will and does violence to the quest for truth in the matter.[4]

But is there any violence to the truth? Is *B* not a cause of *A* simply because *C* is a cause of *B*? When some future position of a planet is predicted with the help of gravitational theory and information about the initial condition of the solar system at some given time, is there ground for skepticism simply because the assumed initial conditions are in turn the outcome of previous ones? These are rhetorical questions, for the answers to all of them are obviously in the negative. Moreover, precisely what is the problem in connection with the Baptist sermon in Atlanta? Is it why a given individual delivered it at a stated time and occasion,

[4] Beard, C. A. *The Discussion of Human Affairs*. New York: Macmillan, 68–69 (1936).

or why he chose a particular text and theme, or why that occasion happened to arise, or why Baptists flourished in Atlanta, or why they developed as a Protestant sect, or why the Protestant Reformation occurred, or why Christianity arose in antiquity? These are all quite different questions, and an adequate answer for one of them is not even relevant as a proposed solution for the others. The supposition that, when a problem is made definite a regressive chain of answers must be sought if any one answer is to be objectively warranted, is patently self-contradictory. On the other hand, the fact that one problem may suggest another, and so lead to a possibly endless series of new inquiries, simply illustrates the progressive character of the scientific enterprise; that fact is no support for the claim that unless the series is terminated, every proposed solution to a given problem is necessarily a mutilation of the truth.

Skepticism concerning the possibility of objectively warranted explanations in human history takes a more empirical turn when it bases its negations on the influence of personal and social bias upon such inquiry. The doubt embodied in the *aperçu* that history is written by the survivors is by no means a novelty; but in recent years it has been deepened and given a radical form by many sociologists of knowledge. According to some of them, all thought is conditioned and controlled by the "existential situation" in which it occurs; and, especially when thinking is directed to human affairs, the interpretation of observed facts, the selection of problems for inquiry and the methods employed for resolving them, and the standards of validity accepted are all functions of the thinker's unconscious value commitments and world outlook, his social position, and his political and class loyalties. Every cognitive claim concerning matters of vital human interest is therefore said to be valid only within the particular social setting in which it emerges; and the belief that it is possible to obtain explanations that are "true" for everyone, irrespective of his position in a given society, is declared to be part of the self-deception (or "ideology") of a culture.

There appear to be four distinct issues raised by this form of skepticism. In the first place, the choice of particu-

lar problems for study, especially inquiries into human affairs, is undoubtedly controlled by the character of a given
culture, and sometimes by the status of the student in that
culture. An investigation of traffic problems is not likely to
be made in an agricultural society, and a man's interest in
labor history may very well be causally related to his social
position. But, as has already been seen, this form of selective activity on the part of an inquirer does not necessarily
jeopardize the objectivity of his findings.

In the second place, no inquiry takes place in an intellectual vacuum, and every investigator approaches his task
with information and guiding ideas derived in large measure from his culture. But it does not follow from this circumstance alone that the conscious and unconscious value
commitments associated with the social status of an investigator inevitably influence his acceptance of one conclusion rather than another. The preconceptions he brings to
the analysis of a given problem may be neutral to all differences in social values, even when that problem is concerned with human affairs. And, in point of fact, there are
many questions in the social as well as in the natural
sciences upon which there is complete agreement among
students, despite their different social positions and loyalties.

It is undoubtedly the case, in the third place, that the
standards of validity operative in an inquiry are *causally*
related to other cultural traits, and that social status, class
and national bias, and general world perspectives frequently influence what conclusions a man accepts. For example, the degree of precision currently demanded in
experimental work is certainly not independent of the current state of technology; and a comparison of Southern and
Northern histories of the period of reconstruction following
the American Civil War makes amply clear the force of
sectional and race bias. This is an area of study that has
not yet been systematically exploited, although sociologists
of knowledge have already illuminated the genesis of many
ideas and the manner in which social pressures enforce their
acceptance. In any event, biased thinking is a perennial
challenge to the critical historian of human affairs; and research into the causal determinants of bias is of undoubted

value for recognizing its occurrence and for mitigating if not always eliminating its influence. The very fact that biased thinking may be detected and its sources investigated shows that the case for objective explanations in history is not necessarily hopeless. Indeed, the assertion that a historian exhibits bias assumes that there is a distinction between biased and unbiased thinking, and that the bias can be identified—for otherwise the assertion would at best be simply futile name-calling. In consequence, it is possible, even if frequently difficult, to correct the bias and to obtain conclusions in better agreement with the evidence. Accordingly, if doubt concerning the objectivity of a historical explanation is based on considerations relating to the causal influence of various social factors upon the evaluation of evidence, it is often salutary and well taken; but it does not entail a wholesale skepticism concerning the possibility of such explanations.

This brings me to the final issue. It is sometimes argued that the social perspective of a student of human affairs is not only causally influential upon his inquiry, but is *logically* involved both in his standards of validity as well as in the meaning of his statements. And it is also maintained that one must therefore reject the thesis that "the genesis of a proposition is under all circumstances irrelevant to its truth."[5] On the other hand, the radical skepticism concerning objective explanations of human affairs that results is qualified by the further claim that a "relational" type of objectivity can nevertheless be achieved. Thus, students who share the same social perspective and employ the same conceptual and categorical apparatus will allegedly arrive at similar conclusions on any problem when the standards characteristic of their common perspective are correctly applied. And students operating within different social perspectives can attain objectivity in a "roundabout fashion" by construing their inevitable differences in the light of the differences in the structures of their perspectives.

There are, however, grave factual and dialectical difficulties in these several claims. There is no factual evidence to

[5] Mannheim, K. *Ideology and Utopia*. New York: Harcourt, Brace, 243, 259 (1936).

show that the "content and form" of statements, or the standards of validity employed, are *logically* determined by the social perspective of an inquirer. The facts commonly cited establish no more than some kind of causal dependence between these items. For example, the once much-publicized view that the "mentality" or logical operations of "primitive" social groups are different from those typical of European civilization—a difference that was once attributed to institutional differences in the societies compared—is now generally recognized to be without foundation. Moreover, even the most extreme proponents of the sociology of knowledge admit that there are many assertions (those usually mentioned come from mathematics and the natural sciences) which are neutral to differences in social perspective and whose genesis is irrelevant to their validity. Why cannot assertions about human affairs exhibit the same neutrality? If, as no one seems to doubt, the truth of the statement that two horses can in general pull a greater load than either horse alone is logically independent of the social status of the one who asserts it, what inherent social circumstance precludes such independence for the statement that two laborers can in general dig a ditch of given dimensions more quickly than either laborer working alone?

Second, what is the logical status of the claim that social perspectives enter essentially into the content and warrant of all assertions about human affairs? Is the claim itself meaningful and valid only for those occupying a certain social status? In that case, its validity is narrowly self-limited, no student with a different social perspective can properly understand or evaluate it, and it must be dismissed as irrelevant by most inquirers into social questions. Or is the claim peculiarly exempt from what it asserts, so that its meaning and truth are not logically dependent upon the social status of those who assert it? In that case, then, there is at least one conclusion about human affairs which may be "objectively valid" in the usual sense of this phrase; and if there is one such conclusion, there is no clear reason why there may not be others.

Finally, the relational type of objectivity which the claim

admits as attainable is nothing other than objectivity in the customary sense, which the claim appears to deny as possible. A translation formula which renders the "common denominator" of seemingly diverse conclusions stemming from differing social perspectives, cannot in turn be "situationally determined" in the sense under dispute. Indeed, the search for such formulas is but a well-known phase of theoretical research in all areas of inquiry. It is a search for objective invariants in numerically and qualitatively distinct processes; and when the quest is successful, as it often is, it terminates in laws of greater or less generality, with whose help what is relevant to the occurrence of an event or to the continuance of a process can be distinguished from what is not.

In brief, therefore, although the historian is undoubtedly selective in the conduct of his inquiries, and although personal and social bias frequently color his judgment and control what conclusions he accepts, none of these facts precludes the possibility of warranted explanations for the events he studies.

### 10.

*I have concluded this prolonged debate between historians and philosophers with a brief excerpt from* Introduction to Philosophy of History *by W. H. Walsh, who is a Fellow and Lecturer in Philosophy in the University of Oxford and does not quite belong to either side. It is a succinct and perceptive summary of the major issues involved in this controversy; and I personally subscribe to the conclusion that—as yet—"moral and metaphysical preconceptions" impose limits upon the goal of achieving objectivity in history which are not to be found in the sciences.*[1]

*The moral issue or the conflict of values, as we have seen, has come up in several selections as a possible source*

[1] It is only fair to add that the "prima facie case for an ultimate historical scepticism," on which Mr. Walsh concludes in this excerpt, does not express his own views on the subject as developed in a later section of this chapter.

*for conflicting interpretations of history. This issue is the topic of Part III.*

## W. H. WALSH

### CAN HISTORY BE OBJECTIVE?*

I suggest that the main factors which actually make for disagreement among historians[1] may be grouped under the following four heads. First, personal likes and dislikes, whether for individuals or classes of person. Historian A (Carlyle would be an example) admires great men; historian B (e.g., Wells) has a strong antipathy to them. Historian A, in consequence, makes his whole narrative centre round the ideas and actions of his hero, which he presents as decisive for the history of the time; historian B goes out of his way to write down the same actions as (for example) muddled, insincere, vicious or ineffective. Secondly, prejudices or, to use a less colourful word, assumptions associated with the historian's membership of a certain group: the assumptions he makes, for example, as belonging to this or that nation, race or social class, or again as professing this or that religion. Thirdly, conflicting theories of historical interpretation. Historian A is a Marxist and sees the ultimate explanation of all historical events in the operation of economic factors; historian B (Mr. Russell is an example) is a pluralist and refuses to regard any single type of causal factor as decisive in history. Whilst agreeing with some Marxist conclusions there are others which he cannot bring himself to accept. Fourthly, basically different moral beliefs, conceptions of the nature of man or, if the term is

---

* In *Introduction to Philosophy of History* (London: Hutchinsons University Library, 1951), pp. 100–11. I have reprinted only #3 of Mr. Walsh's chapter, and I have cut a few references to other parts of the book. H.M.

[1] I must make clear that the kind of disagreement with which I am concerned in what follows is not disagreement about what conclusions to draw from a given body of (often inadequate) evidence, but rather disagreement about the proper interpretation of the conclusions drawn . . .

preferred, *Weltanschauungen*. The influence of this last group is perhaps most readily illustrated in the different results produced by those who approach history with a background of Christian beliefs and those whose approach is "rationalist" in the eighteenth-century sense.

Without enquiring into the adequacy or exhaustiveness of this classification, I shall proceed at once to make some remarks on each of the four groups of factor, with a view to determining, if possible, which should claim our special attention in the present discussion.

*Personal bias.* The position in regard to this is, I think, comparatively simple. There is, of course, plenty of evidence of the influence of personal likes and dislikes both in the judgments historians make and (more important) in their general presentation of facts, but it is doubtful, all the same, whether we should regard bias of this kind as a serious obstacle to the attainment of objective truth in history. It is doubtful for the simple reason that we all know from our own experience that this kind of bias can be corrected or at any rate allowed for. Once we recognize our own partialities, as we certainly can, we are already on our guard against them, and provided that we are sufficiently sceptical they need hold no further terrors for us. And we do hold that historians ought to be free from personal prejudice and condemn those historians who are not. It is a common reproach to Thucydides, for instance, that his dislike of Cleon led him to give an inaccurate account of the political history of his time. He could not help his feelings about the man, but they ought not to have been imported into his history. The same would be said, *mutatis mutandis,* about cases where the object of an historian's enthusiasm or aversion is a whole class of person—clerics, or scientists, or Germans, for example. Wells' antipathy to all notable military figures in his *Outline of History* is universally condemned as bad history on just these grounds.

*Group prejudice.* In principle the same account must be given of the factors which fall under this heading as of those in our first class, though with certain important reservations. The reservations arise in the first place from the obvious fact that assumptions we make as members of a group are less easy to detect and therefore to correct than are our personal likes and dislikes. They are more subtle and widespread in their operation, and just because of their general acceptance in the group there is less urge for us to become conscious of them and so overcome them. Moreover, there is a difficulty about some of the factors in this class which is not found at all in the first. Our personal likes and dislikes rest primarily on our feelings, but it would be claimed that some of our group assumptions are of another character altogether: they have rational warrant, and so are not strictly matters of prejudice, but of principle. We should all say, for instance, that a man's religious opinions ought not to influence his history to the extent of making him incapable of doing justice to the actions of men who did not share them; but many would add that it would be absurd to require him to abstract from them altogether in what he writes. The case for that view would rest on the contention that, despite much facile assumption on the point, religious beliefs are not obviously the product of irrational prejudice only, but may be held as a matter of rational conviction. And if this is so it is not only inevitable but perfectly proper that they should exert an influence on the historian's thinking.

I do not wish to argue this particular case for its own sake, but only to make the general point. Its existence, however, should not jeopardize our main contention about this class of subjective factor, which we can put as follows. The assumptions which historians make as (for example) patriotic Englishmen, class-conscious members of the proletariat or staunch Protestants must be such as they can justify on rational grounds, or they must be extruded from their history. And we all believe the extrusion possible, in principle at least. To claim this is indeed to claim no more than that rational thinking is possible, that our opinions can be grounded as well as caused. It is true that the claim is one which would be dogmatically rejected in many quarters today: Marxists and Freudians, in their different ways, have taught us all to look for non-rational causes for ideas and beliefs which on the surface look perfectly rational, and have convinced some that rational thinking as such is an impossibility. But though we cannot (and should not) return to the naïve confidence of our grandfathers in these matters, it must none the less be pointed out that the anti-rationalist case here cannot be stated without contradiction. It undermines not only the theories of which its proponents disapprove, but itself as well. For it asks us to believe, as a matter of rational conviction, that rational conviction is impossible. And this we cannot do.

*Conflicting Theories of Historical Interpretation.* By a theory of historical interpretation I mean a theory of the relative importance of different kinds of causal factor in history. It is plain enough that historians do employ such theories even when they do not explicitly formulate them, and again that there is no agreement among them about which of the many possible theories of this kind is correct. Conflicting theories of historical interpretation are thus an important source of historical disagreement. And at first sight at least they present a more serious problem than the two classes of subjective factor we have so far considered. We have argued that historians can, if they make the effort, overcome the effects of personal bias and group prejudice. But we cannot urge the same solution of the difficulties which now confront us, by telling the historian to dispense with any theory of historical interpretation. For some such theory he must have, if he is to make any sense of his facts.

We may well be told at this point that our difficulties are more imaginary than real, because a theory of historical interpretation, if it is to claim any justification, must be a well-established empirical hypothesis, based on a close study of the actual facts of historical change. If no such theory has yet succeeded in winning universal acceptance, it can only be a matter of time before one does, and when it does this particular source of disagreement will disappear. But it is by no means certain that this optimistic attitude can be sustained. The paradox of the situation lies, indeed, just in this: that while those who put forward comprehensive theories of this sort profess to derive them from the facts, they hold them with greater confidence than they should if they were merely empirical hypotheses. They are prepared to stand by them even in the face of unfavourable evidence, to accord them the status not so much of hypotheses as of revealed truths. The behaviour of Marxists in regard to the theory of historical materialism is the most obvious illustration of this point, but parallels to it could be found in that of other schools too.

What is the source of the obstinate conviction with which the theories we have mentioned are held or repudiated? In many cases it is no doubt little more than vulgar prejudice. A particular theory strikes us as emotionally as well as intellectually attractive or repulsive, and our attitude to it henceforth is less that of an impartial observer than of a partisan. Our final reason for accepting or rejecting the theory is that we *want* it to be true or false. But it is not clear that this type of explanation covers all cases, and it would certainly not be accepted by sophisticated Marxists, for example. Historical materialism, these would claim, even if not simply grounded in the facts, is none the less capable of rational defence, because we can show it to be bound up with a certain conception of the nature of man and his relation to his environment, a general philosophy whose truth is confirmed in many fields. It is to this philosophy that Marxists make implicit appeal in the course of their historical work, and it is on its validity that the value of their interpretations must finally rest.

If this is correct, it appears that the conflict between different theories of historical interpretation raises no special problems for our purposes. Certainly it is a potent source of disagreement among historians, but the centre of the disagreement, where it cannot be found in simple prejudice, must be looked for in differing philosophical conceptions. Consideration of this third class of subjective factor therefore leads on directly to consideration of the fourth group, to which I shall turn without delay.

*Underlying Philosophical Conflicts.* Since the very title of this section will be viewed with suspicion by hard-headed persons, I must begin by trying to specify more fully what factors fall within the group. What I have in mind are, to make no bones about it, moral and metaphysical beliefs. By the former term I intend to refer to the ultimate judgments of value historians bring to their understanding of the past, by the latter to the theoretical conception of the nature of man and his place in the universe with which these judgments are associated. The two sets of beliefs are, I should say, closely bound up together, though not all who hold them are explicitly aware of the fact.

The suggestion I am making is that historians approach the past each with his own philosophical ideas, and that this has a decisive effect on the way they interpret it. If I am right, differences between historians are in the last resort differences of philosophies, and whether we can resolve them depends on whether we can resolve philosophical conflicts. But I can well imagine that these assertions will involve some strain on the reader's credulity. "Are you seriously suggesting," I shall be asked, "that *all* historians import moral and metaphysical prejudices into their work, thus as it were contemplating the past through spectacles which cannot be removed? And if you are, are you not confusing what is true of history at a crude and unscientific level only with what is true of all history? No doubt ethical, religious or, if you like, metaphysical prejudices can be shown to mar popular historical works of all kinds; but can the same be said of the writings of reputable historians? Is it not apparent that historical thinking can be effective only so far as the historian forgets the ethical, religious and metaphysical outlook of his own age and tries to see his facts in the way those he was writing of did? Must he not read the past in terms, not of his own conception of what human nature is or ought to be, but in terms of the ideas held by those who were alive at the time he is studying? And do we not differentiate good and bad work in history by examining how far particular writers have done just this —by seeing how far they have freed themselves from their own preconceptions and contrived to put themselves in the places of the persons whose actions they are recounting?"

There is obviously much sense in this criticism, yet I doubt even so if it is wholly effective. Certainly there is a difference of the kind indicated between good and bad work in history, a difference we bring out by describing the former as "authentic" and the latter as "unimaginative." Exercising the imagination is an important part of historical thinking, and it does consist in trying, so far as we can, to put ourselves in the places of those whose actions we are studying. But, as we saw before, there are very real difficulties in holding that putting oneself in another man's place is a simple intuitive process: it seems rather to depend on the accumulated experience of the person who carries it out. And when we speak of "experience" here I think we must recognize that this too is not a simple term. My understanding of the ancient world depends on what I have myself experienced or assimilated from the experience of others; but . . . there seems to be in all such experience a subjective or *a priori* element contributed by myself. When I try to put myself in the place of an ancient Greek or a medieval cleric or a Victorian parent, in order to write the history of the ancient world or the medieval church or the Victorian family, I must certainly put aside, so far as I can, the moral and metaphysical preconceptions of my own time. But I cannot escape, if I am to make any sense of my material, making some general judgments about human nature, and in these I shall find my own views constantly cropping up. I shall find myself involuntarily shocked by this event and pleased by that, unconsciously seeing this action as reasonable and that as the reverse. And however much I tell myself to eschew my own prejudices and concentrate on understanding what actually happened, I shall not succeed in carrying out the injunction to the letter, since understanding itself is not a passive process but involves the judging of evidence by principles whose truth is independently assumed.

The point I am making here will perhaps become plainer for some readers if I try to connect it with the classical discussions of historical testimony to be found in Hume's Essay on Miracles (in his *Enquiry Concerning Human Understanding*) and Bradley's *Presuppositions of Critical History*.[2] Neither Hume nor Bradley is concerned with the whole question of historical objectivity: each of them has in mind only the narrower problem of whether we can believe stories of miraculous events. Even so, their conclu-

[2] *Collected Essays,* Vol. I.

sions bear closely on the present discussion. Hume says, in effect, that we cannot give credence to accounts of events in the past the occurrence of which would have abrogated the laws of physical nature; Bradley, urging much the same conclusion, says we can believe about the past only that which bears some analogy to what we know in our own experience. The points in which the present account attempts to go beyond Hume and Bradley are two. First, in suggesting that if we accept Bradley's formula for history we must understand by "experience" not merely experience of physical nature, but experience of human nature too. And secondly, in maintaining that such experience is not all given, but includes in addition an *a priori* element.

(1) The first of these points should be clear enough from the discussions of [a previous chapter], where we tried to show that it was generalizations about human nature which ultimately lay behind historical explanations. It depends on the assertion there made that the proper subject-matter of history is human actions in the past. If this is so it is clear that we must have some knowledge of human nature to make sense of history at all.

(2) The crucial question is, however, what knowledge we need to have. Here what I am suggesting is that whilst a large part of the content of our conception of human nature is drawn from experience, and alters as our experience is added to, it remains true that there is a hard core in it which is not come by in the same way. This hard core I connect with our moral and metaphysical beliefs. When we look at the past, what understanding we gain of it depends primarily on the extent to which we succeed in identifying ourselves with the subjects of our study, thinking and feeling as they thought. But we could not even begin to understand unless we presupposed some propositions about human nature, unless we applied some notion of what is reasonable or normal in human behaviour. It is here that our own outlook exercises its effect and colours the interpretation we give.

No doubt it is a wise piece of practical advice to historians to tell them to become aware of their own moral and metaphysical preconceptions, and to be on their guard

against reading them naïvely into their history. But to draw
from that the conclusion that historians have only to make
the effort to be able to contemplate the past without any
preconceptions, allowing their minds to be coloured solely
by what they find there, is surely excessively sanguine. It
would certainly be wrong at this stage to infer that objective understanding of the past is impossible, on the ground
that we all look at it through our own moral and metaphysical spectacles: the possibility of a synthesis of different
points of view, and of the inclusion of one in another, remains to be discussed. Nevertheless, there is without doubt
some *prima facie* case for an ultimate historical scepticism,
a case which the spectacle of actual differences among historians greatly strengthens. To ignore this case altogether is
to bury one's head in the sand.

# PART III

# History and Morality

"*There is a popular saying of Madame de Staël,*" Lord Acton said in his Inaugural Lecture at Cambridge in 1895, "*that we forgive whatever we really understand. The paradox has been judiciously pruned by her descendant, the Duke de Broglie, in the words: 'Beware of too much explaining, lest we end up by too much excusing.' History, says Froude, does teach that right and wrong are real distinctions. Opinions alter, creeds rise and fall, but the moral law is written on the tablets of eternity. And if there are moments when we may resist the teaching of Froude, we have seldom the chance of resisting when he is supported by Mr. Goldwin Smith: 'A sound historical morality will sanction strong measures in evil times; selfish ambition, treachery, murder, perjury, it will never sanction in the worst of times, for these are the things that make times evil —Justice has been justice, mercy has been mercy, honour has been honour, good faith has been good faith, truthfulness has been truthfulness from the beginning.' The doctrine that, as Sir Thomas Browne says, morality is not ambulatory, is expressed as follows by Burke, who, when true to himself, is the most intelligent of our instructors: 'My principles enable me to form my judgments upon men and actions in history, just as they do in common life, and are not formed out of events and characters, either present or past. History is a preceptor of prudence, not of principles.*"

*The principles of true politics are those of morality en-
larged; and I neither now do, nor ever will admit of any
other.'* "[1]

A stanch advocate of passing judgment on men and ideas
(including the doctrine of papal infallibility, which he opposed as a Catholic), Lord Acton conducted an interesting
correspondence on the subject with Bishop Creighton, the
author of a historical work on the papacy, parts of which
are reprinted in the volume from which I have just quoted.

This is not the place to discuss the nature of morality;
but, as we have seen in the previous part, moral issues and
conflicts of values permeate history as they do ordinary
life. No special problem arises over the interests and values
which the historian finds in his material; presumably, he
treats them, as Mr. Nagel suggested, like any other "fact."
But history throws a more disturbing shadow upon morality
in two respects: (a) with regard to the vexing problem of
moral relativism; (b) with regard to the propriety of moral
judgments by the historian.

As to the former, the question is whether moral principles are written "on the tablets of eternity" or whether a
"historical consciousness," as Dilthey said, reveals "the relativity of every metaphysical or religious doctrine" and
leaves us to contemplate sadly "a vast field of ruins of religious traditions, metaphysical positions, demonstrated systems, and possibilities of all sorts." As to moral judgments,
the question is whether they are legitimate or not, and what
their effect is upon the "truth" of a historical narrative.

It is this last question which is discussed first in the following two selections. Mr. Butterfield, Professor of Modern
History in the University of Cambridge, takes the position
of Madame de Staël, but from a Christian point of view.
Sir Isaiah Berlin, Professor of Social and Political Theory in
the University of Oxford, reaffirms the views of the Duke de
Broglie and Burke, but in the context of an analysis of
"ordinary language" which is the characteristic style of Oxford philosophy in the present, post-Wittgenstein period.

Butterfield argues that the historian should not indulge

[1] Lord Acton, *Essays on Freedom and Power*, ed. by G. Him-
melfarb (New York: Meridian, 1955).

*in moral judgments, partly because we know so little about the secret motives hidden in the human heart, partly because of the Christian maxim: Judge not lest ye be judged!* Berlin replies that the historian *must* judge, whether he wants to or not, partly because moral categories are as deeply embedded in the structure of our language as are the physical categories of space, time, or causality, partly because it is morally monstrous to say that we cannot judge a Nero, Tamerlane, or Hitler.

Implicit in either view is a special conception of history. Butterfield pleads for the "technical historian," whose job is similar to the detective's, as Collingwood said. Both try to discover the truth, not the grounds for praise and blame. The primary function of the historian is to reconstruct the past in its own context, not in ours; to recover, by "sympathetic understanding," what actually happened, in Ranke's sense. To fulfill this task he must be capable of an "act of self-emptying,"[2] of divesting himself precisely of those preconceptions, whether moral, political, or religious, which are characteristic of our judgments in ordinary life. He must discover a "deeper kind of truth" lying behind the conflicting values which, say, Catholics or Protestants ordinarily bring to an interpretation of the Reformation. Thus moral judgments are "irrelevant," "alien," or "an actual hindrance to inquiry."

Berlin, in turn, rests his case primarily on the grounds that to exclude moral judgments from history is to confuse "the aims and methods of the humane studies with those of natural science." The latter, obviously, do not use moral categories; but history is not a science—the believers in the alleged laws of history to the contrary notwithstanding. The belief in "vast impersonal forces" guiding the course of history according to laws of their own is an illusion; history has not even developed any significant concepts of its own; its method and language are primarily those of common sense. In general, "we explain and elucidate in history . . . as in ordinary life." Ordinary language, however, can no more dispense with moral judgments than with causal

[2] Cf. Professor Lovejoy's phrase "effort of self-transcendence," p. 180 above.

*statements. Or, our moral concepts are no more flexible
than our physical ones—and just as legitimate in the life of
the ordinary man and historian. To suppress them would
be both unnatural and impossible.*

*Two other points may be noted briefly. (1) Professor
Butterfield's case against moral judgments in historical
works does not, for him, rule out "morality in life" or even
a belief in "the hand of God in history." (2) Professor Berlin's case for moral judgments implies that the agent (or
patient) in history is endowed with an inalienable sense of
personal freedom and responsibility. Hence, the moral issue reopens the ancient controversy over freedom and determinism with regard to human actions. Sir Isaiah Berlin's
defense of moral judgments, in fact, commits him to a restatement, which goes considerably beyond the province of
ordinary language, of Kant's view according to which the
human agent must be free in some radical, absolute sense,
if moral judgments are to have any meaning.*[3]

1.

## HERBERT BUTTERFIELD

## MORAL JUDGMENTS IN HISTORY*

Those who go to the works of Protestant and Catholic
partisans will find the history of the Reformation staged as
a conflict between right and wrong. If they do not become
war-weary they will soon be somewhat bewildered; and
they will yearn on occasion for a more humdrum narrative
—one which will make clear the ascertained data and not
harass the mind too severely by entangling the argument
with the evidence. What they will hanker after, strangely
enough—though they might be shocked to see the matter
so expressed—is the technical historian who may be a Cath-

[3] For a technical discussion of this crucial point, see below,
pp. 246–47; see also *Historical Inevitability*, p. 253, footnote 1.
  * In *History and Human Relations* (London: Collins, 1931),
pp. 101–30; reprinted by permission of William Collins Sons &
Co. Ltd.

olic or a Protestant but is willing to jettison for the time
being his private views and personal valuations. He performs an act of self-emptying in order to seek the kind of
truths which do not go further than the tangible evidence
warrants, the kind of truths which the evidence forces us
to believe whether we like them or not. Though this kind
of history is more limited in some respects than a Protestant
version of the story (which will be packed with Protestant
evaluations and judgments) it is richer and more far-reaching in other ways, for it is calculated to carry the student
to higher altitudes and it can lead him to a further range of
discoveries. It may enable him, for example, to get behind
the very conflict that divides Protestant and Catholic, and
learn why Western Christendom ever came to such a state
of dissension. This, then, is what we mean by "technical
history"—the sort of history which is the subject of a high
and austere academic discipline. It may never exist in its
absolute purity. But its assertions have a higher authenticity in so far as the ideal is attained.

Men who in centuries long past were firmly convinced
that an outbreak of plague was the manifestation of the
handiwork of God would still seem to have been capable
of noting on occasion the observable connections between
events and the operation of intermediate causes. Those who
have believed that a war came as a judgment from Heaven
have still been able to observe and discuss the activity of
the human instruments of the divine Providence. A natural
scientist is pledged to work in the way Gibbon purported
to do; that is to say, he confines his explanations to the
causes that are "under God", and he would be committing
an act of sabotage if he brought God into his scientific argument. It would be wrong to infer that because he sub-
mits to this discipline he is necessarily an unbeliever. The
historian may be convinced that the will of God is in every
step and motion of the drama, every pulse-beat of the centuries. As a technical student, however, he is under the obligation to perform the particular act of self-emptying that
has been described. He is committed to an attempt to learn
all that can be learned by the scientific study of just the
observable interconnections of events.

If we consider these facts, if we note the nature of the questions which the technical procedure of the historian is intended and qualified to answer, if we bear in mind the intellectual realm in which that kind of question is appropriately discussed, we are in a position to embark upon an estimate of the place which moral judgments ought to have in history. And in view of the situation that has been described, it may be possible to reduce the shock sometimes produced by the thesis which denies any ethical character (in the usual sense of the words) to the technical historian's universe. The thesis may be asserted in so far as it means that moral judgments on human beings are by their nature irrelevant to the enquiry and alien to the intellectual realm of scientific history. It has practical significance in that, granted such a view of the matter, these moral judgments must be recognised to be an actual hindrance to enquiry and reconstruction; they are in fact the principal reason why investigation is so often brought to a premature halt. Yet we do not deny the importance of morality in life any more than we deny the hand of God in history, if we decide to conduct technical history without this postulate. On the contrary we shall find that, at the last stage of the argument, the historical realm emerges as a moral one in what we may regard as a higher sense of the word altogether.

Indeed we may say that precisely because all men are sinners and precisely because the rest of the truth about the matter cannot be disentangled short of the Judgment Day, the vindication of the moral element in history neither requires nor permits the separation of the sheep from the goats by the technical historian. Precisely because the issue is so important and precisely because life is a moral matter every inch of the way (while no historian can keep his ethical vigilance continuous or trouble to be making moral judgments absolutely all the time)—precisely for these reasons the occasional dip into moral judgments is utterly inadequate to the end it purports to serve. The effect of the whole situation is to make the judgments in question depend on the historian's unconscious selection of the moments at which he will think fit to raise the moral issue. There have been liberal historians who would tend to fix upon religious persecution as the topic which called for the particular act of judgment, as though it were the test case in ethics. It has even happened that the devout and reasonably virtuous person, who at certain periods would have needed exceptional saintliness or real originality of mind to break away from the prevalent principles of persecution, has suffered greatly at the hands of such historians, while the irreligious scoundrel, pursuing toleration from worldly-mindedness and motives of *realpolitik*, has been able to emerge with undeserved honours. Moral judgments are the more apt for this reason to be political ones in disguise—the historian is seeking to add a sort of supercharge to his condemnation of a certain policy. Some Whig historians would seem to have reserved the severest judgment for the men who support what they describe as "absolutism"; and the rest of the wide world of moral action that is open to a man seems either to be ignored, as a mere matter of private life, or is reserved for a concession made in parenthesis. It is difficult to see how anybody who surveys historical literature—even leaving out of the reckoning the vast amount of writing which patently misuses the occasion for polemical purposes—could feel that justice is done to the place of morality in life by those spasmodic incursions into the field of ethics.

It would be foolish to take arms against the mere *obiter dicta* of historians, however, or against the incidental utterance of personal opinions. These things have a way of leaking into a narrative, and they are not to be taken as part of the structure of the history. We can accept them as the addition of a sort of colouring matter, while refusing to construe them seriously or to admit any pontifical claim that may be put forward on their behalf. A greater danger arises, however, if moral judgments are incorporated in the structure of the narrative, if they control the mounting of the story, and if they become embedded in the very fabric of our historical thinking. Above all it is necessary to resist those who claim for the historian the solemn role of moral arbiter, and particularly those who transfer this ethical preoccupation into the reconstruction of the whole course of ages. Important issues are raised if the struggle of Whigs and Tories is ranged into an epic conflict of the righteous against the unrighteous. Those who pitch their claim so high are tempting the technical student to a dangerous form of self-aggrandisement and do violence to the character of academic history. In their whole presentation of the human drama throughout the ages the conflict between good and evil is wrongly placed.

## II

It may help us to keep our balance in our analysis of the question if we take note that even in the ordinary course of life the issues of morality are often settled with very little thought. Granting the all-importance of our ethical principles and ethical teaching—granting also the momentousness of the obligation that we are under to follow righteousness in our own conduct—we might wonder whether in reality there is any meaning or purpose in ethical judgments directed against actual people in respect of an action once that action has been done. In fact it is questionable whether any retrospective ethical judgment—I mean the kind of judgment which is directed against a personality—is worth anything, except in the form of the judgment that all men are, and men always have been, sinners. And this particular thesis owes its power and authenticity to the fact that in reality it is translatable for each of us into a self-judgment. For my own part I am willing to say that religious persecution is always wrong. It is wrong even when it is committed by people who are unaware that it is wrong. In other words I believe that it is essential to treat this planet as the kind of world in which men are allowed to "choose" the God they will serve and the moral end for which they live. Granted that there is only one religion—namely the right one—this religion will be the one to suffer in the long run if that sphere of freedom is brought under the rule of force. I should hope, then, to go to the last limits along with anybody who refuses to countenance religious persecution for any reason. From this it will be clear that clarity or firmness in one's principles of conduct is not by any means the point which is at issue; and if there is question of a man who is about to persecute, we can all agree that he ought to be beset behind and before with the moral argument. From the same standpoint it is easy to say that an action is wrong therefore—the action itself is wrong even if the man who performs it is unaware that it is wrong. Such a judgment is almost a piece of tautology—it is merely a restatement of the original ethical principle. On the other hand, to denounce those who *have* persecuted; to condemn them in terms that suggest them to have been inhuman; to assume that they in turn did not have an ethical principle; and to assert or imply that they were more wicked than I am—all this is improper in itself and is a formidable obstruction to historical understanding.

As a preliminary to the discussion of the problem that concerns the historian, it will possibly serve a purpose to put forward certain general theses relating to the administration of moral judgments in the world at large. Such theses will help to define a mode of approach to this subject and will provide a framework for the argument that is to follow. If they give offence, however, they can be rendered otherwise harmless by the addition of the proviso that even if they fail to secure acceptance—even if a great wind comes to blow them all off the face of the earth—still, so far as I can see, this fact ought not to weaken the main argument which follows them, and to which they serve as a background.

The first point, then, is the belief that to some degree men are responsible for themselves and for their actions; but that all men are imperfect and that human suffering is greatly increased and multiplied by this general fact.

The second is the thesis that the difference between the wickedness and responsibility of one man and those of another, in the general world of nature (where it must be recognised that good fortune or adverse conditions play a great but still unmeasured part in the development of human beings), is so idle a question and so nice a point that it is not worth the wear of our fine intellects to discuss it in any imaginable conjuncture of life or history. Indeed, since human responsibility is so subtle a substance, presenting itself with vividness inside me, but not open to my vision at all inside another man—in other words, since I know that I could have done better than I did do while I can never tell what allowances I ought to make for other people—it is impossible to think one man essentially more wicked than another save as one might say: "All men are sinners and I the chief of them". It follows from this that moral judgments of actual people cannot defensibly or usefully exist in concrete cases save in the form of self-judgments.

Thirdly, though I, looking to the immediate future, must regard myself as a responsible person who may do things that are moral and immoral, and may follow or betray a law which is written on my conscience or a law that I have imposed upon myself; yet in regard to other people (who may think earnestly and differ from me about the law itself) and in regard to other people's actions once they are done (so that I cannot now prevent them), the passing of what purports to be a moral judgment—particularly a judgment which amounts to the assertion that they are worse men than I am—is not merely irrelevant, but actually immoral and harmful, not merely dangerous to my soul but unfitted for producing improvement in human nature anywhere.

Fourthly, granted that the State is under the necessity of punishing crimes, and granted that in the case of crime the offence is not merely technical but has moral implications (though sometimes the implications are not so assured or so direct as the world would like to believe), still we are not justified in expanding a legal verdict into a final judgment on a personality, or in assuming that because our own sins do not happen to have been also technical offences they are less morally blameworthy. If a man is sent to gaol, in fact, both the judge and the gaoler are to be interpreted as saying to him: "Look here, old sport, we know that you may be a better man than we are, but since we can't tell what to do in order to save society, we have to resort to force". If it is necessary to hang murderers, we must be sure that we are doing it because of a necessity and not out of moral indignation. And when we have done it we shall do well to reflect sadly on the bitterness of the necessity, and say: "There, but for the grace of God, go I".

Fifthly, since moral indignation corrupts the agent who possesses it and is not calculated to reform the man who is the object of it, the demand for it—in the politician and in the historian for example—is really a demand for an illegitimate form of power. The attachment to it is based on its efficacy as a tactical weapon, its ability to rouse irrational fervour and extraordinary malevolence against some enemy. As in such cases its efficacy is not lessened even when it is used unfairly and unscrupulously against those who have done no great harm, the argument for the use of this weapon is valid also for the unscrupulous use of it. The passage from the one to the other is indeed one of the most regular conjuring-tricks in the world.

Finally—so far as these statements of principle are concerned—I should say that, though I assume there are limits, I do not know where to place the limits to the operation of the truth that we condemn where we do not understand. This is tantamount to the assertion that the kind of ethical judgments which historians like Lord Acton have been so anxious to achieve are possible only to God.

All these principles are ultimately referable to the good old-fashioned doctrine that in the created world nothing really matters except live human beings. They would be inconsistent with anything like a Nazi view of human beings or the State or the *Volk*. They could not survive in a world that believed a society or corporation to represent the genuine whole, the authentic Person, with individual people as mere limbs of that body. They become submerged altogether if the State is regarded as the ethical end, and actual living people are construed as merely the means to an end. The principles imply that the biography of the worst of murderers could conceivably be written in such a way that he would be what in a technical sense we call the "hero" of the story, so that our pity and sympathy would be around him as we followed him up from childhood. By the same argument what we should desire even in the case of a man like Hitler is not a mere angry denunciation. What would prove of incomparable value, if it

were possible, would be an intimate account of him by a
person who did not hate him too much—an account which
would enable us to see how a lump of human nature (how
a boy playing in a field) could ever have come to be *like
that*. Best of all for the good of our souls would be an account such as would be written by a mother who was compelled to watch helplessly through the years while this child
of hers took to terrible ways. But if it is objected that all
this implies too delicate a regard for the effect of conditions
on the development of human beings—if it is asserted that
it seems to transform men into mere puppets, mere victims of circumstance—a counter-thesis must be stated in
terms so uncompromising as to leave no doubt of a man's
ultimate responsibility. It must be asserted that neither the
outcasts nor the pillars of respectability can in reality escape judgment if judgment is going to be pressed for. Indeed, if we are writing the life of a person whom we think
the best of human beings, we may make him the "hero"
of the story, but this can only be in the technical sense
again; we cannot pretend that he is a spotless saint. That
is why we must go further than Lord Acton, who was inclined to feel that all the great men of history were bad
men. If we want human responsibility we can only save it
by something like the general dogma that levels all men—
the doctrine that all are sinners, all are responsible for not
being better than they are. In other words, none is completely excused if he has allowed even a bad education or
the most adverse circumstances to corrupt his character.
None is completely free and unconfined, but none is to be
regarded as the absolute slave of conditions.

The principles that have been put forward would have
to be defended in the last resort on the ground that these,
and nothing less than these, enable us to do full justice
to the authenticity of other people's personalities in a world
where we cannot see inside other people. The theses would
be inescapable if one went further and accepted the ultimate principle that no law of God or man, and no alleged
utility, can supersede the law or transcend the utility of
extending charity to all men, or can set imaginable limits
to the law of charity.

Supposing, however, that these statements of principle fail to win acceptance, it may be pointed out that the issue with which we are concerned does not require that we shall commit ourselves to them at the moment. As a view of life they may be brushed aside, but the matter which does immediately concern us is the fact that in any case we must still adopt this point of view and transfer it into the very structure of our story of the past, the moment we undertake the work of the historian. In other words, if these theses and maxims are not true in the present world they are a necessary part of the structure of the realm of history. For in this latter realm, certainly, no ethical principle can be alleged to override the primary duty of extending charity, that is to say, increasing human understanding by an effort which always requires the expansion of sympathy.

## III

In the conduct of life we shall often find it the case that the world condenses its assessment of a personality into something which it would not be unjust to describe as rather an aesthetic than a moral judgment. The question of a man's charm and his general demeanour, his bravery and the tact which he shows in the conduct of affairs—all these may be rolled up with our moral approval in what is really a judgment of the total product in so far as it is observable to an outsider. It cannot be denied that this over-all judgment of personalities—which is inclined to regard itself as a moral judgment, and as the final summing-up of the matter—tends to award medals to many of those qualities of personality which bloom more readily in the warmth of favourable circumstance. Here, where we applaud a certain nobility of mind or a niceness of disposition in a man, we are not unaware that fortune itself may have had a part in producing the attractive result. There, on the other hand, where we see forms like blasted oaks, we know that fine shapes of men have perhaps been devastated as by a flash of lightning. There is much of what we might call the broken crockery of human nature, where sometimes the fractures and deformities mark the effects of a not quite successful struggle with heredity and environment. Human beings are responsible at some point for the use which they make of the materials at their disposal—otherwise there is no sense in a discussion of moral judgments at all. But genuine ultimate assessments of worthiness are beyond the power of our mathematics to calculate. It is well that the ordinary verdicts of the world should be quasi-aesthetic ones and that we should realise them to be such.

Now the limitation of the historian, when he passes verdict on personalities, is that he is so liable to be satisfied in a similar way with the kind of judgment that is much less truly ethical than it pretends to be. Much of the benefit which is supposed to result from the whole practice is nullified by the deplorable fact that the moral judgments of historians are so often taken at a low level; we might even say that these things are almost invariably more rough-and-ready than anything else in the whole complicated fabric of historical writing. In reality they are pseudo-moral judgments, masquerading as moral ones—mixed and muddy affairs, part prejudice, part political animosity—with a dash of ethical flavouring wildly tossed into the concoction. They come blithely from impetuous adjudicators who have a rough idea of Henty heroes shining brightly against the background of something which is not cricket. Against such purveyors of rough justice Acton wrote much of his argument on this subject and made a justifiable protest; and it was in this context that he used the terminology of one who is protesting against a debasement of the currency.

In any case, in the world of pseudo-moral judgments there is generally a tendency on the one hand to avoid the higher regions of moral reflection and on the other hand to make moral issues out of what are not really moral issues at all. And if some may think that this is a laudable symptom of ethical zeal, they are mistaken. Even in the world at large it is rather a decline in genuine fervour which produces the desire to make gratuitous moral issues where such issues ought not really to be drawn. This is the method by which conflicts and controversies between human beings are rendered bitter and cut-throat and incapable of compromise. Against the argument that German historians in recent generations did great harm by avoiding moral judgments, it is possible to assert that these historians did harm, not through abstention and austerity, but precisely because they were not sufficiently reserved. They inserted pseudo-moral judgments and approvals, mixed ethics with reason-of-state, and tended to ratify and confirm Frederick the Great and Bismarck at the critical points. Indeed it has been commonly the case that those who were most eager to demand moral judgments in history—and who generally insist on the lower kind of pseudo-moral judgments, since a more delicate handling of the matter would hardly serve their purpose—have on the whole been politicians, or men with a more or less direct political purpose, men with an axe to grind, who have rightly seen that moral judgments in history represent a considerable form of power. When Acton was confronted with the claim that the historian should forgo judgments on people, he betrayed on more than one occasion the fact that what preoccupied him was the fear that those bugbears of his, the wicked Ultramontanes, would in such a case get off scot-free.

Indeed, when the historian asserts the case for moral judgments on people, he is always bound to retreat and turn it into a case for the kind of verdict which pretends to be an "approximation". Only the latter—only the judgment which is mixed with a good deal of earth—will serve the militant purposes of the man who has a polemical intent. In any case, the lofty heights of the former are closed to the historian, whose apparatus and evidence are not qualified to carry him to such rarefied realms. The historian can never quite know men from the inside—never quite learn the last secret of the workings of inspiration in a poet or of piety in a devout religious leader. For the same reason he can never quite carry his enquiries to that innermost region where the final play of motive and the point of responsibility can be decided. The historian fails to pierce the most inward recesses and the essential parts of a man; and all he can depend on is a general feeling for human nature, based ultimately on self-analysis, but further enlarged in a general experience of life. Much can be achieved by a constant practice of that kind of imaginative sympathy which works on all types and varieties of men and acquires a certain feeling for personality. But the only understanding we ever reach in history is but a refinement, more or less subtle and sensitive, of the difficult—and sometimes deceptive—process of imagining oneself in another person's place.

Equipped with this general knowledge of human nature, the historian, when he deals with an historical character, examines external acts, thoughts that happen to have been put into writing, medical evidence, official records, perhaps the impressions of friends. Always he has to work on external data which he combines with all that he had previously learned concerning the interior of a human personality. He does not study human nature, therefore, in the way that an omniscient deity might observe it, with an eye that pierces our unspoken intentions, our thick folds in insincerity and the motives that we hardly avow to ourselves. It is true that an historian may feel that by imaginative sympathy he has almost completed the gaps in his picture of some historical personage, almost achieved what we might call an internal knowledge of the man. By great insight and by running all his molten experience into the mould that has been presented to him, he may feel that he has found the essential clue to a character—even to a man who has hitherto baffled the interpreters. Even this degree of knowledge fails, however, in that innermost region of all, which has to be reached before a personality can be assessed in a moral judgment. The genuine utility of such knowledge lies in the opposite direction altogether. In reality it adds more than anybody would have imagined to the wealth of historical explanation which can be assembled around a human action or a personality. And that enrichment of historical explanation is liable to be the thing which complicates or undermines the simple moral judgment which originally we might have been tempted to make.

When Lord Acton issued his justifiable protests against the slackness of the current ideas on the subject of moral judgments, the critical point in his argument had reference to the difficulty that arises from the inevitable incompleteness of the historian's knowledge. Rightly indignant against the casual handling of such important questions, he was

wrongly severe, however, in the remedy which he proposed
to administer. He approved the principle that we should beware of too much explaining lest we end by excusing the
men of the past. Lack of knowledge in his opinion did not
justify a suspension of judgment; he thought that the cause
of morality would be better served if the historian erred
rather by excessive severity. In the famous controversy with
Creighton on the subject of the *History of the Papacy* it
is apparent that the heart of the difficulty lay at the same
point in the argument. Creighton was surely right when
he said—after second thoughts on the subject—that he, for
his part, could not bring himself to be the judge of Pope
Alexander VI and must make allowances for time and circumstance. Acton, on the other hand, must have been right
in believing that the historian does not know enough to exonerate such a man, and that, whatever might be dis-
counted for the age of the Renaissance, the ethics of the
New Testament had at any rate been in circulation for
nearly fifteen hundred years. It is not to be presumed that
either of these historians hesitated to agree that certain actions were wrong—that lying and poisoning were immoral.
The dispute concerned the assessment of an historical personality, the verdict of posterity and of the last judgment
—it was a question of the allowances to be made in the
summing-up of a man. The truth was that Creighton could
not know enough to exonerate. Neither, on the other hand,
did Acton in reality know enough to condemn the man himself. It would have been better to recognise that the historian is not competent to make the necessary calculations,
and that he carries the whole issue into a different realm of
thought. It is not for him to steal the mantle of the ancient
prophets; and it is more fitting that he should keep within
the limits that his apparatus and evidence have set for him.
Within these limits he has indeed a more important task;
for Creighton and Acton had not even said the last word as
yet towards the settlement of the question whether Alexander VI had actually committed all the deeds imputed to
him. Beyond that, it is the real service of the historian to
assemble all that can be gathered—everything relating to
situation, circumstances, limiting conditions and preceding

events—all that will throw a further explanatory light upon the conduct of this Pope. The historian will never be able to settle the controversy between Creighton and Acton or to determine whether Alexander VI had more than his fair share in man's universal sin—more responsibility than the rest of human nature. His function is to surround the man with all that can be gathered in the way of historical explanation.

## IV

Working upon a given historical event, then, the historian knits around it a web of historical explanation. If the event happens to be one so anomalous that it has no meaning for us, or so alien to our experience that it leaves us cold, the explanation—which in reality is its reintegration in its context—will establish, so to speak, a means of communication with it. The follies, the crimes and the wilfulnesses that were unspeakable will not be turned into virtues but will at least become humanly understandable. When we think of the men who believed that the sun went round the earth and that Intelligencies moved the planets, we shall no longer brush these fools aside as though they had nothing to do with us. When we hear of pious men who persecuted their neighbours in the sixteenth century, we shall cease to turn our backs on them and bluntly dismiss the affair as a case of ordinary crime. The total result of such habits and procedures is to lessen the inclination to declare in an impetuous way that this man is a fool, that man a criminal, that other one a representative of a vested interest. The effect, therefore, should be from one point of view a greater urbanity; and from another point of view a recognition of wider fields for the exercise of charity. What is essential to the whole task is the realisation that a special effort is needed to comprehend the men who are not like-minded with oneself. There are those who think that there can be too much charity, too much human understanding, in the relations of man with man. All that we can do with these is to say that the time has come when this particular issue should be clearly drawn.

Some kinds of history do not operate in the way that has been described. We can discover that it is in their intention —it is considered their virtue—that they should rather kindle the anger and awaken the indignation of men. Such history has played a great part in the generation of the national animosities of our time. And, since all can find something wicked that another Power has done, our continent has seethed with a terrifying passion for justice and redress— seethed with that kind of indignation which feels itself only too righteous, only too sincere. What must be noted in the case of the conflicts that take place between either nations, or parties, or regimes or ideologies, is the fact that each can be fertile and ingenious in its "historical explanation" of one part of the story, while in the other part nothing more is necessary but to bring the effort of understanding to a halt—the mind can rest satisfied for it can clinch the matter with a moral judgment instead. So the Whig historians were not at fault in that they found historical explanation for the conduct of the Whigs. They were wrong because they could not enter with that same *élan* into the sympathetic understanding of the other party.

It can hardly have escaped notice, especially in recent years, how men sympathetic to Communism, when they were confronted by some crime on the part of Russia, were eager to assemble around it what we have called "the historical explanation" of the event. They were right in this, though, as we have seen, they were wrong if they imagined that such explanatory data could have the effect of authorising the exoneration of the culprits. What is remarkable, however, is the fact that when confronted by the identical crime in a follower of Franco, the identical atrocity in the ranks of the Nazis, they pursued a totally different course, closed down on all historical explanation and insisted on the moral issue clear and clean. Having taken this stand they were able to expose all other people's attempts at historical explanation as a crime against morality, and the sleight-of-hand was hardly detectable. One witness tells us that English soldiers, fighting the E.L.A.S. in Greece, declared the atrocities of the rebels to be so appalling as to make the armies of Germany appear comparatively clean. In the House of Commons debate on the trouble in Greece, Mr. Gallagher made the point that the outcry against atrocities can itself be unfair—that even the atrocities are to be envisaged with reference to their historical explanation. What the men of the Left Wing will do for the revolutions of the Left the men of the Right will do for the revolutions of the Right; and here is the formula for one of the modern forms of deadlock. It is curious that the world should have been content for so long to allow itself to be entertained by a conjuring-trick so transparent—the hen that has a black patch on the Right Wing seething with moral indignation against the hen that has a black patch on the Left.

The truth is that, as we have seen already, we need no help from the historian to bring us to the recognition of the criminality of religious persecution or wholesale massacre or the modern concentration camp or the repression of dissident opinions. And those who do not recognise that the killing and torturing of human beings is barbarity will hardly be brought to that realisation by any labels and nicknames that historians may attach to these things. There is one way in which the historian may reinforce the initial moral judgment and thereby assist the cause of morality in general; and that way lies directly within his province, for it entails merely describing, say, the massacre or the persecution, laying it out in concrete detail, and giving the specification of what it means in actuality. It is possible to say that one of the causes of moral indifference is precisely the failure to realise in an objective manner and make vivid to oneself the terrible nature of crime and suffering; but those who are unmoved by the historical description will not be stirred by any pontifical commentary that may be superadded. If historical analysis begins to move further than this exposure of the wickedness of the action itself, however—if it directs our attention to the doers of the action and turns the enquiry into an examination of these— then complications are liable to occur. The offence itself is no less horrifying, but judgment is liable to be affected if it transpires that the perpetrators are African tribesmen driven into a desperate position by white exploiters; or if the case turns out to be one of direct reprisal, instituted to check atrocities against one's own people. In this manner history draws us further away from our original simple judgment, if only because it tends to reveal the intricate cross-currents and qualifying circumstances.

Let us take the case of the massacre of St. Bartholomew and imagine that we have traversed the whole range of accompanying facts and conditioning circumstances. Let us say that we have assembled around Catherine de' Medici everything that may have reference to the affair—all that we can discover of her predicament at the time, of preceding events, of her own constitution and structure, of her views, her intentions and motives, as well as all that we can discover of the range of options which was open to her at the decisive moment. Assisted by all this material and by all the humanity we possess, we are now called to resurrect the whole occasion and to see with Catherine, feel with her, hold our breath with her, and meet the future with all her apprehensions. If by imaginative sympathy we can put ourselves in her place in this way, not only envisaging the situation in all its detail but apprehending it in all its vividness and intensity until we reach the point at which we could almost conceive ourselves making the drastic decision, or at least have a sense of just what it would take to carry us across the border to such a decision—then we are historians indeed. In such a case it is in our power to add something to human understanding, though such a contribution would certainly not come in the form of moral judgments. On the other hand, if we cannot achieve this sort of thing at all, if we cannot bring our imagination to such an endeavour, we are in no state to give the measure of a moral judgment either. Nor does it help matters if we pretend to assert: "We cannot enter imaginatively into this particular case because Catherine de' Medici was wicked beyond all imagination". The most that we can say in this respect is that either Catherine was wicked beyond any man's imagination or else we ourselves are deficient in this particular quality—either one of the two alternatives may be true. Those who ask themselves which of these two ills of the world they are going to attack had better set about

remedying that deficiency of imagination which exists here
and now. For Catherine de' Medici, since she is dead, is
out of our hands and after all we are not children playing
with shadows. She can wait till the Judgment Day.

Some people who wish not merely to condemn massacre
as such (which is always legitimate) but to dispose of a
whole class of human beings at the same time, attempt to
use the case of St. Bartholomew to show that there is an
organic connection between Roman Catholicism and atrocity as such, just as people will assume that there is an
organic connection between a particular nationality and
atrocity, though the nationality does not remain the same
in successive centuries of history. One of the great needs
of the twentieth century is a scientific study of atrocity and
of the moral issues involved.

It has been rightly pointed out that, while men are able
so often to be indifferent, or only faintly stirred, or mildly
deprecating, when atrocities are committed against the
weak or the poor, the fires of our moral indignation will
burn to a passionate intensity if they are stoked not merely
by our altruism but also by our self-interest—when we have
the good fortune to know that it is an enemy nation, a hostile party, or a business rival that commits the crime. When
life is so complicated as this, and the historian himself is in
the arena—subject to aberrations much more serious than
mere intellectual errors—moral judgments are a loophole
for every abuse in historical study. The very dispenser of
moral judgments is himself caught in the net—beat upon by
the self-same forces that he pretends to survey from the
point of view of sovereign mind.

## V

It may be objected that the problem of moral judgments
is of minor significance, since the historian, without step-
ping a foot beyond the frontiers of his science, is in a position to cover the requirements of the case. It is his function
to describe faithfully the men of the past; and if a politician
is regularly drunk or beats his wife or makes money by
revealing Cabinet secrets, these very tangible points, which

are controllable through specific kinds of evidence, will become part of the description of the personality. Even at a further remove, if a man is delineated as weak in character, or as subject to violent moods, or as having become hardened during his tenure of power, all this, though it is purely descriptive and avoids the pitfalls of moral judgment, leaves us without illusions on the subject of the person in question. Since the historian in his capacity as detective can prove that a man has lied with considerable regularity, what does it matter whether the same historian, in the capacity of judge, has power to measure the actual guilt of this, or to decide upon the culprit's real deserts?

It matters because the historian who leaves the realm of explanation and description, and moves into the world of moral judgments, is in reality trying to take upon himself (and to claim for his intellectual system) a new dimension. Very quickly this has its effect on the whole shape and setting which he gives to the course of things in time, and on his whole conception of the drama of human life in history. The morality comes to be worked into the organisation of the narrative and the structure of the historical scene in a manner that is illegitimate. What is projected across the length and breadth of the centuries is the pattern of a universe in which the good men are fighting the bad from one generation to another; so that the whole historical fabric, at whatever point we choose to observe it, is shot through with the colourful contrast of divine right and diabolical wrong. It transpires that the fabric is in truth like a piece of shot silk, for the colour of its parts seems to depend very largely on the way the observer looks at them, after all; and for one historian the Catholic or the royalist or the capitalist or the aristocratic cause may seem to be the absolutely virtuous one, while for another historian only the Protestant or the parliamentarian or the Liberal or the Socialist is on the side of righteousness. Not only does that magnificent war of Right versus Wrong come to look suspiciously political therefore, but historiography itself is seen to be split from top to bottom, so that what some men regard as the good is for others the seat of all the evil in the universe. In other words, the very aggrandisement that was to have made history the moral arbiter has in reality degraded it into an instrument of the partisan. Each side seeks to extract the maximum firing-power from the weapon by advertising the solemnity and the pontifical character of the moral judgments of history. In times of war and revolution these arguments possess redoubled force, with unfortunate consequences for the cause of historical science.

It is not always remembered that apart from the fervour of the Cavalier and the Roundhead there can be such a thing as a sheer historian's zeal, a passion for the past which does not subordinate itself to militant causes. Besides the ardour for the Whig or Tory or Socialist programme, there can be another kind of flame which is simply a compassion for human beings. It is possible for Catholic and Protestant, each locked in his separate universe, to construct his separate history of the sixteenth century, so that two mutually exclusive narrative structures incorporate alternative wars of Right versus Wrong to suit the taste of the reader. Yet historians who pursue questions belonging to a different order of thought may make discoveries that are equally valid for both religious parties; they may reach something of that deeper kind of truth which embraces and helps to explain even the antitheses. Such historians are drawing together again the torn fabric of historic life, and healing the wounds of mankind and deepening our insight into human destiny. We are right if we wish to see human history in moral terms, but we are running to myth if we mount the story on the pattern of the conventional war for righteousness.

It is perhaps not too much to say that in the fifty years since the death of Lord Acton the moral constitution of the historian's universe—if we leave out of account the literature which is incident to revolution and war—has been changing its character in a subtle manner. The change may be due to the fact that, whereas in former times men built up their picture of human advance from the study of mighty episodes like the Renaissance, the Reformation and the French Revolution, the more meticulous study of the broad intervening spaces—the central period of the eighteenth century for example—has shown us since that time how much progress is due to the gradual development of things in times of peace and stability, when passions subside and human beings are able to grow in reasonableness. It would perhaps be true to say that, ever since the time of Acton, therefore, a different kind of historical analysis has shown to what a great degree the advances that have mattered in the world have in a certain sense been the co-operative achievement of the whole human race—not so much the result of the victory that one set of men secured over another. The Aristotelians of Padua as well as the Platonists of Renaissance Florence contributed to the development of the scientific revolution. English liberty has been enriched in recent centuries because of the refusal to divide the country irredeemably by the trenchant assertiveness of Revolution—the refusal to carry the issue to the point of a "war for righteousness". The really important things (like the spread of education and enlightenment) have been advanced by a process which can best be described as the work of the leaven that gradually leavens the whole lump.

## 2.

## SIR ISAIAH BERLIN

## HISTORICAL INEVITABILITY*

The proposition that everything that we do and suffer is part of a fixed pattern; that Laplace's observer (supplied with adequate knowledge of facts and laws) could at any moment of historical time describe correctly every past and future event including those of 'inner' life, that is, human thoughts, feelings, acts, and so on, has often been entertained, and different implications have been drawn from

* Sections III and IV of *Historical Inevitability* (London—New York: Oxford University Press, 1954), pp. 30–54; reprinted by permission of the Oxford University Press. I have deleted some footnotes and several passages without, I hope, impairing the substance of Professor Berlin's argument. I have also taken the liberty of introducing a few paragraphs which do not appear in the original. H.M.

it; belief in its truth has dismayed some and inspired others. But whether such determinism is a valid theory or not, it seems clear that acceptance of it does not in fact colour the ordinary thoughts of the majority of human beings, nor those of historians, nor even those of natural scientists outside the laboratory. For if it did, the language of the believers would reflect this fact and be very different from that of the rest of us. There is a class of expressions which we constantly use (and can scarcely do without) like 'you should not (or need not) have done this'; 'why did you make this terrible mistake?'; 'I could do it, but I would rather not'; 'why did the King of Ruritania abdicate?', because, unlike the King of Abyssinia, he lacked the strength of will to resist'; '*must* the Commander-in-Chief be quite so stupid?' Expressions of this type plainly involve the notion of more than the merely logical possibility of the realization of alternatives other than those which were in fact realized, namely of differences between situations in which individuals can be reasonably regarded as being responsible for their acts, and those in which they can not. For no one will wish to deny that we do often argue about the best among the possible courses of action open to human beings in the present and past and future, in fiction and in dreams; that historians (and judges and juries) do attempt to establish, as well as they are able, what these possibilities are; that the ways in which these lines are drawn mark the frontiers between reliable and unreliable history . . . It seems superfluous to add that all the discussions of historians about whether a given policy could or could not have been prevented, and what view should therefore be taken of the acts and characters of the actors, are intelligible only on the assumption of the reality of human choices. If determinism were a valid theory of human behaviour, these distinctions would be as inappropriate as the attribution of moral responsibility to the planetary system or the tissues of a living cell. These categories permeate all that we think and feel so pervasively and universally, that to think them away, and conceive what and how we should be thinking, feeling, and talking without them, or in the framework of their opposites, is psychologically well-nigh impossible—as impracticable as, let us say, to pretend that we live in a world in which space, time, or number in the normal sense no longer exist. . . .

If the belief in freedom—which rests on the assumption that human beings do occasionally choose, and that their choices are not wholly accounted for by the kind of causal explanations which are accepted in, say, physics or biology —if this is a necessary illusion, it is so deep and so pervasive that it is not felt as such. No doubt we can try to convince ourselves that we are systematically deluded. But unless we attempt to think out the implications of this possibility, and alter our modes of thoughts and speech to allow for it accordingly, this hypothesis remains hollow; that is, we find it impossible even to entertain it seriously, if our behaviour is to be taken as evidence of what we can and what we cannot bring ourselves to believe or suppose not merely in theory, but in practice. My submission is that to make a serious attempt to adapt our thoughts and words to the hypothesis of determinism is scarcely feasible, as things are now, and have been within recorded history. The changes involved are too radical; our moral categories are, in the end, not much more flexible than our physical ones; we cannot begin to think out in real terms, to which behaviour and speech would correspond, what the universe of the genuine determinist would be like, any more than we can think out, with the minimum of indispensable concrete detail (i.e. begin to imagine) what it would be like to be in a timeless world, or one with a seventeen-dimensional space. Let those who doubt this try for themselves; the symbols with which we think will hardly lend themselves to the experiment; they, in their turn, are too deeply involved in our normal view of the world, allowing for every difference of period and clime and culture, to be capable of so violent a break . . . Hence the ancient controversy between free will and determinism, while it remains a genuine issue for theologians and philosophers, need not trouble the thoughts of those whose concern is with empirical matters—the actual lives of human beings in the space and time of normal experience. For historians determinism is not a serious issue.

Yet, unthinkable as it may be as a theory of human action, specific forms of the deterministic hypothesis have played an arresting, if limited, role in altering our views of human responsibility. The irrelevance of this general hypothesis to historical studies must not blind us to its importance as a specific corrective to ignorance, prejudice, dogmatism, and fantasy on the part of those who judge the behaviour of others. For it is plainly a good thing that we should be reminded by social scientists that the scope of human choice is a good deal more limited than we used to suppose; that the evidence at our disposal shows that many of the acts too often assumed to be within the individual's control are not so; that man is an object in nature to a larger degree than has at times been supposed, that human beings more often than not act as they do because of characteristics due to heredity or physical or social environment or education, or biological laws or physical characteristics or the interplay of these factors with each other, and with the obscurer factors loosely called psychical characteristics; and that the resultant habits of thought, feeling, and expression are as capable of being classified and made subject to hypotheses and systematic prediction as the behaviour of material objects. And this certainly alters our ideas about the limits of freedom and responsibility. If we are told that a given case of stealing is due to kleptomania, we protest that the appropriate treatment is not punishment but a remedy for a disease; and similarly, if a destructive act or a vicious character is ascribed to a specific psychological or social cause, we decide, if we are convinced that the explanation is valid, that the agent is not responsible for his acts and consequently deserves therapeutic rather than penal treatment. It is salutary to be reminded of the narrowness of the field within which we can begin to claim to be free; and some would claim that such knowledge is still increasing, and the field still contacting. Where the frontier between freedom and causal laws is to be determined is a crucial practical issue; knowledge of it is a powerful and indispensable antidote to ignorance and irrationality, and offers us new types of explanation—historical, psychological, sociological, biological—which previous generations have lacked. What we cannot alter, or can alter less than we had supposed, can hardly be used as evidence for or against us as free moral agents; it can cause us to feel pride, shame, regret, interest, but not remorse; it can be admired, envied, deplored, enjoyed, feared, wondered at, but not praised or condemned; our tendency to indignation is curbed, we desist from passing judgment. 'Je ne propose rien, je ne suppose rien, je n'impose rien . . . J'expose,' is a proud saying, and such *exposition* means the treatment of all events as natural phenomena, as scientific material to the exclusion of moral judgment. Historians of this persuasion, anxious to avoid all personal, above all, all moral judgments, tend to emphasize the immense predominance of impersonal factors in history, of the physical media in which life is lived, the power of geographical, psychological, social factors which are not, at any rate consciously, man-made, and often beyond human control.[1] This does tend to check our arrogance, to induce humility by forcing us to admit that our own outlook and scales of value are neither permanent nor universally accepted, that the over-confident, too-complacent moral classifications of past historians and of their societies sprang all too obviously from specific historical conditions, specific forms of ignorance or vainglory, or from particular temperamental traits in the historian, or from countless other causes and circumstances which, from our vantage point, we perceive to belong to their own place and time, and to have given rise to interpretations which today seem idiosyncratic, inadequate, and often grotesque in the light of our own standards of accuracy or objectivity . . . Have we learned nothing from the intolerable moral dogmatism and the mechanical classifications of those historians and moralists and politicians whose views are now so dated, so obsolete, and so justly discredited? And, indeed, who are we to make such a parade of our personal opinions, to give such importance to what are no more than symptoms of our own ephemeral

---

[1] To this may be added the views of those who claim that whatever the case with regard to individuals, the behaviour of groups of sufficient size can often be predicted with a statistical probability approaching virtual certainty.

outlook? And what right, in any case, have we to sit in judgment on our fellows whose moral codes are the products of their specific historical environments, as our own are of ours? Is it not better to analyse, to describe, to present the events, and then withdraw and let them 'speak for themselves', refraining from the intolerable presumption of awarding marks, meting out justice, dividing the sheep from the goats according to our own personal criteria, as if these were eternal and not, as in fact they are, neither more nor less valid than those of others with other interests, in other conditions?

Such advice to us to retain a certain scepticism about our own powers of judgment, especially to beware of ascribing too much authority to our own moral feelings, comes to us . . . from at least two quarters; from those who think that we know too much, and from those who think that we know too little. We know now, say the former, that we are as we are, and our moral and intellectual criteria are what they are, in virtue of the evolving historical situation. Let me once more remind you of their varieties. Some among them, who feel sure that the natural sciences will in the end account for everything, explain our behaviour in terms of natural causes. Others, who accept a more metaphysical interpretation of the world, explain it by speaking of invisible powers and dominions, nations, races, cultures; the spirit of the age, the 'workings', overt and occult, of 'the Classical Spirit', 'the Renaissance', 'the Mediaeval Mind', 'the French Revolution', or 'the Twentieth Century', conceived as impersonal entities, at once patterns and realities, in terms of whose 'structure' or 'purpose' their elements and expressions—men and institutions—must behave as they do. Yet still others speak in terms of some teleological procession or hierarchy, whereby each man, country, institution, culture, age, fulfil their part in some cosmic drama, and are what they are in virtue of the part cast for them, but not by them, by the divine dramatist Himself. From this it is not far to the views of those who say that History is wiser than we, and its purposes are unfathomable to us, that we are but the means, the instruments, the manifestations, worthy or unworthy, of some vast all-embracing schema of eternal human progress, or of the German Spirit, or of the Proletariat, or of post-Christian civilization, or of Faustian man, or of Manifest Destiny, or of the American Century, or of some other myth or mystery or abstraction. To know all is to understand all; it is to know why things are and must be as they are; therefore the more we know the more absurd we must think those who suppose that things could have been otherwise, and so fall into the irrational temptation to praise or blame.

*Tout comprendre, c'est tout pardonner* is transformed into a mere truism. All forms of moral censure—the accusing finger of historians or publicists or politicians, and indeed the agonies of the private conscience too—tend, so far as possible, to be explained away as sophisticated versions of primitive taboos or psychical tensions or conflicts, now appearing as moral awareness, now as some other sanction, growing out of and battening upon that ignorance which alone generates fallacious beliefs in free will and uncaused choice, doomed to disappear in the growing light of scientific truth. Or, again, we find that the adherents of a sociological or historical or anthropological metaphysics tend to interpret the sense of mission and dedication, the voice of duty, all forms of inner compulsion of this type, as being an expression within each individual's conscious life of the 'vast impersonal forces' which control it, and which speak 'in us', 'through us', 'to us', for their own inscrutable purposes. To hear is then literally to obey—to be drawn towards the goal that belongs to our 'real' self, or its 'natural' or 'rational' development—that to which we are called by belonging to this or that class, or nation, or race, or church, or station in society, or tradition, or age, or character. The explanation, and in some sense the weight of responsibility, for all human action is (at times with ill-concealed relief) transferred to the broad backs of these vast impersonal forces—institutions or historic trends—better made to bear such burdens than a feeble, thinking reed like man . . .

This is a doctrine which lies at the heart equally of scientific attempts to explain moral sentiments as psychological or sociological 'residues' or the like, and of the metaphysical vision for which whatever is—'truly' is—is good. To understand all is to see that nothing could be otherwise than as it is; that all blame, indignation, protest is mere complaint about what seems discordant, about elements which do not seem to fit, about the absence of an intellectually or spiritually satisfying pattern. But this is always mere evidence of failure on the part of the observer, of his blindness and ignorance; it can never be an objective assessment of reality, for in reality everything necessarily fits, nothing is superfluous, nothing amiss, every ingredient is 'justified' in being where it is by the demands of the transcendent whole; and all sense of guilt, injustice, ugliness, all resistance or condemnation, is only proof of lack of vision, of misunderstanding, subjective aberration. Vice, pain, folly, maladjustment, all come from failure to understand, from failure, in Mr. E. M. Forster's celebrated phrase, 'to connect'. This is the sermon preached to us by thinkers of very different outlooks, by Spinoza and Godwin, by Tolstoy and Comte, by mystics and rationalists, theologians and scientific materialists, metaphysicians and dogmatic empiricists, American sociologists, Russian Marxists, and German historicists alike. Thus Godwin tells us that to understand a human act we must always avoid applying general principles but examine each case in its full individual detail. When we scrupulously examine the texture and pattern of this or that life, we shall not, in our haste and blindness seek to condemn or to punish; for we shall see why this or that man was caused to act in this or that manner by ignorance or poverty or some other moral or intellectual or physical defect, as we always (Godwin optimistically supposes) can see, if we arm ourselves with sufficient patience, knowledge, and sympathy, and we shall then blame him no more than we should an object in nature; and since it is axiomatic that we cannot both act upon our knowledge, and yet regret the result, we can and shall in the end succeed in making men good, just, happy, and wise. So, too, Condorcet and Henri de Saint-Simon and their disciple, Auguste Comte, starting from the opposite conviction, namely that men are not unique, or in need of individual treatment, but, on the contrary, like the inhabitants of the animal, vegetable and mineral kingdom, belong to types and obey general laws, maintain no less stoutly that once these laws have been discovered (and therefore applied) this will of itself lead to universal felicity.

This belief in the one true answer has since been echoed by many idealistic liberals and rationalists, planners, technocrats, positivists and believers in the scientific organization of society; and in very different keys by theocrats, neomedieval romantics, authoritarians, and political mystics of many faiths. This, too, is in substance the morality preached by Marx, by Engels, by Prussian nationalist historians, by Spengler, and by many another thinker who believes that there is a pattern which he has seen that others have not seen, or at least not so clearly seen, and that by this vision men may be saved. Know and you will not be lost. What it is that we must know differs from thinker to thinker, differs as views of the nature of things differ. Know the laws of the universe, animate and inanimate, or the principles of growth, or of evolution or of the rise and fall of civilizations, or the goals towards which all creation tends, or the stages of the Idea, or something less tangible still. Know, in the sense of identifying yourself with it, realizing your oneness with it, for, do what you may, you cannot escape from the laws to which you are subject, of whatever kind they may be, 'mechanistic', 'vitalistic', causal, purposive, imposed, transcendent, immanent, or the 'myriad' impalpable strands which bind you to the past—to your land and the dead, as Barrès declared; to the milieu, the race, and the moment, as Taine asserted; to Burke's great society of the dead and living, who have made you what you are; so that the truth in which you believe, the values in terms of which you judge, from the profoundest principles to the most trivial whims, are part and parcel of the historical continuum to which you belong. Tradition or blood or class or human nature or progress or humanity; the *Zeitgeist* or the social structure or the laws of history, or the true ends of life; know these—be 'true' to them—and you will be free.[2] From Plato to Lucretius, from the Gnos-

---

[2] And not only free but victorious. The feeling or belief that, whatever the appearances, the universe is on your side, and will fulfil your innermost wishes, is an unexampled source of strength

tics to Leibniz, from Thomas Aquinas to Lenin and Freud, the battle-cry has been essentially the same; the object of knowledge, the methods of discovery have often been violently opposed, but that reality is wholly knowable, and that knowledge and only knowledge liberates, and absolute knowledge liberates absolutely[3]—that is common to all these doctrines which are so large a part of Western civilization.

To explain is to understand, and to understand is to justify. The notion of individual responsibility is a delusion; the farther we are from omniscience, the larger our notion of our responsibility, that product of ignorance and fear which populates the unknown with terrifying fictions. Personal freedom is a noble and socially valuable fiction, for society might have crumbled without it; it is a necessary deception—one of the greatest devices of 'The Cunning of Reason' or of History, or of whatever other cosmic force we may be invited to worship. But a delusion however noble, useful, metaphysically justified, historically indispensable, is still a delusion. And so individual responsibility, the perception of the difference between right and wrong actions, between avoidable evil and misfortune, are mere symptoms of our vanity, evidences of our imperfect adjustment, of our inability to face the truth. The more we know, the greater the relief from the burden of choice; we forgive others for what they cannot avoid being, and by the same token we forgive ourselves. In ages in which the choices seem peculiarly agonizing, when strongly held ideals cannot be reconciled and collisions cannot be averted, such doctrines seem peculiarly comforting. We escape moral dilemmas by denying their reality; and, by directing our gaze towards the greater wholes, we make them responsible in our place. All we lose is an illusion, and with it the painful and superfluous emotions of guilt and remorse. Freedom notoriously involves responsibility, and it is for many spirits a source of welcome relief to lose both, not by some ignoble act of surrender, but by daring to con-

---

to some natures. Few great political or religious movements have been without apocalyptic moments of this kind.

[3] Hence for those who believe that only God is omniscient only He is wholly free.

template in a calm spirit things as they are; for this is to be truly philosophical. Thereby we reduce history to a kind of physics; as well blame the galaxy or gamma-rays as Genghis Khan or Hitler. 'To know all is to forgive all' turns out to be, in Professor Ayer's striking phrase (used in another context) nothing but a dramatized tautology.

We have spoken thus far of the view that we cannot praise or blame because we know, or shall soon know, or at any rate could know, too much for that. By a queer paradox the same position is reached by those who hold what seems at first the diametrical opposite of this position, that we cannot praise or blame, not because we know too much, but because we know too little. Historians imbued with a sense of humility before the scope and difficulties of their task, viewing the magnitude of human claims and the smallness of human knowledge and wisdom, warn us sternly against setting up our parochial values as universally valid and applying what may, at most, hold for a small portion of humanity for a brief span, in some insignificant corner of the universe, to all beings in all places and at all times. Tough-minded realists influenced by Marxism and Christian apologists differ profoundly in outlook, in method, in conclusions, but they are at one in this. The former[4] tell us that the social or economic principles, which, for example, Victorian Englishmen accepted as basic and eternal, were but the interests of one particular island community at one particular moment of its social and commercial development, and the truths which they so dogmatically bound upon themselves and upon others, and in the name of which they felt justified in acting as they did, were but their own passing economic or political needs and claims, masquerading as universal truths, and rang progressively more hollow in the ears of other nations with increasingly opposed interests, as they found themselves frequently the losers in a game where the rules had been invented by the stronger side. Then the day began to dawn when they in

[4] See, for example, the impressive and influential writings of Mr. E. H. Carr on the history of our time.

their turn acquired sufficient power, and turned the tables, and transformed international morality, albeit unconsciously, to suit themselves. Nothing is absolute, moral rules
vary directly as the distribution of power: the prevalent
morality is always that of the victors; we cannot pretend
to hold the scales of justice even between them and their
victims, for we ourselves belong to one side or the other;
*ex hypothesi* we cannot see the world from more than one
vantage point at a time. If we insist on judging others in
terms of our transient standards we must not protest too
much if they, in their turn, judge us in terms of theirs,
which sanctimonious persons among us are too swift to denounce for no better reason than that they are not ours.

Some Christian opponents of this position, starting from
very different assumptions, see men as feeble creatures
groping in darkness, knowing but little of how things come
about, or what in history inexorably causes what, and how
things might have turned out, but for this or that scarcely
perceptible, all but untraceable, fact or situation. Men, they
argue, often seek to do what is right according to their
lights, but these lights are dim, and such faint illumination
as they give reveal very different aspects of life to different
observers. The English follow their own traditions; the
Germans fight for the development of theirs; the Russians
to break with their own and those of other nations; and the
result is often bloodshed, widespread suffering, the destruction of what is most highly valued in the various cultures
which come into violent conflict. Man proposes, but it is
cruel and absurd to lay upon him—poor, fragile creature,
born to sorrows—responsibility for many of the disasters
that occur. For these are entailed by what, to take a Christian historian of distinction, Professor Herbert Butterfield
calls the 'human predicament' itself—wherein we seem
to ourselves virtuous enough, but being imperfect, and
doomed to stay so by Man's original sin, being ignorant,
hasty, vainglorious, self-centred, lose our way, do unwitting
harm, destroy what we seek to save and strengthen what
we seek to destroy. If we understood more, perhaps we
could do better, but our intellect is imperfect. For Professor
Butterfield, if I understand him correctly, the 'human pre-

dicament' is a product of the complex interaction of innumerable factors, few among them known, fewer still controllable, the greater number scarcely recognized at all. The
least that we can do, therefore, is to acknowledge our condition with due humility; and since we are involved in a
common darkness, and few of us stumble in it to much
greater purpose than others (at least in the perspective of
the whole of human history), we should practise understanding and charity. The least we can do as historians,
scrupulous to say no more than we are entitled to say, is
to suspend judgment; neither praise nor condemn; for the
evidence is always insufficient, and the alleged culprits are
like swimmers for ever caught in cross-currents and whirl-
pools beyond their control.

A not dissimilar philosophy, it seems to me, is to be
found in the writings of Tolstoy and other pessimists and
quietists, both religious and irreligious. For these, particularly those conservatives of our own day who echo Hume
or Burke or Taine, life is a stream moving in a given direction, or perhaps a tideless ocean stirred by occasional
breezes. The number of factors which cause it to be as it
is, is very great, but we know only a small number of them.
To seek to alter things radically in terms of our knowledge
is therefore often unrealistic to the point of absurdity; we
cannot resist the central currents, for they are stronger than
we, we can only tack, trim to the winds and avoid collisions with the great fixed institutions of our world, its
physical and biological laws, and the great human estab-
lishments with their roots deep in the past—the empires,
the churches, the settled beliefs and habits of mankind. For
if we resist these our small craft will be sunk, and we shall
lose our lives to no purpose. Wisdom lies in avoiding situations where we may capsize, in using the winds that blow
as skilfully as we can, so that we may last at any rate our
own time, preserve the heritage of the past, and not hurry
towards a future, which will come soon enough, and may
be darker even than the gloomy present. On this view, more
common, perhaps, in our time than in the past, it is the
human predicament—the disproportion between our vast
designs and our feeble means—that is responsible for most

of the suffering and injustice of the world. Without help, without divine grace, or one or other form of divine intervention, we shall not, in any case, succeed. Let us then be tolerant and charitable and understanding, and avoid the folly of accusation and counter-accusation, which will expose us to the laughter or pity of later generations. Let us seek to discern what we can—some dim outline of a pattern—in the shadows of the past, for even so much is surely difficult enough.

In one important sense, of course, such hard-boiled realists and Christian historians are right. Censoriousness, recrimination, moral or emotional blindness to the ways of life and outlooks of others, intellectual or ethical fanaticism, are vices in the writing of history, as in life. No doubt Gibbon and Michelet and Macaulay and Carlyle and Treitschke and Trotsky (to mention only the dead) do try the patience of those who do not accept their opinions, almost beyond endurance. Nevertheless this corrective to dogmatic partiality, like its opposite, the doctrine of inevitable bias, by shifting responsibility on to human weakness and ignorance, and identifying the human predicament itself as the ultimate central factor in human history, in the end leads us by a different road to the very same position as the doctrine that to know all is to forgive all; only for the latter it substitutes the formula that the less we know the fewer reasons we can have for just condemnation; for knowledge can only lead to a clearer realization of how small a part men's wishes and even their unconscious desires play in the life of the universe, and thereby reveals the absurdity of placing any serious responsibility upon the shoulders of individuals, or, for that matter, of classes, or states, or nations.

Two separate strands of thought are involved in the modern plea for a greater effort at understanding and the fashionable warnings against censoriousness, moralizing, and partisan history. There is, in the first place, the view that men and nations always, or at any rate more often than not, aim at what seems to them desirable; but owing to ignorance, or weakness, or the complexities of the world which mere human insight and skill cannot adequately understand or control, they feel and act in such a manner that the result is too often disastrous both for themselves and for others, caught in the common human predicament. Yet it is not individuals but the human predicament itself —man's imperfection—that is largely to blame for this. There is, in the second place, the further thesis that in attempting to explain historical situations and to analyse them, to unwind their origins and trace their consequences, and, in the course of this, to fix the responsibility for this or that element in the situation, the historian, no matter how detached, clear-headed, scrupulous, dispassionate, however skilled at imagining himself in other men's shoes, is nevertheless faced with a network of facts so minute, connected by links so many and complex, that his ignorance must always far outweigh his knowledge; consequently his judgment, particularly his moral judgment, must always be founded on insufficient data; and if he succeeds in casting even a little light upon some small corner of the vast and intricate pattern of the past, he has done as well as any human being can ever hope to do. The difficulties of disentangling even a minute portion of the truth are so great that he must, if he is an honest and serious practitioner, soon realize how far he is from being in a position to moralize. Consequently to praise and blame, as historians and publicists do so easily and glibly, is presumptuous, foolish, irresponsible, unjust.

This *prima facie* very convincing thesis is, however, not one but two: It is one thing to say that man proposes, but the consequences are too often beyond his control or powers of prediction or prevention; that since human motives have so seldom had any decisive influence on the actual course of events, they should not play any great part in the accounts of the historian; and that since the historian's business is to discover and describe what occurred, and how and why, therefore if he allows his moral opinions of men's characters and motives—those least effective of all historical factors—to colour his interpretations, he is thereby exaggerating their importance for purely subjective or psychological reasons; for to treat what may be morally significant as *eo ipso* historically influential is to distort the facts. That

is a perfectly clear position. Quite distinct from it is the
other thesis, namely, that our knowledge is never sufficient
to justify us in fixing responsibility, if there is any, where
it truly belongs. An omniscient being could do so, but we
are not omniscient, and our attributions are therefore ab-
surdly presumptuous; to realize this and feel an appropriate
degree of humility is the beginning of historical wisdom.
It may well be that both these theses are true. And it may
further be that they both spring from the same kind of pessimistic conviction of human weakness, blindness and ineffectiveness both in thought and in action. Nevertheless,
these melancholy views are two, not one: the first is an
argument from ineffectiveness, the second from ignorance:
and either might be true and the other false. Moreover,
neither seems to accord with common belief, nor with the
common practice of either ordinary men or of ordinary historians; each seems plausible and unplausible in its own
way, and each deserves its own refutation. And I should
like to draw attention to an implication common to them:
in both these doctrines individual responsibility is made to
melt away. We may not applaud nor condemn individuals
or groups either because they cannot help themselves (and
all knowledge is a growing understanding of precisely this),
or conversely because we know too little to know either this
or its opposite. But then neither may we bring charges of
moralism or bias against those historians who are prone to
praise and blame, because we are all in the same boat together, and no one standard can be called objectively superior to any other. For what, on this view, could 'objective'
mean? and by what standard do we measure its degrees?
It is plain that there can exist no 'super-standard' for the
comparison of entire scales of value, which itself derives
from no specific set of beliefs, no one specific culture. All
such tests must be internal, like the laws of a state that
apply only to its own citizens. The case against the notion
of historical objectivity is like the case against international
law or international morality: that it does not exist. And
more than this: that the very notion has no meaning, because ultimate standards are what we measure things by,

and cannot by definition themselves be measured in terms of anything else.

This is indeed to be hoist by one's own petard. Because all standards are relative, to condemn bias or moralism in history or to defend them, turn out themselves to be attitudes which, in the absence of a super-standard, cannot be rationally defended or condemned. All attitudes turn out to be morally neutral; but even this cannot be said, for the contradictory of this proposition cannot be refuted. Hence nothing on this topic can be said at all. This is surely a *reductio ad absurdum* of the entire position. A fallacy must be lurking somewhere in the argument of the anti-moralistic school.[5]

Let us consider the normal thoughts of ordinary men on this topic. In normal circumstances we do not feel that we are saying something hazardous or questionable if we praise

[5] The paradox arising out of general scepticism about historical objectivity may perhaps be put in another fashion. One of the principal reasons for complaining about the moralistic attitude of this or that historian is that his scale of values is thought to distort his judgments, to cause him to pervert the truth. But if we start from the assumption that historians, like other human beings, are wholly conditioned to think as they do by specific material (or immaterial) factors, however incalculable or impalpable, then their so-called bias is, like everything else about their thought, the inevitable consequence of their material or 'ontological' predicament, and so, equally, are our objections to it—our own ideals of impartiality, our own standards of objective truth in terms of which we condemn, say, nationalistic or Marxist historians, or other forms of animus or *parti pris* . . . In this relativistic view the very notion of an absolute standard, presupposing as it does the rejection of all specific vantage points as such, must, of course, be an absurdity. All complaints about partiality and bias, about moral (or political) propaganda seem . . . beside the point. Whatever does not agree with our views we call misleading, but if this fault is to be called subjectivism, so must the condemnation of it . . . On this view all that we do when we reject this or that historian as a conscious or unconscious propagandist, is solely to indicate our own moral or intellectual or historical distance from him; nothing more: we are merely underlining our personal position. And this seems to be a fatal internal contradiction within the system of those who believe in the historical conditioning of historians and yet protest against moralizing by them, whether ironically like Mr. Carr, or sorrowfully like Professor Butterfield.

or condemn Cromwell for what he did for the English, or
if we describe Pasteur as a benefactor of mankind or Hitler
as an evil-doer. Nor do we feel that we are saying something strange if we maintain that, let us say, the late Mr.
Belloc or Lord Macaulay do not seem to apply the same
standards of objective truth, or apply them as impartially,
as did, let us say, Ranke, or Bishop Creighton, or M. Elie
Halévy. In saying this, what are we asserting? Are we
merely expressing our private approval or disapproval of
Cromwell's acts or Pasteur's purposes or our distaste for
Hitler's character or activities? Are we merely saying that
we agree with Ranke's conclusions or M. Halévy's general
tone, that they are more to our taste, please us better (because of our own outlook and temperament) than the tone
and conclusions of Macaulay or Mr. Belloc? Yet if there
is an unmistakable tinge of reproach in our assessment of,
say, Cromwell's policies or of Mr. Belloc's account of those
policies, is that no more than an indication that we are not
favourably disposed towards one or other of them, that our
moral or intellectual ideals differ from what we take to be
theirs, with no indication that we think that they could,
and moreover should, have acted differently? And if we do
imply that their behaviour might, or should, have been different, is that merely a symptom of our psychological inability to realize that they could not (for no one can) have
acted differently, or of an ignorance too deep to entitle us
to tell how they could, let alone should, have acted? With
the further implication that it would be more civilized not
to say such things, but to remember that we are all equally,
or almost equally, deluded, and remember, too, that moral
responsibility is a fiction, that with the increase of knowledge and a more scrupulous and appropriate use of language, such quasi-ethical expressions, and the false notions
of human freedom on which they rest, will, it is to be
hoped, finally disappear from the vocabulary of civilized
human beings? For this seems to me to follow directly from
the doctrines outlined above. Determinism, whether benev-
olent or malevolent, no less than the view that our moral
judgments are rendered absurd either because we know too
much or because we know too little, all seem to point to

this: it is a view that in its various forms has been held by many civilized and sensitive persons. Nevertheless it rests on beliefs about the world and about human beings which are too difficult to accept; which are unplausible because they render illegitimate certain basic distinctions which we all draw—distinctions which are inevitably reflected in our everyday use of words. If such beliefs were true, too much that we accept without question would turn out to be sensationally false. Yet these paradoxes are urged upon us although there is no evidence to force us to embrace them.

It is part of the same tendency to maintain that even if total freedom from moralizing is not to be looked for in this world (for all human beings inevitably live and think by their own varying moral or aesthetic or religious standards) yet, as historians, an effort must be made to repress such tendencies. As historians it is our duty only to describe and explain, not to pronounce verdicts. The historian is, we are told, not a judge but a detective; he provides the evidence, and the reader, who has none of the professional responsibilities of the expert, can form what moral conclusions he likes. As a general warning against moralistic history this is, particularly in times of acute partisan emotion, timely enough. But it must not be interpreted literally. For it depends upon a false analogy with some among the more exact of the natural sciences. In these last objectivity has a specific meaning. It means that methods and criteria of a less or more precisely defined kind are being used with scrupulous care; and that evidence, arguments, conclusions are formulated in the special terminology invented or employed for the specific purpose of each science, and that there is no intrusion (or almost none) of irrelevant considerations, or concepts or categories, i.e. those specifically excluded by the canons of the science in question.

I am not sure whether history can usefully be called a science at all, but certainly it is not a science in this sense. For it employs few, if any, concepts or categories peculiar to itself, but broadly speaking, only those of common sense, or of ordinary speech. The central concepts of history—the ways in which events or situations are 'explained', are shown

to be connected or unconnected with one another—the use
of such crucial terms as 'because' and 'therefore', 'inevitable'
and 'possible' and 'probable', 'surprising' and 'unexpected',
'influential' and 'trivial', 'central' and 'accidental', and so
forth, is much the same as that which it has in ordinary,
non-technical thought and speech. As history becomes
specialized, e.g. in such disciplines as the history of science
or of commerce or of art, technical terms do begin to make
their appearance, and to that degree something approaching, but still somewhat remotely, the natural sciences, begins to occur, and the elimination of a good many of the
normal moral and psychological concepts of daily speech
becomes possible and, according to some, desirable and
perhaps even indispensable. But in the realm of general history, social, political, and cultural—what goes by the name
of history without specific qualification—this is not so. There
we explain and elucidate as we explain and elucidate in
ordinary life. We account for the French Revolution or the
character of Napoleon or the behaviour of Talleyrand as
we would account for the behaviour of our own contemporaries and events in our own lives, public and private,
with the same rich, scarcely analysable mixture of physiological and psychological, economic and biographical, aesthetic and ethical, causal and purposive concepts, which
provide what we regard as normal and sufficient answers to
our normal questions about how and why things or persons
act as they do. All attempts to construct special sets of concepts and special techniques for history (e.g. by Marxists)
have broken down because they proved sterile, for they
either misdescribed—overschematized—our experience, or
they were felt not to provide answers to our questions. We
can accuse historians of bias, or inaccuracy, or stupidity, or
dishonesty, as we can accuse one another of these vices in
our ordinary daily intercourse; and we can praise them for
the corresponding virtues; and usually with the same degree of justice and reason. But just as our ordinary speech
would become fantastically distorted by a conscious effort
to eliminate from it some basic ingredient—say, everything
remotely liable to convey value judgments, our normal,

scarcely noticed, moral or psychological attitudes—and just as this is not regarded as indispensable for the preservation of what we should look upon as a normal modicum of objectivity, impartiality, and accuracy, so, for the same reason, no such radical remedy is needed for the preservation of a reasonable modicum of these qualities in the writing of history. There is a sense in which a physicist can, to a large degree, speak with different voices, as a physicist, and as a human being; although even there the line between the two vocabularies is anything but clear or absolute. It is possible that this may in some measure be true of economists or psychologists; it grows progressively less true as we leave mathematical methods behind us, for example, in palaeography, or the history of science or that of the woollen trade; and it comes perilously near an absurdity when demanded of social or political historians, however skilled in the appropriate techniques, however professional, however rigorous. History is not identical with imaginative literature, but it is certainly no more free from what, in a natural science, would be rightly condemned as unwarrantably subjective or personal. Except on the assumption that history must deal with human beings purely as material objects in space—must, in short, be behaviourist—its method can scarcely be assimilated to the standards of an exact natural science.[6] The invocation to historians to suppress even that minimal degree of moral or psychological evaluation which is necessarily involved in viewing human beings as creatures with purposes and motives (and not merely as causal factors in the procession of events), seems to me to rest upon a confusion of the aims and methods of the humane studies with those of natural science. It is one of the greatest and most destructive fallacies of the last hundred years.

[6] That history is in this sense different from physical description, is a truth discovered long ago by Vico, and most imaginatively and vividly presented by Herder and his followers, and, despite the exaggerations and extravagances to which it led some nineteenth-century philosophers of history, still remains the greatest contribution of the Romantic movement to our knowledge . . .

3.

*I have radically reversed the chronological order by putting
the following essay by Jacob Burckhardt (1818–97) in this
place. Burckhardt's "Fortune and Misfortune in History"
(1871) is the only selection that belongs to the nineteenth
century. I have taken this course for two reasons: In the
first place, Burckhardt's views resemble those of Professor
Butterfield. For Burckhardt also ascribed moral judgments
to an "optical illusion," also called them "the deadly enemies of true historical insight," and concluded that we
could, and should, do without them because "there is
enough hypocrisy in the world as it is." This helps to show
how history is beset, like philosophy, by perennial problems of its own, and that it is precisely these problems
which are the most interesting. In the second place, Burckhardt also discusses a different question which takes us into
the subject of Part IV below. For he argues not only against
bringing moral judgments to history; he also repudiates the
view that we can learn a moral lesson from history, or that
we can use history as a source of moral comfort.*

*This repudiation, as we have seen, is part of the heritage
of modern historicism. The moral law may be written "on
the tablets of eternity"; but this only means that it is beyond history. On the tablets of time, moral beliefs are
erased and replaced as are the people holding them.*

*History, however, may still be used as a justification for
morality if we believe that the course of history as a whole
conveys a moral message or discloses moral progress. This
belief, as I tried to show in the general introduction, is an
essential component of the quest for a "meaning" in history.
It is a belief that dies hard, which may indicate either that
it is not altogether unfounded or that the wish behind the
thought is indestructible.*

*Burckhardt's remarks are addressed to this "theory of
perfection (so-called progress) in favor of the present or
the future"; in other words, to the belief that what comes
later, in the evolutionary or historical development of man,*

*is better in terms of human perfection and happiness. His-
torical progression—say, toward industrialism, nationalism,
liberalism, or totalitarianism—is interpreted as moral progress.*

*This view, of course, need hardly be refuted; for the
moral question posed by any historical development is obviously whether it is good or bad. Besides, it is easier for
us today to sympathize with nineteenth-century "pessimists" like Burckhardt than with his optimistic contemporaries in the party of progress. The wars, gas chambers,
and mushroom clouds of our own century have been more
persuasive in refuting the naïve correlation between historical progression and moral progress than any logical arguments.*

*Burckhardt does not deny that there are criteria accord-
ing to which we may speak of "fortune" and "misfortune,"
progress and regress in history.[1] What he does deny is the
view that what is called "fortune" or "progress" be simply
equated with happiness. In other words, he raises, and rejects, the view that mankind is made happier as a result of
what is called progress in history. "Evil is . . . assuredly a
part of the great economy of world history."*

*In this argument Burckhardt reflects the Christian and
Hegelian message on the meaning of history. The religious
message—whether it refers to "the last things" beyond history or to the eternal possibility of "being in Christ" in this
life—does promise the believer ultimate redemption from
all evil; but it is sin, suffering, and death, not happiness,
which are his lot in the sorry spectacle of human history.
Similarly, Hegel envisaged objective moral ends in history,
freedom, self-consciousness, or a rational society in which
all evil was transcended; but this ultimate meaning of history was achieved at a great price. "World history is not
the theatre of happiness"; on the contrary, it is "a pan-
orama of sin and suffering." Thus for Christianity, as for
Hegel, Burckhardt—and even for Freud—the price of prog-*

---

[1] For a similar point, cf. the essay by Karl Jaspers, Part IV,
pp. 336–38 below.

*ress in history is paid by forfeiting human happiness[2]—a melancholy conclusion which may serve as a transition to the "meaning of history" discussed in the last part.*

## JACOB BURCKHARDT

## ON FORTUNE AND MISFORTUNE IN HISTORY*

In our private lives, we are wont to regard our personal fate under the two categories "fortunate" and "unfortunate," and we transfer these categories without hesitation to history.

Yet from the outset we should feel misgivings, since, in our own affairs, our judgment may change radically with age and experience. Not until the last hour of our lives can we pronounce a final judgment on the men and things we have known, and that judgment may be totally different according to whether we die in our fortieth or our eightieth year. It has, moreover, no objective validity but only a subjective validity for ourselves. This is the common experience of any man whose youthful desires appear to him folly in later life.

Nevertheless, historical judgments of good and evil fortune in the past have been pronounced both on isolated events and on whole epochs and conditions of life, and it is mainly modern times that are prone to pronounce them.

There are, of course, older expressions of opinion. The well-being of a class with slaves at its command is apparent here and there for instance in the *Skolion* of Hybreas. Machiavelli praises the year 1298, though only as a contrast to the revolution which immediately followed, and Justinger gives a similar picture of old Berne about 1350.

[2] This sentence is Freud's in *Civilization and Its Discontents*. Instead of "evil" or "sin," Freud uses the concept of guilt: for him happiness is lost "through the heightening of a sense of guilt."

* In *Force and Freedom*, ed. by James H. Nichols (New York: Pantheon Books, Inc., 1943), Chapter VI; reprinted by permission of Pantheon Books, Inc. I have deleted four footnotes appearing in the original. H.M.

All these judgments are, of course, much too local, and the happiness they praise was in part based on the sufferings of others; nevertheless, they are at least ingenuous, and were not devised to throw light on world history.

We, however, judge as follows:

It was fortunate that the Greeks conquered Persia, and Rome Carthage;

unfortunate that Athens was defeated by Sparta in the Peloponnesian War;

unfortunate that Caesar was murdered before he had time to consolidate the Roman Empire in an adequate political form;

unfortunate that in the migrations of the Germanic tribes so many of the highest creations of the human spirit perished, but fortunate that they refreshed the world with new and healthy stock;

fortunate that Europe, in the eighth century, on the whole held Islam at bay;

unfortunate that the German Emperors were defeated in their struggle with the Papacy and that the Church was able to develop its terrible tyranny;

unfortunate that the Reformation triumphed in only half of Europe and that Protestantism was divided into two sects;

fortunate that first Spain, then Louis XIV were eventually defeated in their plans for world dominion, etc.

The nearer we come to the present, of course, the more opinions diverge. We might, however, reply that this does not invalidate our right to form an opinion which, as soon as a wider survey in time enables us to assess at their true value causes and effects, events and their consequences, finds its justification.

By an optical illusion, we see happiness at certain times, in certain countries, and we deck it out with analogies from the youth of man, spring, sunrise and other metaphors. Indeed, we imagine it dwelling in a beautiful part of the country, a certain house, just as the smoke rising from a distant cottage in the evening gives us the impression of intimacy among those living there.

Whole epochs, too, are regarded as happy or unhappy. The happy ones are the so-called high epochs of man. For instance, the claim to such happiness is seriously put forward for the Periclean Age, in which it is recognized that the life of the ancient world reached its zenith in the State, society, art and poetry. Other epochs of the same kind, e.g. the age of the good Emperors, have been abandoned as having been selected from too one-sided a standpoint. Yet even Renan says of the thirty years from 1815 to 1848 that they were the best that France, and perhaps humanity, had ever experienced.

All times of great destruction naturally count as eminently unhappy, since the happiness of the victor is (quite rightly) left out of account.

Judgments of this kind are characteristic of modern times and only imaginable with modern historical methods. The ancient world believed in an original golden age, with respect to which the world had steadily deteriorated. Hesiod paints the "present" age of iron in sinister tints of night. In our day, we may note a theory of perfection (so-called progress) in favor of the present and the future. Discoveries in pre-history reveal at least this much—that the pre-historical epochs of the human race were probably spent in profound torpor, half-animal fear, cannibalism, etc. In any case, those epochs which have hitherto been regarded as the youth of the individual peoples, namely those in which they can first be recognized, were actually very derivative and late epochs.

But who is, as a rule, responsible for such judgments? They arise from a kind of literary consensus which has gradually taken shape out of the desires and arguments of the Age of Reason and the real or imagined conclusions of a number of widely read historians.

Nor do they spread haphazard. They are turned to journalistic uses as arguments for or against certain trends of the time. They form part of the fussy baggage of public opinion and, in part, bear very clearly in the very violence, not to say crudity, of their appearance, the impress of the time from which they issue. They are the deadly enemies of true historical insight.

And now we may enquire into some of their separate sources.

The most important of these is *impatience*, and it is the writer and the reader of history who are most subject to it. It supervenes when we have had to spend too long a time on a period, and the evidence—or perhaps our own effort— is inadequate to enable us to form an opinion. We wish things had moved more quickly, and would, for instance, willingly sacrifice one or two of the twenty-six dynasties of Egypt if only King Amasis and his liberal reform would at last carry the day. The Kings of Media, though only four in number, make us impatient because we know so little about them, while that great mover of the imagination, Cyrus, seems to be already waiting at the door.

In short, we take sides for what our ignorance finds interesting against the tedious, as if for happiness against unhappiness. We confuse what was desirable to remote epochs (if anything was) with the pleasures of our imagination.

From time to time we try to delude ourselves with an apparently nobler explanation, but our only motive is one of retrospective impatience.

We pity for their unhappiness past ages, peoples, parties, creeds and so on which pass through long struggles for a higher good. Today we should like to see the aims with which we sympathize triumph without a struggle, and pluck victory without effort; and we transfer the same wish to the past. We pity, for instance, the Roman plebeians and the pre-Solonian Athenians in their century-long struggle with the hard-hearted patricians and Eupatridae and the pitiless debtors' law.

Yet it was only the long struggle which made victory possible and proved the vitality and great worth of the cause.

But how short-lived was the triumph, and how ready we are to side with one decadence against another! Through the victory of democracy, Athens declined into political impotence; Rome conquered Italy, and ultimately the world, at the cost of infinite suffering to the nations and great degeneration at home.

The state of mind which would like to spare the past its troubles, however, comes out most strongly in connection with the wars of religion. We are indignant that any truth (or what we regard as such) should have only been able to make headway by material force, and that it should be suppressed if that force proved inadequate. And it is true that truth infallibly sacrifices something of its purity and sanctity during prolonged struggles, owing to the worldly intentions of its representatives and devotees. Thus it seems to us a misfortune that the Reformation had to contend with a terrible material opposition and hence had to be represented by governments whose heart was in the property of the Church rather than in religion.

Yet in struggle, and in struggle alone, and not in printed polemics, does the full, complete life develop that must come of religious warfare. Only struggle makes both sides fully conscious. Only through struggle, at all times and in all questions of world history, does mankind realize what it really wants and what it can really achieve.

Firstly, Catholicism again became a religion, which it had almost ceased to be. Then men's minds were opened in a thousand directions, political life and culture were brought into all kinds of contact and contrast with the religious conflict, and ultimately the world was transformed and spiritually vastly enriched. None of these things could have come about in mere smooth obedience to the new creed.

Then comes the judgment according to *Culture*. It consists in appraising the felicity and morality of a people or a state of life in the past by the diffusion of education, of general culture and comfort in the modern sense. Here nothing stands the test and all past ages are disposed of with more or less commiseration. For a time, the "present" was literally synonymous with progress, and the result was the most ridiculous vanity, as if the world were marching toward a perfection of mind or even morality. Imperceptibly, the criterion of security, which will be discussed later, creeps in, and without security, and without the culture just described, *we*, at any rate, could not live. But a simple, strong mode of life, with the physical nobility of the race still intact, and the people perpetually on its guard against enemies and oppressors, is also culture, and possibly productive of a superior quality of feeling. Man's mind was complete early in time. And the enquiry as to "moral progress" we may justifiably leave to Buckle, who was so naïvely astonished that there is none to be found, forgetting that it is relevant to the life of the individual and not to whole epochs. If, even in bygone times, men gave their lives for each other, we have not progressed since.

Now follows the judgment by *personal taste*, under which we may group a number of factors. It regards such times and peoples as happy in and among whom precisely that element was predominant which lies nearest the heart of whoever is passing judgment. According as feeling, imagination or reason is the central value of life, the palm will go to those times and peoples in which the largest possible number of men were seriously occupied with spiritual things, or in which art and poetry were the reigning powers, and the greatest possible amount of time was free for intellectual work and contemplation, or in which the greatest number of people could earn a good livelihood and there was unimpeded activity in trade and traffic.

It would be easy to make the representatives of all these three categories realize how one-sided is their judgment, how inadequately it comprehends the whole life of the age concerned, and how intolerable, for many reasons, they themselves would have found life in that age.

Judgment by *political sympathy* is also common. To one, only republics were happy; to another, only monarchies. To one, only times of great and incessant unrest; to another, only times of calm. We might here quote Gibbon's view of the age of the good Emperors as the happiest the human race had ever lived through.

Even in the cases already mentioned, and more especially in the case of judgment by *culture*, the criterion of *security* creeps in. According to this judgment, the prime condition of any happiness is the subordination of private purposes to a police-protected law, the treatment of all questions of property by an impartial legal code and the most far-reaching safeguarding of profits and commerce. The whole morality of our day is to a large extent oriented toward this security, that is, the individual is relieved of the most vital decisions in the defense of house and home, in the majority of cases at any rate. And what goes beyond the power of the State is taken over by insurance, i.e., the forestalling of definite kinds of misfortune by a corresponding annual sacrifice. As soon as a livelihood or its revenues has become sufficiently valuable, the neglect to insure it is considered culpable.

Now this security was grievously lacking at many times which otherwise shine with an immortal radiance and till the end of time will hold a high place in the history of man.

Piracy was of everyday occurrence, not only in the age which Homer describes, but obviously in that in which he lived, and strangers were quite courteously and ingenuously questioned on the subject. The world was swarming with murderers, voluntary and involuntary, who sat at kings' tables, and even Odysseus, in one of his fictitious stories of his life, lays claim to a murder. And yet what simplicity and nobility of manners those people knew! And an age in which the epic lay was the common property of many singers, and moved from place to place, the common delight of nations, is for ever enviable for its achievements, its emotions, its strength and its simplicity. We have only to think of the figure of Nausicaa.

The Periclean Age in Athens was in every sense of the word an age in which any peaceful and prudent citizen of our time would refuse to live, in which he could not but be mortally unhappy, even if he was neither a member of the slave-majority nor a citizen of a city under the Attic hegemony, but a free man and a full citizen of Athens itself. Huge contributions levied by the State, and perpetual inquisitions into the fulfilment of duties toward the State by demagogues and sycophants, were the order of the day.

Yet the Athenians of that age must have felt a plentitude of life which far outweighed any security in the world.

A very popular judgment in our day is the judgment by *greatness*. Those who pass such judgment cannot, of course, deny that great political power rapidly acquired, whether by the State or by the individual, can only be bought at the cost of untold sufferings to others. But they ennoble the character of the ruler and those about him to the utmost limit, and attribute to him the prophetic vision of all the great and good results which later came of his work. Finally, they assume that the spectacle of genius must have transfigured and made happy the people he had to deal with.

They dismiss the sufferings of the multitude with the utmost coolness as a "temporary misfortune"; they point to the undeniable fact that settled conditions, i.e., subsequent "happiness," have only been established when terrible struggles have bestowed power on one side or the other. As a rule, the origin and life of the man who applies this standard is based on conditions established in that fashion, hence his indulgence.

And now at last the common source trickling through all these judgments, and long since perceptible in them, the judgment by *egoism*. "We" judge thus and thus. It is true that somebody else, who is of the contrary opinion—perhaps out of egoism too—also says "we," while in the absolute sense as much is achieved by both as by the prayers of the individual farmer for sun or rain.

Our profound and utterly ridiculous self-seeking first regards those times as happy which are in some way akin to our nature. Further, it considers such past forces and individuals as praiseworthy on whose work our present existence and relative welfare are based.

Just as if the world and its history had existed merely for our sakes! For everyone regards all times as fulfilled in his own, and cannot see his own as one of many passing waves. If he has reason to believe that he has achieved pretty nearly everything that lay in his power, we can un-

derstand his standpoint. If he looks for change, he hopes
that he will soon see it come, and may help to bring it
about.

But every individual—we too—exists not for his own sake,
but for the sake of all the past and all the future.

In face of this great, grave whole, the claims of peoples,
times and individuals to happiness and well-being, lasting
or fleeting, is of very subordinate importance, for since the
life of humanity is one whole, it is only to our frail powers
of perception that its fluctuations in time or place are a
rise and fall, fortune and misfortune. The truth is that they
are governed by a higher necessity.

We should try to rid the life of nations entirely of the
word "happiness" and replace it by some other, while, as
we shall see later, we cannot do without the word "unhappiness." Natural history shows us a fearful struggle for life,
and that same struggle encroaches far upon the historical
life of nations.

"Happiness" is a desecrated word, exhausted by common
use. Supposing that there was a world plebiscite to decide
on the definition of the word. How far should we get?

And above all, only the fairy-tale equates changelessness
with happiness. From its childish standpoint it may strive
to hold fast to the image of a permanent, joyous well-being
(about half-way between Olympus and the Land of Cock-
ayne). But even the fairy-tale does not take it really seriously. When the wicked magician at last lies dead and the
wicked fairies are punished, Abdullah and Fatima live happily ever after into a ripe old age, but imagination, their
trials over, forthwith dismisses them, to claim our interest
for Hassan and Zuleika or Leila, or some other couple. The
end of the *Odyssey* is so much nearer the truth. The trials
of him who has suffered so much are to continue, and he
must at once set out on a grievous pilgrimage.

The conception of a happiness which consists in the permanence of certain conditions is of its very nature false. The
moment we set aside a primitive state, or state of nature,
in which every day is like every other day, and every century like every other century, until, by some rupture, his-

torical life begins, we must admit that permanence means paralysis and death. Only in movement, with all its pain, is life. And above all, the idea of happiness as a positive feeling is false in itself. Happiness is mere absence of pain, at best associated with a faint sense of growth.

There have been, of course, arrested peoples who present the same general picture for centuries and hence give the impression of tolerable contentment with their fate. As a rule, however, that is the product of despotism, which inevitably appears when a form of State and society has been achieved (presumably at great cost) and has to be defended against the rise of opposing forces, and with all available measures, even the most extreme. The first generation must, as a rule, have been very unhappy, but succeeding ones grow up in that order of ideas, and ultimately they pronounce sacred everything that they cannot and do not wish to change, praising it perhaps as supreme happiness. When Spain was on the point of material extinction, she was still capable of deep feeling as soon as the splendor of the Castilian name came into question. The oppression of the government and the Inquisition seems to have been powerless to humiliate her soul. Her greatest artists and poets belong to that age.

These stationary peoples and national epochs may exist in order to preserve definite spiritual, intellectual and material values from earlier times and to pass them on uncontaminated as a leaven to the future. And their calm is not absolute and deathly; it is rather of the nature of a refreshing sleep.

There are other ages, peoples, men, on the other hand, which at times spend their strength, indeed their whole strength, in rapid movement. Their importance resides in the destruction of the old and the clearing of the way for the new. But they were not made for any lasting happiness, or indeed for any passing joy, save for the short-lived rejoicing of victory. For their power of regeneration is born of perpetual discontent, which finds any halt tedious and demands to advance.

Now this striving, however important its consequences,

however great its political consequences may be, actually
appears in time in the garb of the most unfathomable human egoism, which must of necessity subdue others to its
will and find its satisfaction in their obedience, yet which
is insatiable in its thirst for obedience and admiration and
claims the right to use force in all great issues.

Now evil on earth is assuredly a part of the great economy of world history. It is force, the right of the stronger
over the weaker, prefigured in that struggle for life which
fills all nature, the animal and the vegetable worlds, and is
carried on in the early stages of humanity by murder and
robbery, by the eviction, extermination or enslavement of
weaker races, or of weaker peoples within the same race,
of weaker States, of weaker social classes within the same
State and people.

Yet the stronger, as such, is far from being the better.
Even in the vegetable kingdom, we can see baser and
bolder species making headway here and there. In history,
however, the defeat of the noble simply because it is in the
minority is a grave danger, especially in times ruled by a
very general culture which arrogates to itself the rights of
the majority. The forces which have succumbed were perhaps nobler and better, but the victorious, though their
only motive was ambition, inaugurate a future of which
they themselves have no inkling. Only in the exemption of
States from the general moral law, which continues to be
binding on the individual, can something like a premoni-
tion of it be divined.

The greatest example is offered by the Roman Empire,
inaugurated by the most frightful methods soon after the
end of the struggle between the patricians and plebeians in
the guise of the Samnite War, and completed by the sub-
jection of East and West in rivers of blood.

Here, on the grand scale, we can discern a historical purpose which is, to us at any rate, plainly apparent, namely
the creation of a common world culture, which also made
possible the spread of a world religion, both capable of being transmitted to the Teutonic barbarians of the Völkerwanderung as the future bond of a new Europe.

Yet from the fact that good came of evil, and relative happiness of misery, we cannot in any way deduce that evil and misery were not, at the outset, what they were. Every successful act of violence is evil, and at the very least a dangerous example. But when that act was the foundation of power, it was followed by the indefatigable efforts of men to turn mere power into law and order. With their healthy strength, they set to work to cure the State of violence.

And, at times, evil reigns long as evil on earth, and not only among Fatimids and Assassins. According to Christian doctrine, the prince of this world is Satan. There is nothing more un-christian than to promise virtue a lasting reign, a material divine reward here below, as the early Church writers did to the Christian Emperors. Yet evil, as ruler, is of supreme importance; it is the one condition of selfless good. It would be a horrible sight if, as a result of the consistent reward of good and punishment of evil on this earth, all men were to behave well with an ulterior motive, for they would continue to be evil men and to nourish evil in their hearts. The time might come when men would pray Heaven for a little impunity for evildoers, simply in order that they might show their real nature once more. There is enough hypocrisy in the world as it is.

Let us now try to see whether the consolation we have divined will stand the test of a few of the most justified indictments of history.

Firstly, by no means every destruction entails regeneration. Just as the destruction of a finer vegetation may turn a land into an arid waste forever, a people which has been too brutally handled will never recover. There are (or at any rate there seem to be) absolutely destructive forces under whose hoofs no grass grows. The essential strength of Asia seems to have been permanently and for ever broken by the two periods of Mongol rule. Timur in particular was horribly devastating with his pyramids of skulls and walls of lime, stone and living men. Confronted with the picture of the destroyer, as he parades his own and his people's self-seeking through the world, it is good to realize the ir-

resistible might with which evil may at times spread over
the world. In such countries, men will never again believe
in right and human kindness. Yet he may have saved Europe from the Osmanlis. Imagine history without him, and
Bajazet and the Hussites hurling themselves simultaneously
on Germany and Italy. The later Osmanlis, people and sul-
tans, whatever terror they may have meant for Europe,
never again approach the climax of power represented by
Bajazet I before the battle of Angora.

Even ancient times present a picture of horror when we
imagine the sum of despair and misery which went to establish the old world Empires, for instance. Our deepest
compassion, perhaps, would go out to those individual peoples who must have succumbed to the Kings of Persia, or
even to the Kings of Assyria and Media, in their desperate
struggle for independence. All the lonely royal fortresses
of individual peoples (Hyrcanians, Bactrians, Sogdanians,
Gedrosians) which Alexander encountered marked the
scenes of ghastly last struggles, of which all knowledge has
been lost. Did they fight in vain?

We feel quite differently about the peoples whose last
struggle and end are known to us; that of the Lydian cities
against Harpagus, Carthage, Numantia, Jerusalem against
Titus. They seem to us to have taken their place in the
ranks of those who have been the teachers and examples
of mankind in the one great cause—that all must be staked
on the cause of the whole and that individual life is not
the supreme value. And thus, of their despair, a happiness,
harsh but sublime, is born for all the world.

And if Persian tablets should be discovered bringing us
greater knowledge of the end of those peoples in the Eastern provinces, were they only conceived in the bombastic
Ormuzd style of the mindless victor, they would go to swell
the number of those great memories.

We may here leave out of account the consolation we
derive from the thought that without such temporary de-
stroyers as Assyria and Persia, Alexander could not have
borne the elements of Greek culture so far into Asia. Be-

yond Mesopotamia it had little influence. We must always be on our guard against taking our historical perspectives for the decrees of history.

One thing, however, must be said of all great destructions: since we cannot fathom the economy of world history, we never know what would have happened if some event, however terrible, had not occurred. Instead of one wave of history which we know, another, which we do not know, would have risen; instead of one evil oppressor, perhaps one still more evil.

Yet no man of power should imagine that he can put forward for his exculpation the plea: "If we do not do it, others will." For then every crime would be justified. (Such men in any case feel no need of exculpation, but say: "What *we* do turns out well because *we* do it.")

It may be, too, that if those who succumbed had lived longer, they would no longer have seemed worthy of our compassion. A people, for instance, that succumbed early in the glorious struggle might later not have been very happy, not very civilized, early corrupted by its own iniquity and deadly to its neighbors. But, having perished in the flower of its strength, we feel toward it as we feel toward exceptional men who have died young; we imagine that, had they lived, they could not but have progressed in good fortune and greatness, while perhaps their meridian already lay behind them.

Consolation comes from another direction in the mysterious law of compensation, which becomes apparent in one point at least, namely in the increase of populations after great plagues and wars. There seems to be a total life of humanity which makes losses good.

Thus it is not certain, yet it appears to us probable, that the retreat of culture from the eastern half of the Mediterranean in the fifteenth century was made good, spiritually and materially, by the expansion overseas of the peoples of Western Europe. The accent of the world shifted.

Thus as, in the one case, another manner of death would have come instead of the one we know, in this case the vital power of the world replaces a vanished life by a new one.

The compensation, however, must not be taken as a substitute for suffering, to which its originator might point, but only as a continuance of the life of wounded humanity with its center of gravity shifted. Nor must we hold it out to the sufferers and their dependents. The Völkerwanderung was a great rejuvenation for the moribund Roman Empire, but if we had asked the Byzantine, living under the Comneni in the twelfth century in the Eastern remnant of it, he would have spoken with all the pride in the world of the continued life of Rome on the Bosphorus, and with an equal contempt of the "renewed and refreshed" Occident. Even the Greco-Slav of our day under the Turks does not consider himself inferior to, and probably not more unhappy than, the man of the West. Indeed, if the people were consulted, they could not pay for the greatest regeneration in the world, if the price were their own end and the influx of savage hordes.

The theory of compensation is, after all, generally the theory of desirability in disguise, and it is and remains advisable to be exceedingly chary in the use of such consolation as is to be gained from it, since we cannot finally assess these losses and gains. Bloom and decay are certainly the common lot, but every really personal life that is cut off by violence, and (in our opinion) prematurely, must be regarded as absolutely irreplaceable, indeed as irreplaceable even by one of equal excellence.

Another variant of compensation is the postponement of an event which seemed imminent. From time to time a great event, ardently desired, does not take place because some future time will fulfil it in greater perfection. In the Thirty Years' War, Germany was twice on the point of union, in 1629 by Wallenstein, in 1631 by Gustavus Adolphus. In both cases a terrible, unbridgeable breach would have remained in the nation. The birth of the nation was postponed for 240 years, and came at a moment when that breach had ceased to be a menace. In the realm of art we may say that Pope Nicholas V's new St. Peter's would have been immeasurably inferior to the St. Peter's of Bramante and Michelangelo.

Another variant is the substitution of one branch of culture for another. In the first half of the eighteenth century, when poetry was almost completely negligible and painting half dead, music reached its sublimest heights. Yet here too there are imponderabilia which we must not play off against each other too glibly. The one thing certain is that *one* time, *one* people cannot possess everything at the same time, and that a great many talents, of themselves indeterminate, are attracted by the art that has already reached its zenith.

The most justified indictments which we seem to have the right to bring against fate are those which concern the destruction of great works of art and literature. We might possibly be ready to forgo the learning of the ancient world, the libraries of Alexandria and Pergamum; we have enough to do to cope with the learning of modern times, but we mourn for the supreme poets whose works have been lost, and the historians too represent an irreparable loss because the continuity of intellectual tradition has become fragmentary over long and important periods. But that continuity is a prime concern of man's earthly life, and a metaphysical proof of the significance of its duration, for whether a spiritual continuity existed without our knowledge, in an organ unknown to us, we cannot tell, and in any case cannot imagine it, hence we most urgently desire that the awareness of that continuity should remain living in our minds.

Yet our unfulfilled longing for the lost is worth something too. We owe to it, and to it alone, the fact that so many fragments have been rescued and pieced together by incessant study. Indeed, the worship of relics of art and the indefatigable combination of the relics of history form part of the religion of our day.

Our capacity for worship is as important as the object we worship.

It may be, too, that those great works of art had to perish in order that later art might create in freedom. For instance, if, in the fifteenth century, vast numbers of well-preserved Greek sculptures and paintings had been discovered, Leo-

nardo, Raphael, Titian and Correggio would not have done
their work, while they could, in their own way, sustain the
comparison with what had been inherited from Rome. And
if, after the middle of the eighteenth century, in the en-
thusiastic revival of philological and antiquarian studies,
the lost Greek lyric poets had suddenly been rediscovered,
they might well have blighted the full flowering of German
poetry. It is true that, after some decades, the mass of rediscovered ancient poetry would have become assimilated
with it, but the decisive moment of bloom, which never
returns in its full prime, would have been irretrievably past.
But enough had survived in the fifteenth century for art,
and in the eighteenth for poetry, to be stimulated and not
stifled.

Having reached this point, we must stop. Imperceptibly
we have passed from the question of good and evil fortune
to that of the survival of the human spirit, which in the
end presents itself to us as the life of *one* human being.
That life, as it becomes self-conscious *in* and *through* history, cannot fail in time so to fascinate the gaze of the
thinking man, and the study of it so to engage his power,
that the ideas of fortune and misfortune inevitably fade.
"Ripeness is all." Instead of happiness, the able mind will,
*nolens volens*, take knowledge as its goal. Nor does that
happen from indifference to a wretchedness that may be-
fall us too—whereby we are guarded against all pretense
of cool detachment—but because we realize the blindness
of our desires, since the desires of peoples and of individuals
neutralize each other.

If we could shake off our individuality and contemplate
the history of the immediate future with exactly the same
detachment and agitation as we bring to a spectacle of nature—for instance, a storm at sea seen from land—we should
perhaps experience in full consciousness one of the greatest
chapters in the history of the human mind.

At a time when the illusory peace of thirty years in which
we grew up has long since utterly vanished, and a series
of fresh wars seems to be imminent;

when the established political forms of the greatest civilized peoples are tottering or changing;

when, with the spread of education and communications, the realization and impatience of suffering is visibly and rapidly growing;

when social institutions are being shaken to their foundations by world movements, not to speak of all the accumulated crises which have not yet found their issues;

it would be a marvelous spectacle—though not for contemporary earthly beings—to follow with enlightened perception the spirit of man as it builds its new dwelling, soaring above, yet closely bound up with all these manifestations. Any man with such a vision in mind would completely forget about fortune and misfortune, and would spend his life in the quest of that knowledge.

# PART IV

# The Meaning of History

*I have dealt with this problem at length in the general introduction to this volume. There I suggested:*

*First, that the phrase "the meaning of history" contains two separate components that were invariably conjoined in the traditional literature on the subject: (a) the theoretical assertion that there is some unified meaningful structure, or law, in history; (b) the moral assertion that the course of human history was moving toward a goal that would make good the evil of history.*

*Second, that both the religious and the philosophical approach to the study of history, from St. Augustine to Hegel, tried to satisfy these two conditions in different ways.*

*Third, that this tradition, for a variety of reasons, suffered a serious decline in the nineteenth century and a virtual eclipse since.*

*Fourth, that the current attitude toward this tradition is either (a) that the quest for a meaning is both useless and hopeless or (b) that the sickness of modern man, caused by the failure to discover such a meaning, can be cured only by a return to theology.*

1.

*The essay by Mr. Bullock, Professor of History in the University of Oxford, is a mild version of the view that the*

*quest for meaning in the traditional sense is useless and
irrelevant. It is a critique of "metahistory"; i.e., the attempt
to elicit from history a metaphysical system à la Hegel and
Spengler. The historian's purpose is both more modest and
empirical, "not to form general propositions about revolutions or civilizations as such, but to give an account of the
French or the Russian revolution, to trace the rise and fall
of the Hellenistic or Chinese civilizations." In short, his purpose is not to generalize but to narrate; and we are trans-
ported back to issues discussed in earlier parts of this volume: a plea, like Butterfield's, for an interest in the past
for its own sake, not for ours; the distrust of converting
history into science or philosophy; and the affinity of history with great literature and drama. Yet there is also a
plea for a critical apparatus which distinguishes history
from fiction and for the need of a critical awareness of one's
"own assumptions and preconceptions." These are familiar
themes, as are many of the names cited.*

## ALAN BULLOCK

## THE HISTORIAN'S PURPOSE:
## HISTORY AND METAHISTORY*

Since Hegel delivered his lectures on the Philosophy of
History in Berlin, he has had many imitators. Not that
Hegel was the first to make the attempt at reading the
meaning of history, but since his time historical prophecy
has established its own apostolic succession from Hegel
himself and Marx to Spengler and Wells, Croce and Toynbee. These interpretations are various and contradictory,
but they have this in common: they are all attempts to
discover in history patterns, regularities and similarities on
whose recurrence is built a philosophical explanation of human existence, or at the very least a panoramic view of the
stages of its development. It is this sort of *Weltanschauung*
—metahistory, to borrow a phrase of Mr. Isaiah Berlin's—

* In *History Today*, Vol. 7 (February 1951), pp. 5–11; reprinted by permission of the editor and the author.

which is the fascination and justification of historical study to many people.

Equally obviously, it is not what most historians themselves mean by history. On the contrary, this is a kind of speculative activity which many professional historians eye with distrust and dislike. When G. N. Clark delivered his Inaugural Lecture as Regius Professor at Cambridge, he said: "To me it seems that no historical investigation can provide either a philosophy, or a religion, or a substitute for religion. . . . I think I should have a general consensus of the working historians with me, if I confined myself to the simpler conclusion that we work with limited aims. We try to find the truth about this or that, not about things in general. Our work is not to see life steadily and see it whole, but to see one particular portion of life right side up and in true perspective." Professor Butterfield, though prepared to assume the rôle of a prophet, was careful to dissociate his speculations from his work as a professional historian. "Those are gravely wrong who regard history as the queen of the sciences" (he wrote in *Christianity and History*), "or think of it as a substitute for religion. . . . Those who complain that technical history does not provide people with the meaning of life are asking from an academic science more than it can give. . . . When we have reconstructed the whole of mundane history it does not form a self-explanatory system, and our attitude to it is a matter not of scholarship, but of religion."

The commonest explanation for the hostility of many professional historians towards philosophical history in the grand style is to put it down to what Carlyle called "the poor, peddling dilettantism of Dryasdust", the contrast between the bold speculations of the philosopher of history and the narrow-mindedness of bloodless academic minds. But not all historians have been pedants or lacking in imagination. Is it true that the historian is confronted with a simple choice between metahistory on the model of Spengler or Toynbee and the desolate wastes of an arid historical erudition? Some historians at any rate—men like Halévy, Pirenne, Mathiez, Marc Bloch—seem to have found a way between these two extremes.

The historian, of course, does not live on a desert island.
He is sensitive to the interests and problems of the society
in which he lives. Marc Bloch tells a story of Pirenne, the
great Belgian mediaevalist, when they went together to an
historical congress at Stockholm. As soon as they had un-
packed, Pirenne wanted to go out. *"Qu'allons-nous voir
d'abord? Il paraît qu'il y a un Hôtel de Ville tout neuf. Com-
mençons par lui."* When Marc Bloch expressed his surprise
at such a choice, Pirenne retorted: *"Si j'étais un antiquaire,
je n'aurais d'yeux que pour les vieilles choses. Mais je suis
un historien. C'est pourquoi j'aime la vie."* It is often the
preoccupations and experiences of his own time which suggest to an historian the particular subject or period which
he takes up. But once he begins work, the question he is
trying to answer is: What happened? His interest is in the
past, not in the present or the future.

The historian finds his satisfaction in three things. First,
in searching for and discovering new material to use as evidence. Second, in handling his material when he has found
it, trying to discover whether it is authentic or a forgery—
if so, why it was forged; whether the man who wrote this
document is telling the truth or lies—if so, why he lied;
trying to make it yield unexpected evidence. The third and
supreme satisfaction is to put the evidence together, to produce not only an account of what happened, but a connected account, illuminating the motives and ideas of the
actors, the influence of circumstances, the play of chance
and the unforeseen. What the historian finds fascinating is
to come as close as he can to the concrete and the individual, to try and get inside the skin of *this* man or group of
men, Napoleon, Cromwell, the Jacobins, or the Bolsheviks;
to trace the causes, the connections and consequences of
this particular revolution of 1848, or a particular series of
events like the famines and plagues of the Middle Ages, or
the rise of the English cotton industry.

This is not to identify history with historical research:
that makes as little sense as to confuse literature with textual
criticism. To borrow another quotation from Pirenne: "Historical criticism, or historical erudition, is not the whole of
history. It does not exist for its own sake. . . . Its sole

purpose is the discovery of facts. . . . Criticism provides materials for what is properly called history. . . . Important and indeed essential though it be, its rôle remains subordinate. Once the authenticity of texts has been established, the sources criticized, the chronology of events fixed, there still remains the task of making history. . . . Without hypothesis or synthesis, history remains a pastime for antiquarians; just as without criticism and erudition it loses itself in the realm of fantasy."

Still less am I putting forward an argument in favour of reducing history to chronology, a bare recital of facts. History is always an attempt to explain the sequence and connection of events, to explain why, after the events of 1789, there followed the Revolutionary Wars, the execution of the King, the Jacobin dictatorship, the Terror and the Thermidorian Reaction. Not why they *had* to follow—that is prediction in reverse, and the historian has no business with prediction—but why *in fact* they followed.

Now, the moment the historian begins to explain, he is bound to make use of general propositions of all kinds—about human behaviour, about the effect of economic factors and the influence of ideas and a hundred other things. It is impossible for the historian to banish such general propositions; they are smuggled in by the back door, even when he refuses to admit it. He cannot begin to think or explain events without the help of the preconceptions, the assumptions, the generalization of experience which he brings with him—and is bound to bring with him—to his work. When Mathiez for example began to work on the history of the French Revolution, his mind was not a blank, it was full of views and prejudices about revolutions and their causes, about the way people behave in times of revolution, about how much importance to attach to economic, how much to intellectual factors. The historian gives a false account of his activity if he tries to deny the part that general ideas and assumptions play in his work.

There is, however, a difference between the historian on the one hand and the metahistorian, seeking for patterns of historical evolution, or the sociologist, seeking for general laws governing human development, on the other. This difference lies in their purpose and in the use which they make of such generalizations. What the metahistorian and the sociologist are trying to do is to clear away the confusion of facts and reveal the pattern, or establish the law, which lies beneath. But this is not the historian's purpose: what he wants to know is what happened. For him general propositions are both necessary and illuminating, but they are not the essential purpose of his work. When Marx says "The history of all hitherto existing society is the history of class struggles", Marxism as a system stands or falls by the truth of such a generalization. Its only interest in history is to produce such general propositions. But when Professor Namier says, "The relations of groups of men to plots of land form the basic content of political history", it does not matter whether this is only partially true. It does not invalidate his investigation and interpretation of English politics in the later eighteenth century, and it is this which represents his main purpose, the epigram is thrown off as an aside. For the historian such generalizations are hypotheses which he can use to open up a subject and suggest lines of approach, discarding, adapting, or continuing with them, as they prove fruitful. Few historians to-day, for instance, would fail to make use of the economic interpretation of history as one of the most valuable instruments of historical analysis—but only as one. As an experimental hypothesis, to be dropped or taken up as it fits, it is indispensable; as a dogmatic belief it cramps the mind and forces the historian to distort the evidence. It is in this way, as hypotheses, as the expression of probabilities, of what to look out for, that the historian treats his general propositions; not as the basis of something that can be built up into a general law. His purpose is not to form general propositions about revolutions or civilizations as such, but to give an account of the French or the Russian Revolution, to trace the rise and fall of the Hellenic or Chinese Civilizations.

In such work it is obvious that the first rule of the historian must be to keep a critical eye on his own assumptions and pre-conceptions, lest these should lead him to miss the importance of some piece of evidence, the existence of some connection. His whole training teaches him to break down rather than build up generalizations, to bring the general always to the touchstone of particular, concrete instances. His experience of this discipline and its results makes him cautious and sceptical about the possibility of establishing uniformities and regularities of sufficient generality to bear the weight of the conclusions then built up on them. Probabilities, yes—rules of thumb, the sort of thing you can expect to happen—but not more than this.

When I first came across the bold generalizations of the metahistorian in Spengler's *Decline of the West*, I was bowled over by them. But I have become more wary since, not least because I have encountered many other equally bold but frequently contradictory generalizations. The suspicion has grown that this is to treat history as a ragbag in which every man will find what he wants to find, and what he expects to find. There is indeed no limit to the lessons of history, or to their contradictions.

In short, the historian does not believe that you can annex history to a metaphysical system or turn it into a science on that out-of-date nineteenth century model on which the original expectations of the social sciences were founded. Perhaps, as Marc Bloch suggests in his *Métier de l'Historien*, the temper and attitude of the twentieth century scientist is a good deal closer to that of the historian than the dogmatic assertions of those who have constituted themselves the prophets of science in the past.

There is another objection to be met, however. Professor Butterfield, for instance, might well agree with a good deal of what has been said so far. "Nothing" (he wrote in *Christianity and History*), "can exceed the feeling of satisfaction that many people have when they meet some system which helps them through the jungle of historical happenings, and gives them an interpretation of the story seen as a whole. In such cases, however, our interpretation is a thing which we bring to history and superimpose upon it. We cannot say that we obtained it as technical historians by inescapable inferences, from the purely historical evidence. Therefore the Liberal, the Jesuit, the Fascist, the Communist, and all the rest may sail away with their militant versions of history, howling at one another across the interstellar spaces, all claiming that theirs is the absolute version. . . ."

But Professor Butterfield seems to feel that, deprived of these broad sweeps and metaphysical perspectives, the historian's work must be very limited in scope and interest. The historian emerges from Professor Butterfield's pages as a poor creature, blinkered and earth-bound, labouring to produce the fragments which the metahistorian combines into the glittering pattern of his mosaic.

I find it hard to believe, however, that if history cannot be made to bear the weight of the systems of moral absolutism after which so many people hanker, that it must therefore be regarded as a study which is either dull or meaningless. It is too easily assumed that the only approach to knowledge and understanding of human life and behaviour is by the search for general factors, regularities and uniformities, which can be reduced to formulas and general propositions. This is not a popular objection to raise. I can still remember the look of horror on the face of a young sociologist when I suggested there was more to be learned from Dostoievski's novels or Shakespeare's plays, with their series of individual portraits, than from the abstract and meagre generalizations of his own study. In that preference for the concrete and the particular, that distrust of the abstract and general which is the characteristic of many historians, there may be something akin to the approach of the painter and the novelist—think of Proust, for instance, and his incomparable re-creation of the past.

Probably it is a question of temperament, of the way your mind works. But behind the historian's distrust of the metahistorians and the dogmatists there often lies an instinctive feeling that, alongside the approach to knowledge of human nature and human behaviour represented by the attempt to frame general laws and trace broad general patterns of historical development, there is another approach, equally legitimate and to some people's way of thinking more fruitful. That is, by studying and trying to penetrate in all its individuality and uniqueness the development of one society, or one civilization, the behaviour not of men and women in general, but of one particular group in a given period of time. And it is a fair question to ask—who sees the more—the airman who flies continually across several countries five thousand feet up, from where he can see the land for miles and miles, or the countryman who has lived in one place all his life but knows the valleys, the woods and lanes of his own countryside like the back of his hand?

## 2.

*I hesitated long before including the following selection; but I finally pushed aside my personal misgivings for two reasons: First, Professor Popper's views on history have gained considerable notoriety in wide circles, and I thought they should be represented in a cross section of contemporary thought about history. Secondly, his statement is an extreme version of the thesis that "history has no meaning" precisely because there is neither a fixed universal law nor an inexorable direction toward a moral end in history.*

*Now Mr. Popper, Professor of Logic and Scientific Method at the University of London, has adopted a highly idiosyncratic terminology. He has attached the label of "historicism" to any theory, such as Plato's, Hegel's, or Marx's, which believes in inevitable cyclical, dialectical, or evolutionary trends in history analogous to a universal determinism in nature.[1] In the excerpt below, he speaks of a "theistic historicism," by which he means a conception of history in the Augustinian tradition; i.e., the belief that the course of history is set and determined by the will of God.*

*Everybody, of course, has a right to coin neologisms; but to apply the term "historicism," by arbitrary fiat and for the purpose of a historical analysis, to something with which it has nothing to do in history—this is, to say the least, quite odd and misleading. The issue involves more then an exercise in semantics. To have a target to shoot at, Mr. Popper has set up a false image of historicism. What*

[1] For a similar point of view, cf. Professor Berlin's arguments in the above selection, p. 257.

*he has criticized as "the poverty of historicism" is a parody
of historicism. It has nothing to do with the movement of
historicism as defined and analyzed in the classic work of
Friedrich Meinecke nor with the modern historicism of
Dilthey and his successors.[2] Instead, it is a critique of religious and philosophical interpretations of history, as represented by Plato, St. Augustine, Hegel, Marx, or Comte,
which radically differed from historicism both in its
methods and in its conclusions.*

*To put it more crudely: the critic is flogging a dead
horse; for what he calls "historicism" has been a dead issue
in historical theory—though not in practical politics—for a
long time. The issue involves more than an exercise in semantics. For by still tilting windmills with Hegel, Marx,
and Comte, this type of philosophical analysis reveals its
own poverty: it ignores the historical record—as if we had
suddenly discovered that Plato, Hegel, or Marx were vul-
nerable to criticism—and it declines to come to terms with
the problems raised by the genuine historicism of our times.
Dilthey, it must be remembered, was an empirical, analytic
thinker. Neither he nor Croce nor Collingwood believed in
determinism, inevitability, or teleology in history. What
they and their successors did believe (and rightly so, I
think) was that the empirical facts and the analytic techniques in history were sufficiently different from those in
philosophy and the general sciences that they deserved a
special inquiry and that they yielded a "logic" of their own.
Their work may be fragmentary and unsatisfactory, but it
constitutes the main stream of modern historicism.*

*The semantic confusion turns into something of an aca-
demic farce when it "develops," as in his discussion of historical interpretations, that Mr. Popper himself subscribes
to the views of a modern historicism. Thus he admits that
history is always written from a present standpoint: that
"each generation has . . . its own interests, its own point
of view"; that history is always an answer to needs "arising
out of the practical problems and decisions we face"; that
there is no history as it actually happened; that there are*

---

[2] Cf. my introductory survey and the description of historicism
in Mr. Barraclough's essay, p. 27 ff. above.

*no "final interpretations", but only different perspectives; that history is not a science and that our moral decisions, and judgments, invariably contain subjective, emotive components. In short, he endorses the typical relativistic theses of historicism with regard to knowledge and values.*

*Mr. Popper's denial of a religious, rational, or teleological design of "meaning" in history goes together with an activist, existentialist affirmation of meaning: "Although history has no meaning, we can give it a meaning." And the same formula is applied to "the meaning of life." Les extrêmes se touchent: logical empiricism and existentialism have both discovered the loss of meaning in life and history.*

## KARL POPPER

## HAS HISTORY ANY MEANING?*

. . . It is important to see that many 'historical theories' (they might perhaps be better described as 'quasi-theories') are in their character vastly different from scientific theories. For in history (including the historical natural sciences such as historical geology) the facts at our disposal are often severely limited and cannot be repeated or implemented at our will. And they have been collected in accordance with a preconceived point of view; the so-called 'sources' of history only record such facts as appeared sufficiently interesting to record, so that the sources will, as a rule, contain only facts that fit in with a preconceived theory. And since no further facts are available, it will not, as a rule, be possible to test that or any other subsequent theory. Such untestable historical theories can then rightly be charged with being circular in the sense in which this charge has been unjustly brought against scientific theories. I shall call such historical theories, in contradistinction to scientific theories, *'general interpretations.'*

* In *The Open Society and Its Enemies,* one vol. ed. (Princeton, N.J.: Princeton University Press, 1950), pp. 449–63. I have deleted several passages, as indicated, without, I hope, impairing the substance of Mr. Popper's argument. H.M.

Interpretations are important since they represent a point of view. But we have seen that a point of view is always inevitable, and that, in history, a theory which can be tested and which is therefore of scientific character can only rarely be obtained. Thus we must not think that a general interpretation can be confirmed by its agreement even with all our records; for we must remember its circularity, as well as the fact that there will always be a number of other (and perhaps incompatible) interpretations that agree with the same records, and that we can rarely obtain new data able to serve as do crucial experiments in physics. Historians often do not see any other interpretation which fits the facts as well as their own does; but if we consider that even in the field of physics, with its larger and more reliable stock of facts, new crucial experiments are needed again and again because the old ones are all in keeping with both of two competing and incompatible theories (consider the eclipse experiment which is needed for deciding between Newton's and Einstein's theories of gravitation), then we shall give up the naïve belief that any definite set of historical records can ever be interpreted in one way only.

But this does not mean, of course, that all interpretations are of equal merit. First, there are always interpretations which are not really in keeping with the accepted records; secondly, there are some which need a number of more or less plausible auxiliary hypotheses if they are to escape falsification by the records; next, there are some that are unable to connect a number of facts which another interpretation can connect, and in so far 'explain.' There may accordingly be a considerable amount of progress even within the field of historical interpretation. Furthermore, there may be all kinds of intermediate stages between more or less universal 'points of view' and those specific or singular historical hypotheses mentioned above, which in the explanation of historical events play the role of hypothetical initial conditions rather than of universal laws. Often enough these can be tested fairly well and are therefore comparable to scientific theories . . .

I said before that interpretations may be incompatible; but as long as we consider them merely as crystallizations of points of view, then they are not. For example, the interpretation that man steadily progresses (towards the open society or some other aim) is incompatible with the interpretation that he steadily slips back or retrogresses. But the 'point of view' of one who looks on human history as a history of progress is not necessarily incompatible with that of one who looks on it as a history of retrogression; that is to say, we could write a history of human progress towards freedom (containing, for example, the story of the fight against slavery) and another history of human retrogression and oppression (containing perhaps such things as the impact of the white race upon the colored races); and these two histories need not be in conflict; rather, they may be complementary to each other, as would be two views of the same landscape seen from two different points. This consideration is of considerable importance. For since each generation has its own troubles and problems, and therefore its own interests and its own point of view, it follows that each generation has a right to look upon and reinterpret history in its own way, which is complementary to that of previous generations. After all, we study history because we are interested in it, and perhaps because we wish to learn something about our own problems. But history can serve neither of these two purposes if, under the influence of an inapplicable idea of objectivity, we hesitate to present historical problems from our point of view . . . The main thing is to be conscious of one's point of view, and critical, that is to say, to avoid, as far as this is possible, unconscious and therefore uncritical bias in the presentation of the facts. In every other respect, the interpretation must speak for itself; and its merits will be its fertility, its ability to elucidate the facts of history, as well as its topical interest, its ability to elucidate the problems of the day.

To sum up, there can be no history of 'the past as it actually did happen'; there can only be historical interpretations, and none of them final; and every generation has a right to frame its own. But not only has it a right to frame its own interpretations, it also has a kind of obligation to do so; for there is indeed a pressing need to be answered . . . Instead of recognizing that historical interpretation should answer a need arising out of the practical problems and decisions which face us, the historicist believes that in our desire for historical interpretation, there expresses itself the profound intuition that by contemplating history we may discover the secret, the essence of human destiny. Historicism is out to find The Path on which mankind is destined to walk; it is out to discover The Clue to History (as J. Macmurray calls it), or The Meaning of History.

But is there such a clue? *Is there a meaning in history?*

I do not wish to enter here into the problem of the meaning of 'meaning'; I take it for granted that most people know with sufficient clarity what they mean when they speak of the 'meaning of history' or of the 'meaning of life.' And in this sense, in the sense in which the question of the meaning of history is asked, I answer: *History has no meaning.*

In order to give reasons for this opinion, I must first say something about that 'history' which people have in mind when they ask whether it has meaning. So far, I have myself spoken about 'history' as if it did not need any explanation. That is no longer possible; for I wish to make it clear that *history in the sense in which most people speak of it simply does not exist;* and this is at least one reason why I say that it has no meaning.

How do most people come to use the term 'history'? (I mean 'history' in the sense in which we say of a book that it is *about* the history of Europe—not in the sense in which we say that it *is* a history of Europe.) They learn about it in school and at the university. They read books about it. They see what is treated in the books under the name 'history of the world' or 'the history of mankind,' and they get used to looking upon it as a more or less definite series of facts. And these facts constitute, they believe, the history of mankind.

But we have already seen that the realm of facts is infinitely rich, and that there must be selection. According to our interests, we could, for instance, write about the history of art; or of language; or of feeding habits; or of typhus fever (see Zinsser's *Rats, Lice, and History*). Certainly, none of these is the history of mankind (nor all of them taken together). What people have in mind when they speak of the history of mankind is, rather, the history of the Egyptian, Babylonian, Persian, Macedonian, and Roman empires, and so on, down to our own day. In other words: They speak about the *history of mankind*, but what they mean, and what they have learned about in school, is the *history of political power*.

There is no history of mankind, there is only an indefinite number of histories of all kinds of aspects of human life. And one of these is the history of political power. This is elevated into the history of the world. But this, I hold, is an offence against every decent conception of mankind. It is hardly better than to treat the history of embezzlement or of robbery or of poisoning as the history of mankind. *For the history of power politics is nothing but the history of international crime and mass murder* (including, it is true, some of the attempts to suppress them). This history is taught in schools, and some of the greatest criminals are extolled as its heroes.

But is there really no such thing as a universal history in the sense of a concrete history of mankind? There can be none. This must be the reply of every humanitarian, I believe, and especially that of every Christian. A concrete history of mankind, if there were any, would have to be the history of all men. It would have to be the history of all human hopes, struggles, and sufferings. For there is no one man more important than any other. Clearly, this concrete history cannot be written. We must make abstractions, we must neglect, select. But with this we arrive at the many histories; and among them, at that history of international crime and mass murder which has been advertised as the history of mankind.

But why has just the history of power been selected, and not, for example, that of religion, or of poetry? There are several reasons. One is that power affects us all, and poetry only a few. Another is that men are inclined to worship power. But there can be no doubt that the worship of power is one of the worst kinds of human idolatries, a relic of the time of the cage, of human servitude. The worship of power is born of fear, an emotion which is rightly despised. A third reason why power politics has been made the core of 'history' is that those in power wanted to be worshipped and could enforce their wishes. Many historians wrote under the supervision of the emperors, the generals, and the dictators.

I know that these views will meet with the strongest opposition from many sides, including some apologists for Christianity; for although there is hardly anything in the New Testament to support this doctrine, it is often considered a part of the Christian dogma that God reveals Himself in history; that history has meaning; and that its meaning is the purpose of God. Historicism is thus held to be a necessary element of religion. But I do not admit this. I contend that this view is pure idolatry and superstition, not only from the point of view of a rationalist or humanist but from the Christian point of view itself.

What is behind this theistic historicism? With Hegel, it looks upon history—political history—as a stage, or rather, as a kind of lengthy Shakespearian play; and the audience conceive either the 'great historical personalities,' or mankind in the abstract, as the heroes of the play. Then they ask, 'Who has written this play?' And they think that they give a pious answer when they reply, 'God.' But they are mistaken. Their answer is pure blasphemy, for the play was (as they know it) written not by God, but, under the supervision of generals and dictators, by the professors of history.

I do not deny that it is as justifiable to interpret history from a Christian point of view as it is to interpret it from any other point of view; and it should certainly be emphasized, for example, how much of our Western aims and ends, humanitarianism, freedom, equality, we owe to the influence of Christianity. But at the same time, the only rational as well as the only Christian attitude even towards the history of freedom is that we are ourselves responsible for it, in the same sense in which we are responsible for what we make of our lives, and that only our conscience can judge us and not our worldly success. The theory that God reveals Himself and His judgment in history is indistinguishable from the theory that worldly success is the ultimate judge and justification of our actions; it comes to the same thing as the doctrine that history will judge, that is to say, that future might is right; it is the same as what I have called 'moral futurism.' To maintain that God reveals Himself in what is usually called 'history,' in the history of international crime and of mass murder, is indeed blasphemy; for what really happens within the realm of human lives is hardly ever touched upon by this cruel and at the same time childish affair. The life of the forgotten, of the unknown individual man; his sorrows and his joys, his suffering and death, this is the real content of human experience down the ages. If that could be told by history, then I should certainly not say that it is blasphemy to see the finger of God in it. But such a history does not and cannot exist; and all the history which exists, our history of the Great and the Powerful, is at best a shallow comedy; it is the opera buffa played by the powers behind reality (comparable to Homer's opera buffa of the Olympian powers behind the scene of human struggles). It is what one of our worst instincts, the idolatrous worship of power, of success, has led us to believe to be real. And in this not even man-made, but man-faked 'history,' some Christians dare to see the hand of God! They dare to understand and to know what He wills when they impute to Him their petty historical interpretations! 'On the contrary,' says K. Barth, the theologian, in his *Credo*, 'we have to begin with the admission . . . that all that we think we know when we say "God" does not reach or comprehend Him . . . , but always one of our self-conceived and self-made idols, whether it is "spirit" or "nature," "fate" or "idea". . . .' (It is in keeping with this attitude that Barth characterizes the 'Neo-Protestant doctrine of the revelations of God in history' as 'inadmissible' and as an encroachment upon 'the kingly office of Christ.') But it is, from the Christian point of view, not only arrogance that underlies such attempts; it is, more specifically, an anti-Christian attitude. For Christianity teaches, if anything, that worldly success is not decisive. Christ 'suffered under Pontius Pilate.' I am quoting Barth again: 'How does Pontius Pilate get into the Credo? The

simple answer can at once be given: it is a matter of date.'
Thus the man who was successful, who represented the
historical power of that time, plays here the purely technical role of indicating when these events happened. And
what were these events? They had nothing to do with
power-political success, with 'history.' They were not even
the story of an unsuccessful nonviolent nationalist revolution (*à la* Gandhi) of the Jewish people against the Roman
conquerors. The events were nothing but the sufferings of
a man. Barth insists that the word 'suffers' refers to the
whole of the life of Christ and not only to His death; he
says: 'Jesus *suffers*. Therefore He does not conquer. He does
not triumph. He has no success. . . . He achieved nothing
except . . . His crucifixion. The same could be said of His
relationship to His people and to His disciples.' My intention in quoting Barth is to show that it is not only my
'rationalist' or 'humanist' point of view from which the worship of historical success appears as incompatible with the
spirit of Christianity. What matters to Christianity is not
the historical deeds of the powerful Roman conquerors but
(to use a phrase of Kierkegaard's) 'what a few fishermen
have given the world.' And yet all theistic interpretation of
history attempts to see in history as it is recorded, i.e. in
the history of power, and in historical success, the manifestation of God's will.

To this attack upon the 'doctrine of the revelation of
God in history,' it will probably be replied that it *is* success,
His success after His death, by which Christ's unsuccessful
life on earth was finally revealed to mankind as the greatest
spiritual victory; that it was the success, the fruits of His
teaching which proved it and justified it, and by which the
prophecy 'The last shall be first and the first last' has been
verified. In other words, that it was the historical success
of the Christian Church through which the will of God
manifested itself. But this is a most dangerous line of defence. Its implication that the worldly success of the
Church is an argument in favor of Christianity clearly reveals lack of faith. The early Christians had no worldly
encouragement of this kind. (They believed that conscience
must judge power, and not the other way round.) Those

who hold that the history of the success of Christian teaching reveals the will of God should ask themselves whether this success was really a success of the spirit of Christianity; and whether this spirit did not triumph at the time when the Church was persecuted, rather than at the time when the Church was triumphant. Which Church incorporated this spirit more purely, that of the martyrs, or the victorious Church of the Inquisition?

There seem to be many who would admit much of this, insisting as they do that the message of Christianity is to the meek, but who still believe that this message is one of historicism. An outstanding representative of this view is J. Macmurray, who, in *The Clue to History*, finds the essence of Christian teaching in historical prophecy, and who sees in its founder the discoverer of a dialectical law of 'human nature.' Macmurray holds that, according to this law, political history must inevitably bring forth 'the socialist commonwealth of the world. The fundamental law of human nature cannot be broken. . . . It is the meek who will inherit the earth.' But this historicism, with its substitution of certainty for hope, must lead to a moral futurism. 'The law *cannot* be broken.' So we can be sure, on psychological grounds, that whatever we do will lead to the same result; that even fascism must, in the end, lead to that commonwealth; so that the final outcome does not depend upon our moral decision, and that there is no need to worry over our responsibilities. If we are told that we can be *certain*, on scientific grounds, that 'the last will be first and the first last,' what else is this but the substitution of historical prophecy for conscience? Does not this theory come dangerously close (certainly against the intentions of its author) to the admonition: 'Be wise, and take to heart what the founder of Christianity tells you, for he was a great psychologist of human nature and a great prophet of history. Climb in time upon the band wagon of the meek; for according to the inexorable scientific laws of human nature, this is the surest way to come out on top!' Such a clue to history implies the worship of success; it implies that the meek will be justified because they will be on the winning side. It translates Marxism . . . into the language of a psychology of human nature, and of religious prophecy. It is an interpretation which, by implication, sees the greatest achievement of Christianity in the fact that its founder was a forerunner of Hegel—a superior one, admittedly . . .

History has no meaning, I contend. But this contention does not imply that all we can do about it is to look aghast at the history of political power, or that we must look on it as a cruel joke. For we can interpret it, with an eye to those problems of power politics whose solution we choose to attempt in our time. We can interpret the history of power politics from the point of view of our fight for the open society, for a rule of reason, for justice, freedom, equality, and for the control of international crime. Although history has no ends, we can impose these ends of ours upon it; and *although history has no meaning, we can give it a meaning.*

It is the problem of nature and convention which we meet here again. Neither nature nor history can tell us what we ought to do. Facts, whether those of nature or those of history, cannot make the decision for us, they cannot determine the ends we are going to choose. It is we who introduce purpose and meaning into nature and into history. Men are not equal; but we can decide to fight for equal rights. Human institutions such as the state are not rational, but we can decide to fight to make them more rational. We ourselves and our ordinary language are, on the whole, emotional rather than rational; but we can try to become a little more rational, and we can train ourselves to use our language as an instrument not of self-expression (as our romantic educationists would say) but of rational communication. History itself—I mean the history of power politics, of course, not the nonexistent story of the development of mankind—has no end nor meaning, but we can decide to give it both. We can make it our fight for the open society and against its enemies (who, when in a corner, always protest their humanitarian sentiments, in accordance with Pareto's advice); and we can interpret it accordingly. Ultimately, we may say the same about the 'meaning of life.' It is up to us to decide what shall be our purpose in life, to determine our ends.

This dualism of facts and decisions is, I believe, fundamental. Facts as such have no meaning; they can gain it only through our decisions . . . This emphasis upon the dualism of facts and decisions determines also our attitude towards such ideas as 'progress.' If we think that history progresses, or that we are bound to progress, then we commit the same mistake as those who believe that history has a meaning that can be discovered in it and need not be given to it. For to progress is to move towards some kind of end, towards an end which exists for us as human beings. 'History' cannot do that; only we, the human individuals, can do it; we can do it by defending and strengthening those democratic institutions upon which freedom, and with it progress, depends. And we shall do it much better as we become more fully aware of the fact that progress rests with us, with our watchfulness, with our efforts, with the clarity of our conception of our ends, and with the realism of their choice.

Instead of posing as prophets we must become the makers of our fate. We must learn to do things as well as we can, and to look out for our mistakes. And when we have dropped the idea that the history of power will be our judge, when we have given up worrying whether or not history will justify us, then one day perhaps we may succeed in getting power under control. In this way we may even justify history, in our turn. It badly needs such justification.

3.

*Reinhold Niebuhr, Professor of Theology at Union Seminary in New York, is the foremost spokesman for a Christian interpretation of history in this country. He has written extensively on the subject; and while his views are not always like those of other religious thinkers, they have been extremely influential and they are very subtle.*

*The following selection deals with three major aspects of "the meaning of history from the standpoint of the Christian faith": (1) the diversity of societies in history, (2) the individual and history, and (3) the unity of history. The discussion of each topic reveals one of the most characteristic traits of Niebuhr's thought. This is the use of a subtle dialectical method: freedom is played against necessity, the individual against the community, Antichrist against Christ, historicity against eternity; all the major issues are viewed as "the product of a tension between natural conditions and the freedom (of man) which transcends nature"; all of them are analyzed, in Hegelian fashion, in terms of the dynamic interaction of opposite concepts. In turn, secular theories of human life and history are criticized because they isolate one pole to the exclusion of the other, because they are satisfied with finite, immanent meanings in history to the exclusion of the transcendent dimension of human existence.*

*This dialectical approach assumes a Christian character, not only because religious concepts like "pride," "sin," "mercy," "grace," or "resurrection" enter into it, but also—and perhaps primarily—I think, because, according to Professor Niebuhr and other Christian thinkers, the historical process is not comprehensible in its own terms. The dialectical components in it are, ultimately, "paradoxical," if the process of history itself is envisaged as guaranteeing "the fulfilment of human life." "There is no escape from the paradoxical relation of history to the Kingdom of God." Dialectical theology, as it is called, solves the historical paradoxes only by an appeal to faith, which is "the fruit of 'grace.'"*

*Thus, for example, the conflict between "finiteness and freedom, which lies at the basis of historical existence, is a problem for which there is no solution by any human power. Only God can solve this problem. From the human perspective it can only be solved by faith. All structures of meaning and realms of coherence, which human reason constructs, face the chasm of meaninglessness when men discover that the tangents of meaning transcend the limits of existence. Only faith has an answer to this problem." Now, "from such a vantage point, history is meaningful, even if it should be impossible to discern any unity in its processes." It is clear that this is a vantage point beyond history. History as well as human life have a meaning only if they be viewed from a transhistorical perspective.*

*That paradox lies at the heart of a Christian view of history is also affirmed by Christopher Dawson from a Catholic point of view. The following passage from his* The Dynamics of World History *is a striking and forthright statement of the elusive ambiguity inherent in this religious outlook: "It is difficult, perhaps even impossible, to explain the Christian view of history to a non-Christian, since it is necessary to accept the Christian faith in order to understand the Christian view of history, and those who reject the idea of a divine revelation are necessarily obliged to reject the Christian view of history as well. And even those who are prepared to accept in theory the principle of divine revelation—of the manifestation of a religious truth which surpasses human reason—may still find it hard to face the enormous paradoxes of Christianity." The critic citing this passage in the London* Times *Literary Supplement (December 27, 1957) makes an appropriate comment: "Presented with such an ultimatum, any conscientious historian" —and one might add, any conscientious philosopher—"may perhaps be excused for protesting that this is having it both ways with a vengeance; not everybody can bring himself to cry* credo quia impossibile est."

## REINHOLD NIEBUHR

## THE DIVERSITY AND UNITY OF HISTORY*

An effort to comprehend the meaning of history from the standpoint of the Christian faith must include three aspects of it: (1) The partial fulfillments and realizations as we see them in the rise and fall of civilizations and cultures; (2) The life of individuals; and (3) The process of history as a whole. In considering these three aspects it will become apparent that the view "from above" must predominate,

* In *The Nature and Destiny of Man*, one vol. ed. (New York: Charles Scribner's Sons, 1953), II, pp. 301–21. I have deleted several lengthy footnotes appearing in the original. H.M.

though it cannot be exclusive, in the consideration of the first two aspects. The view from the "end" must predominate but not be exclusive in viewing history as a whole.

## 1. The Rise and Fall of Cultures and Civilizations

History is filled with many achievements and constructions which "have their day and cease to be." The rise and fall of empires and civilizations are the most obvious examples of the pluralistic aspect of history, but they are not, by any means, the only manifestations of this aspect. The rise and fall of particular governments and oligarchies within a given civilization, the growth and decline of specific cultural traditions, or of eminent families in a community, or of various types of voluntary associations, or of even more minor historical concretions, are equally illustrative of the pluralism of history.

Whatever meaning is to be found in this pageant of recurring life and death must be discerned primarily, though not wholly, "from above." Each historical configuration may be regarded as an integral realm of meaning, for its relation to the whole historical process is minimal or, at any rate, obscure.

The pluralistic interpretation of history has received a new impetus in recent years by the work of Oswald Spengler and, more recently by Arnold Toynbee's monumental inquiry into the rise and fall of civilizations.[1] These and similar pluralistic interpretations conform to Ranke's principles of historical interpretation, summarized in his conception of the equidistance of all temporal events from the eternal. But even historical pluralism cannot escape the question of comprehensive meaning. It seeks to find some principle of coherence in the rise and fall of various civilizations. Spengler believes that the processes of nature are the only clue to the meaning of the growth and decline of various world cultures. According to his thesis there is no unity in history but the common fate of diverse and incommensurate civilizations. This common fate is governed by the

[1] Oswald Spengler, The Decline of the West. Arnold J. Toynbee, The Study of History.

laws of nature. All civilizations pass through ages analogous to spring, summer, autumn and winter; which is to say that historical organisms are equated with natural ones. Thus the freedom of history is regarded as either wholly illusory or at least as completely subordinate to nature. It cannot be denied that, since the freedom of history rises on the ground of nature-necessity, historical destiny is always partly determined by the vitality and decay of the natural factors underlying any historical achievement. Empires and cultures may "grow old"; and fail to survive perils in their age which they could have surmounted in their youth.

Yet, as Toynbee points out, the failure of civilizations always involves something more than mere weakness of age. They perish because they make mistakes in meeting some new challenge or complexity of history. Every civilization makes some fatal mistake in the end and perishes. But these mistakes are not under the law of natural necessity. Unlike individual life, the collective and social organisms of history could ideally be perpetually replenished by new life and strength. But this would require that they be perpetually adapted to new historical situations. Their final failure to do so is always a fate into which they are tempted by their freedom and is not due to natural necessity.[2] Sometimes they perish because pride of power prompts them to extend themselves beyond the limits of human possibilities. Sometimes the oligarchy which has been instrumental in

[2] It is Toynbee's great merit to see this element of tragic destiny in history where Spengler sees only the organic growth and decay of historical organisms. Cf. *The Study of History*, Vol. IV, particularly p. 260 ff. Toynbee unnecessarily emphasizes the rôle of a minority, in the period of creativity; and of the degeneration of this minority into a "dominant" minority, maintained by repression, in a period of decay. There are undoubtedly such minorities in all social and political organisms; and in so far as failure and decay is caused by errors in judgment and action they must be attributed particularly to the portion of the community in which its will and mind are articulated. But the causes of the failure are always many. Could the decay of contemporary France be ascribed to the faults of any particular minority only? Does not history point to a much more complex source of such a breakdown?

organizing a society becomes purely repressive and destroys what it has created. Sometimes the strategies and techniques of yesterday are falsely applied to new situations and problems to which they are not relevant. This mistake may be regarded as a form of the intellectual pride which falsely raises contingent factors in history to the eminence of false absolutes. Sometimes civilizations perish because they are beguiled by philosophies of "detachment." Their spiritual leaders flee prematurely to some illusory realm of supra-historical serenity and equanimity and betray their responsibilities in history.[3] Modern technical civilization may perish because it falsely worshipped technical advance as a final good. One portion of a technical society may harness techniques to the purpose of destruction and vent its fury upon another portion of the civilization, which has grown soft by regarding the comforts yielded in such great abundance by a technical age, as the final good.

If we sought to do full justice to all the various possibilities of decline and causes of decay we would find ourselves merely recapitulating the various types of human sin. They would fall into the two general categories of the sins of sensuality, and the sins of pride. In the former the freedom of history is denied and men creep back to the irresponsibility of nature. In the latter the freedom of man is overestimated. Men seek to complete history without regard to the contingent and finite character of the self, individual or collective, of the culture or civilization, which they make the basis of their pretension. This is the sin of imperialism. Or they seek to abstract human freedom from history. This pride of mystic other-worldliness makes the human spirit,

---

[3] The weaknesses of the rule of Marcus Aurelius in the declining days of Rome belong in this category. It is significant that the most "saintly" of Roman emperors should have hastened, though he certainly did not initiate, the decline of Rome, under the influence of Stoic idealism which made *apatheia* the final good. Some of the "Christian idealism" of our own day, dreaming of a Kingdom of God which is completely irrelevant to the tragic facts and problems of history, stands in the same relation to the decline of Western civilization. There are other, and profounder, causes of our difficulties. But modern "idealism" has certainly aggravated our problems.

not the master of history but the agent of its own emancipation from history.

All these various forms of historical decline and destruction have one common characteristic. They are not merely biological death. The Augustinian dictum: "It is not by death that we sin but by sin that we die," may be partly untrue when applied to individual life; for individual existence is rooted in a natural organism subject to the conditions of finiteness. But it is a very apt description of the death of civilizations. It is by "sin that they die." They are not determined by absolute natural necessity. Their mistakes and errors are made in the same freedom, out of which their creativity arises. The mistakes are never prompted by mere ignorance. The "vain imagination" of sin is in them.

It would be wrong, however, to view the history of the world's many cultures and civilizations with an eye only upon their decline. They die in the end; but they also live. Their life is a testimony of the creativity of history, even as their death is a proof of the sin in history. The vast variety of historic organisms, the richness of their elaborations of human potentialities, the wealth of their many cultural forms and social configurations are as certainly a testimony to the divine providence under which they have grown, as their destruction is a vindication of the eternal judgment, which they are unable to defy with impunity. In their weakness and youth, while making their way in history against all the perils of life, they are revelations of the power of God who "hath chosen . . . the things which are not, to bring to nought things that are."[4] In their glory, when the disintegration of evil is already apparent in their life and yet ultimate destruction is so long postponed, their fate reveals the "longsuffering" of the divine mercy. For God's judgments are never precipitate and the possibilities of repentance and turning from the evil way are many. According to the degree with which civilizations and cultures accept these possibilities of renewal, they may extend their life indeterminately. But at some point or other they make

[4] I Cor. 1:28.

the fatal mistake, or a whole series of fatal mistakes. Then
they perish; and the divine majesty is vindicated in that
destruction.[5]

It is not possible to make some simple distinction between the period of creativity in a civilization and the period of decline, because every civilization and culture, every
empire and nation, reveals destructive elements in its period
of creativity, even as there are creative elements in its period of decline. But we know that there are periods in which
creativity predominates; and other ages in which corruption and destruction predominate.

If the whole of history is viewed from inside a period of
creativity it is given a false meaning; because the entire
historical process is falsely identified with a tangent in a
particular age of a particular culture. If the whole of history is viewed from the vantage point of a period of decline
it is threatened with meaninglessness. For the course of history is falsely identified with the doom of a given civilization. Whatever meaning there is in the rise and fall of civilizations can be known only "by faith"; for it must be
viewed from the vantage point of an eternity above history,
which no man has as a possession but only by faith. From
such a vantage point history is meaningful, even if it should
be impossible to discern any unity in its continuing processes. It is meaningful because eternal principles are vindicated in both the life which overcomes death in rising
civilizations, and in the death which overtakes proud life
in dying ones.

## 2. The Individual and History

The plight of the individual in his relation to the whole
process of history is derived from his twofold relation to the
historical process. His creativity is directed towards the establishment, perpetuation and perfection of historical communities. Therefore the meaning of his life is derived from

[5] Here we must recall the relevance of the prophetic conception of the rise and fall of empires and the belief that their destruction represents a vindication of the divine majesty against
the pretensions of false majesty. Cf. Ezekiel 28:17–18: "Thine

his relation to the historical process. But the freedom which makes this creativity possible transcends all communal loyalties and even history itself. Each individual has a direct relation to eternity; for he seeks for the completion of the meaning of his life beyond the fragmentary realizations of meaning which can be discerned at any point in the process where an individual may happen to live and die. The end of an individual life is, for him, the end of history; and every individual is a Moses who perishes outside the promised land. But each individual also has an indirect relation to eternity. In so far as he takes historical responsibilities seriously he must view the problem of fulfillment from the standpoint of the ultimate and final "end."[6]

If the eternal fulfillment of individual life is comprehended merely from "above," the social and historical meaning of life is destroyed. Individual life is regarded as an end in itself. This is precisely the effect not only of mystic doctrines of fulfillment but also of many orthodox Protestant versions of eschatology, in which the "end" stands only above history and the Biblical idea of the "end" is obscured.[7]

On the other hand modern protests against these Chris-

---

heart was lifted up because of thy beauty, thou hast corrupted thy wisdom by reason of thy brightness: I will cast thee to the ground. . . . I will bring thee to ashes upon the earth in the sight of all them that behold thee." This and many similar predictions of doom upon the various empires is always followed with the refrain: "In that day shall they know that I am the Lord."

[6] The Ezra Apocalypse (Fourth Ezra) states this problem of individual life succinctly: "But lo O Lord thou art ready to meet with thy blessing those that survive *in the end;* but what shall our predecessors do, or we ourselves or our posterity?" (5:41). Or again: "How does it profit us that an eternal age is promised us, whereas we have done works that bring death? And that there is foretold us an imperishable hope, whereas we are so miserably brought to futility?" (7:119–20).

[7] Reformation theology is on the whole defective in failing to preserve the Biblical conception of the end; and modern Barthian eschatology accentuates this defect. It pays little attention to a possible meaning of history as a continuum and speaks of eschatology in terms of the eternity which impinges upon every moment of time.

tian (and sometimes non-Christian) forms of "other-worldliness" make the mistake of trying to fulfill the meaning of
life in the historical process itself. Thereby they not only
obscure the reality of individual freedom in its transcendence over history but also deny the finite character of the
historical process.

In their crudest forms the purely social and historical interpretations of life bid the individual to fulfill his life in
his community. The breadth of the communal life and the
majesty of its power supposedly complete and fulfill the
partial interests and inadequate power of the individual.
The relative immortality of the community is intended to
compensate for the brevity of an individual's life. The difficulty with this solution is that each individual is so much
more, even while he is so much less, than the community.
His years are briefer than those of his community; but both
his memories and anticipations have a longer range. The
community knows only of its own beginnings but the individual knows of the rise and fall of civilizations before
his own. The community looks forward to the victories, and
fears the defeats of history; but the individual discerns a
more final judgment. If the nations stand before that last
judgment too, they do so in the conscience and mind of
sensitive individuals. The brotherhood of the community is
indeed the ground in which the individual is ethically realized. But the community is the frustration as well as the
realization of individual life. Its collective egotism is an of-
fense to his conscience; its institutional injustices negate
the ideal of justice; and such brotherhood as it achieves is
limited by ethnic and geographic boundaries. Historical
communities are, in short, more deeply involved in nature
and time than the individual who constantly faces an eternity above and at the end of the time process.

More refined forms of social and historical schemes of
redemption bid the individual to fulfill his life and compensate for the brevity of his years by his relation, not to
any particular historic community, but to the historical
process itself.[8]

[8] An historian of the eighteenth century describes the substitution of "posterity" for eternity in eighteenth-century thought

We have previously considered the reasons why it is impossible to regard history as redemptive and why the hope of an adequate judgment and a sufficient fulfillment of the life of the individual in the historical process must lead to the most pathetic disillusionment. It may suffice at this point to illustrate and recapitulate previous analyses of this problem by the simple expedient of imagining ourselves the "posterity" to which the eighteenth century appealed and noting the incongruity of being regarded as the "supporters of the oppressed," as "holy and sacred," in short as worthy or capable of being the final judges or redeemers of those who have gone before us. We are furthermore so deeply involved in and preoccupied with our own perplexities that we are as disinclined, as we are unworthy, to act as surrogates for God.

Yet there is always an element of truth in these simple appeals to history as the fulfillment of life; for the meaning of life is to be found partly in man's involvement in historical tasks and obligations.

The New Testament answer to the problem of the individual is given from the standpoint of both the eternity which is "above" and the eternity which is at the end of history. The idea of a "general resurrection," in which all those who perished before the fulfillment of history, are brought back to participate in the final triumph, does justice to both the value of individual life, without which the fulfillment of history would be incomplete; and to the

---

as follows: "For the love of God they substituted love of humanity; for vicarious atonement the perfectibility of man through his own efforts, and for the hope of immortality in another world the hope of living in the memory of future generations. . . . The thought of posterity was apt to elicit from eighteenth-century philosophers and revolutionary leaders a highly emotional and essentially religious response." Carl L. Becker, *The Heavenly City of Eighteenth-Century Philosophers*, p. 130.

The essentially religious character of this appeal to posterity is perfectly expressed in the words of Diderot: "O posterity, holy and sacred! Supporter of the oppressed and unhappy, thou who art just, thou who art incorruptible, thou who wilt revenge the good man and unmask the hypocrite, consoling and certain idea, do not abandon me. Posterity is for the philosopher what the other world is for the religious."

meaning of the whole course of history for the individual, without which his life cannot be fulfilled.

The symbol of the resurrection of the body is, even without the conception of a general resurrection at the end of history, both more individual and more social in its connotations than the alternative idea of the immortality of the soul. It is more individual because it asserts eternal significance, not for some impersonal *nous* which has no real relation to the actual self; but for the self as it exists in the body. This self bears within it the anxiety and insecurity of finite existence on the one hand, and the capacity to touch the horizons of the eternal on the other hand. The hope of the resurrection affirms that ultimately finiteness will be emancipated from anxiety and the self will know itself as it is known.

The idea of the resurrection is more social because the historical constructions of human existence, the cultures and civilizations, the empires and nations and finally the whole historical process, are, just as individual life, the product of a tension between natural conditions and the freedom which transcends nature. The idea of the resurrection implies that the historical elaborations of the richness of creation, in all their variety, will participate in the consummation of history. It gives the struggles in which men engaged to preserve civilizations, and to fulfill goodness in history, abiding significance and does not relegate them to a meaningless flux, of which there will be no echo in eternity.[9]

Neither utopian nor purely other-worldly conceptions of fulfillment do full justice to the paradoxical relation of the individual to the historical process. The individual faces the eternal in every moment and in every action of his life; and he confronts the end of history with his own death. The dimension of his freedom transcends all social realities. His spirit is not fulfilled in even the highest achievements of

---

[9] It is significant that radical sectarianism frequently recognized the relevance and meaning of the idea of the resurrection in its polemic against a too individualistic orthodox Christianity. Cf. particularly *Man's Mortality* by Richard Overton, the leader of seventeenth-century Levellers.

history; his conscience is not eased by even the most unequivocal approbation of historical courts of judgment; nor need it be finally intimidated by historical condemnations. On the other hand the individual's life is meaningful only in its organic relation to historical communities, tasks and obligations.

The relation of the meaning of life to parenthood is a convenient microcosmic example of this double dimension of individual life. No individual parent fulfills the total meaning of his life in his relation to his children. There are innumerable facets of meaning which are comparatively irrelevant to the vocation of parenthood. But on the other hand it is not possible to divorce the meaning of life from the vocation of parenthood. Parents must be "justified" in the lives of their children. But children are hostages held by the future. The fulfillment of the life of the parents depends upon the realization of character in their children. Thus the present must wait upon the future for its final fulfillment.

## 3. *The Unity of History*

However meaningful life may be in the individual patterns and collective configurations which are appreciated "from above," or from the standpoint of their direct relation to the eternal source and end of meaning, history as such represents a total realm of coherence which requires comprehension from the standpoint of its ultimate *telos*.

Even without any explicit principle of comprehension, or any adequate philosophy or theology of history, the most cursory examination of history will yield certain tangents of coherence and reveal minimal relations of unity. A consistently pluralistic conception of history is not tenable, or even plausible. It may be, as Aristotle observed, that the arts are lost and found many times in the course of history. It may be that a Roman civilization must realize certain social standards completely *de novo*, without reference or dependence upon the achievement of these standards in a Babylonian or Egyptian civilization. But on the other hand there is always a residual minimum of social and cultural

experience which is deposited by one civilization and used
by another. The history of science cannot be traced without beginning with the mathematics and astronomy of
Egyptian priests. The science and philosophy of Western
civilization obviously rest upon Greek foundations; and
Western statecraft is inexplicable without an understanding
of its Roman-Stoic presuppositions. The Hebraic-Christian
interpretation of history, which we have sought to elucidate
in these pages, has its roots in Babylonian, Egyptian and
Persian forms of Messianism. There are, in short, cumulative effects in history. Even Spengler is forced to admit that,
when new civilizations are built upon the ruins of old ones,
their character is partly determined by the way new life
absorbs, adapts itself to, and grows around the old ruins.

The inner relation of successive civilizations to each other
may be described as "unity in length" or in time. The inner
relation of contemporary civilizations to each other may be
described as "unity in breadth" or in space. The former
unity is more obvious than the latter one. The history of
Western civilization is, for instance, more clearly related to
Greece and Rome than it is to its own contemporary China.
Yet there are minimal relations of mutual dependence even
in "breadth." While the Western world has elaborated
science and techniques to a greater extent than the oriental
world, it would not be possible to comprehend our Western
scientific development without understanding the contributions of oriental scientific discoveries towards it.

Perhaps the most significant development of our own day
is that the cumulative effects of history's unity in length is
daily increasing its unity in breadth. Modern technical civilization is bringing all civilizations and cultures, all empires
and nations into closer juxtaposition to each other. The fact
that this greater intimacy and contiguity prompts tragic
"world wars" rather than some simple and easy interpenetration of cultures, must dissuade us from regarding a "universal culture" or a "world government" as the natural and
inevitable *telos* which will give meaning to the whole historical process.

But on the other hand it is obvious that the technical
interdependence of the modern world places us under the

obligation of elaborating political instruments which will make such new intimacy and interdependence sufferable. This new and urgent task is itself a proof of the cumulative effects of history. It confronts us with progressively difficult tasks and makes our very survival dependent upon their solution. Thus the development of unity in breadth is one aspect of the unity of length in history.

These facts seem obvious enough to occasion some agreement in their interpretation, even when the presuppositions which govern the interpretations are divergent. It must be agreed that history means growth, however much the pattern of growth may be obscured by the rise and fall of civilizations. Though one age may have to reclaim what previous ages had known and forgotten, history obviously moves towards more inclusive ends, towards more complex human relations, towards the technical enhancement of human powers and the cumulation of knowledge.

But when the various connotations of the idea of "growth" are made more explicit a fateful divergence between the Christian and the modern interpretation of human destiny becomes apparent. As we have previously noted, the whole of modern secular culture (and with it that part of the Christian culture which is dependent upon it) assumes that growth means progress. It gives the idea of growth a moral connotation. It believes that history moves from chaos to cosmos by forces immanent within it. We have sought to prove that history does not support this conclusion. The peril of a more positive disorder is implicit in the higher and more complex order which human freedom constructs on the foundation of nature's harmonies and securities. The spiritual hatred and the lethal effectiveness of "civilized" conflicts, compared with tribal warfare or battles in the animal world, are one of many examples of the new evil which arises on a new level of maturity.

Two other examples of this aspect of history may be cited. The sanity of a mature individual incorporates psychic complexities and tensions into a tolerable unity, richer and finer than the simple unity of childhood. But it is also subject to aberrations to which children are immune. Children may be abnormal but are usually not subject to insanity. The political cohesion of a great national or imperial community has a breadth and extent beyond that of a primitive tribe. Furthermore it embodies social complexities of which tribal unity is innocent. The achievement of unity within this complexity represents growth toward "maturity." But every such realm of political order is filled with tensions which may become overt conflicts if not carefully "managed." The communities of history are political artifacts. They lack the security of nature and are exposed to the perils of human errors, and the aberrations of human freedom. No conceivable historical growth can therefore make a possible world government of the future as stable and secure as the order of a national community; just as no national community is as immune to disorder as the family or the tribe.

The New Testament symbol for this aspect of historical reality, this new peril of evil on every new level of the good, is the figure of the Antichrist. The Antichrist belongs to the *eschata*, to the "last things" which herald the end of history. The most explicit denial of the norm of history must be expected in the most ultimate development of history.[10] Closely related to this idea of the final evil at the end of history, is the general anticipation of evils in the course of history, which believers will understand but by which the world will be taken unawares.

[10] The specific term of Antichrist is found only in the Johannine epistles. I John 2:18; 4:3; II John 7. In these references the figure is not particularly identified with the end. But the Johannine epistles provide an explicit term for a general New Testament idea, which is variously expressed. Jesus' vision of the end includes the appearance of those who "shall come in my name, saying, I am Christ" (Mt. 24:5); and of "false Christs and false prophets" who will "shew great signs and wonders, insomuch that, if it were possible, they shall deceive the very elect" (Mt. 24:24 and Mk. 13:22). Not only the most explicit form of pride, but also final conflicts and wars belong to the end of history (Mt. 24:6).

In the apocalyptic sections of the epistles Christians are assumed to have insights into history which will make it possible for them to understand "sudden destruction" when other men say "peace and safety" (I Thess. 5:2); and "perilous times" are predicted when "men shall be lovers of their own selves, covet-

The New Testament symbol of the Antichrist was appropriated by Catholicism primarily for the purpose of designating potent foes of the church. This polemic use of the symbol obscured the fact that the ultimate evil might be not the denial, but the corruption, of the ultimate truth. This is the point which the Protestant Reformation made in levelling the charge of Antichrist against the church itself. But neither Catholicism nor the Reformation used the symbol of the Antichrist effectively as a principle of general historical interpretation. Modern Protestantism has not understood the significance of the symbol for obvious reasons. It has, therefore, been used and misused primarily by literalists who have sought to prove that some current and contemporary Napoleon, Hitler, or Cæsar conformed to the prophecies of Antichrist or had a name, the letters of which could be tortured to yield the number 666.[11]

The inclination of contemporary millenarian literalism to identify some current embodiment of evil with Antichrist, corresponds to a recurrent tendency in all apocalypses. It is probably as natural for an age to think of the evil against which it contends as the final form of evil as to make the mistake of regarding the good which it embodies as the final good.[12] The belief of an age that it has reached the end of history is pathetic, even though understandable. If we must have such illusions the apocalyptic versions of it have the merit, at least, of picturing history as moving towards a climax, and of regarding the consummation not as

---

ous, boasters, proud," etc. (II Tim. 3:2). Cf. also Revelation 16:16–18; 19:19.

[11] Cf. Rev. 13:18 "Let him that hath understanding count the number of the beast: for it is the number of a man; and his number is six hundred threescore and six." The "Beast" of the book of Revelation is quite rightly related in Christian eschatology to the conception of the Antichrist for it also is a symbol of the final form of evil, demanding blasphemous worship of itself. Cf. Rev. 13:4.

[12] Thus the book of Daniel places the Babylonian Empire in the position of the ultimate evil, believing that, "when the wickedness of the empire has gone so far as to deify itself and deny all reverence to anything higher, it demands and brings the divine intervention. Its hour has struck and with it the hour of the world's salvation." Adam Welch, *Visions of the End*, p. 124.

the mere display of the triumph of the good over evil but
as a desperate conflict between the two.

But an adequate Christian philosophy of history requires
better use of the symbol of the Antichrist than as a polemic
weapon against contemporary foes or as the bearer of in-
advertent insights, scattered among literalistic illusions. In
the New Testament the symbol is integral to a total and
consistent view of history, according to which the future
is never presented as a realm of greater security than the
present or as the guarantor of a higher virtue. The Antichrist stands at the end of history to indicate that history
cumulates, rather than solves, the essential problems of human existence.

This does not mean that evil has its own independent
history, culminating in the final idolatries and blasphemies
of the Antichrist. Both the *civitas Dei* and the *civitas
terrena* grow in history, as Augustine observed. But they
do not have their separate histories. The evil which appears at the end of history is either a corruption of the final
good or it is an explicit denial and defiance of that good
which would be impossible without the juxtaposition of the
good. This is to say that evil is negative and parasitic in
origin, even though its effect is positive and its power something more than inertial resistance. Modern tyrannies are
not the end product of a long history of tyranny in which
ancient evils have been consciously refined to their present
consistency of evil. They are rather characteristic corrup-
tions of a mature civilization in which technical instruments
have become more effective tools of tyrannical purpose.
Modern idolatrous religions, which conform so perfectly to
the vision of the "Beast" who demands religious worship
for himself; and of the "false Christs" who "deceive the

---

In later Jewish and Christian apocalypses it is the Roman,
rather than the Babylonian Empire which has this unenviable
position. In the "Eagle Vision" of the Ezra Apocalypse the sins
of Rome are regarded as embodying and accentuating all previous evils and thus pointing to the end of history (IV Ezra
12:15).

The idea of Marxist apocalypse that capitalism is the final evil,
the defeat of which will mean the destruction of evil in history,
is a secularized version of this same illusion.

very elect," are not the final fruit of an independent history of idolatry. They are explicit forms of self-worship which gain their power by consciously defying higher religious and moral standards. Modern international anarchy is not the fruit of a long history of anarchy. It is, rather, the corruption and disintegration of a system of order. It is so terrible because it presupposes potential or actual mutualities on a larger scale, than those achieved in previous civilizations.

The final evil is thus dependent upon the final good. Either it consciously and explicitly defies the Christ, in which case it requires Christ as a foil; or it is a lesser good, claiming to be the ultimate one, in which case it requires Christ as a cloak. The one form is the Antichrist of the sinners and the other the Antichrist of the righteous. But in either case the force of the Antichrist, though parasitic and negative in origin, is so positive in effect, and so stubborn in purpose that no force, immanent in history, is capable of encompassing its defeat. The Antichrist who appears at the end of history can be defeated only by the Christ who ends history.

All the known facts of history verify the interpretation of human destiny implied in New Testament eschatology. Yet most of the philosophies of history, both ancient and modern, have sought to obscure either one or the other aspect of history which Biblical eschatology illumines. Ancient philosophies of history either denied the meaningfulness of history entirely or they saw only the limited meaningfulness of its allegedly recurring cycles. Modern philosophies have emphasized the unity of history and its cumulative tendencies; but they sought to obscure and deny the perils and evils in the cumulations of history, so that they might regard history itself as the God of redemption.

If we inquire more closely why these mistakes were made, our consideration of the end of human destiny brings us back to the problems of the beginning. For the most plausible explanation of the mistakes is that they were prompted by the desire to find a way of completing human destiny which would keep man's end under his control and

in his power. The ancient world sought to do this by eman-
cipating the spirit of man from the flux of finiteness or by
subordinating his freedom to that flux. The modern world
has sought redemption by regarding the process of history
itself as a guarantor of the fulfillment of human life.

In every case the "vain imagination" of human pride entered into these calculations and determined the result.
"Honest" mistakes may account for some confusion. The
freedom of man transcends the flux of nature in such a way
that the hope of completely severing the spirit from the in-
teguments of nature is an understandable illusion. The processes of growth in history are, furthermore, so obvious that
the modern error of confusing growth with progress may
be regarded as an equally inevitable mistake. Yet both
these mistakes also rested upon a wilful disregard of some
of the obvious evidences. It is obvious that man does not
have the power to extricate himself from flux and finiteness,
as idealists and mystics of the ancient and the modern
world believed. It is equally obvious that history does not
solve the basic problems of human existence but reveals
them on progressively new levels. The belief that man
could solve his problem either by an escape from history
or by the historical process itself is a mistake which is partly
prompted by the most universal of all "ideological" taints:
the pride, not of particular men and cultures, but of man
as man.

For this reason it is possible to make a truer analysis of
human destiny upon the basis of a religious faith which has
disavowed human pride in principle, though it must not be
assumed that any particular Christian analysis will not exhibit in fact what it has disavowed in principle. But if the
Christian faith really finds its ultimate security beyond all
the securities and insecurities of history; if it is really "per-
suaded, that neither death, nor life, nor angels, nor prin-
cipalities, nor powers, nor things present, nor things to
come, nor height, nor depth, nor any other creature, shall
be able to separate us from the love of God, which is in
Christ Jesus our Lord,"[13] it may dissuade men from the

[13] Romans 8:38–39.

idolatrous pursuit of false securities and redemptions in life and history. By its confidence in an eternal ground of existence which is, nevertheless, involved in man's historical striving to the very point of suffering with and for him, this faith can prompt men to accept their historical responsibilities gladly. From the standpoint of such a faith history is not meaningless because it cannot complete itself; though it cannot be denied that it is tragic because men always seek prematurely to complete it.

Thus wisdom about our destiny is dependent upon a humble recognition of the limits of our knowledge and our power. Our most reliable understanding is the fruit of "grace" in which faith completes our ignorance without pretending to possess its certainties as knowledge; and in which contrition mitigates our pride without destroying our hope.

4.

*Professor Niebuhr raised the demand for unity in history as an essential component of its meaning. The same issue is discussed in the following selection. Karl Jaspers is Professor of Philosophy at the University of Basle, Switzerland. A voluminous writer, he has been, beside Heidegger, Sartre, and Marcel, a prominent figure in contemporary existentialism. And the selection reprinted below makes a fitting conclusion to this volume because it returns to some of the major themes which we have encountered in the beginning.*

*Again, the particular is "the yardstick of true historicity"; and historicity is the all-pervasive category of human life and thought. Thus historicism and existentialism complement each other.[1] Moreover, as for Dilthey, the quest for a unified interpretation of history fails. "Every line of development, every typical form, all facts of unity are simplifications within history that become fallacious when they are used as means for seeing through history in its totality.[2] This is shown by a criticism of different attempts to read a meaningful unity out of (or into) history on the basis of*

[1] Cf. p. 57 above.
[2] Cf. the similar argument advanced by Professor Niebuhr in the previous selection.

(1) *man's biological unity*, (2) *psychological and sociological uniformities*, (3) *the idea of progress* (*Jaspers here
is close to Burckhardt and Niebuhr*), (4) *spatial or temporal unities*, (5) *national, cultural, or religious unities*,
(6) *a unity through a goal of history like civilization, liberty, or self-consciousness*, and (7) *a unity through thought
as in the traditional religious and philosophical interpretations of history from St. Augustine to Hegel. The survey
yields a "long list of negations" and failures.*

*What remains, according to Jaspers, is (a) "to appre-
hend the manifoldness of the lines, forms, and unities"
pointing toward, but never encompassing or comprehending, "the always present whole of humanity,"*[3] *and (b) to
look upon the idea of a "universal history as a task" which
is never completed.*

*Jaspers has approached this task by employing "a
schema of world history" which, he believes, is "in closest
accord with openness and unity and empirical reality."
This schema is based upon the idea of a crucial "axis," or
"Axial Period," in world history. These special terms do
not appear in the following selection.*[4] *By "Axial Period"
Jaspers means a secularized version of the Christian idea
according to which world history is both divided and unified by the unique "axis" of the life and death of Jesus
Christ.*[5] *Jaspers has modified this religious conception in
two respects: First, he shifts the center of the axis to
about 500 B.C. (the total span of the Axial Period runs
from 800 to 200 B.C.). Second, his axis does not indicate a
supernatural ingression into time, but a decisive historical
break-through by man, in the basic conditions of his life
and thought, which occurred at this time in all the major
civilizations of the world (China, India, Greece, etc.). This
axis is a kind of watershed in world history: it divides history in that everything preceding this period was but a*

[3] Cf. Dilthey's "Dream".

[4] The idea of an "Axial Period" is discussed in earlier parts of
*The Origin and Goal of History* (cf., especially, Chap. I, pp.
1–21).

[5] For an analysis of the schema of a "Christian axis" in history,
see Oscar Cullmann, *Christ and Time* (Philadelphia, 1950).

*preparation for this break-through; it unifies in that all subsequent history still relates back to this period.*

## KARL JASPERS

## THE UNITY OF HISTORY*

. . . It is the unity of the history of mankind, to which everything that has value and meaning seems to be related. But how are we to think of this unity of the history of mankind? . . .

### A. FACTS THAT POINT TO UNITY

#### 1. *Unity of the human make-up*

We have some such trivial notion of humanity in history as this. Man is a totality of innate tendencies. At any given moment, under the particular conditions, parts of his energies, gifts and impulses are realised, whilst others slumber unawakened. Since, however, man is always the same potentially, everything remains possible at all times. The varying unfoldment of his parts does not mean a difference of nature, but a difference of manifestation. In the collation of all manifestations, as the development to varying degrees of common potentialities, the totality of humanity is first disclosed.

The question of whether man's make-up has been transformed during the few millennia of history, or whether the nature of man has remained the same throughout this period, must be answered by saying that no facts are available in evidence of any such transformation. Any changes that have taken place are rather to be understood in terms of the selection of that which was already present. That which is given in the basic make-up as permanent and unchanging appears at different times, through the agency of varying selection, in quite different directions. At any given

* In *The Origin and Goal of History* (New Haven: Yale University Press, 1953), pp. 247–67. I have deleted several passages, as indicated. H.M.

time those men become visible, successful, and then numerically preponderant whose personal qualities satisfy the particular conditions of the current society and its situation. Conditions may be characterised by the type of human make-up they fostered. With the alteration of conditions, selection changes, and previously hidden types of make-up, which have long been suppressed and reduced to a small number of negative selection, now come to the fore. The varying manifestation of the same nature under ever diverse preconditions, with a diverse selection, is disclosed.

Nevertheless, to this train of thought the rejoinder must be made that the whole of humanity can in no wise be pictured as the totality of innate human tendencies. There is no man who is or can be everything human, neither in reality nor in the projection of an idea of him.

The further objection must be made that the essential variation of the make-up with which an individual is naturally endowed is elemental. Especially when we look at the personal qualities and character traits which already make their appearance in earliest childhood does the ineluctable course taken by the innate disposition become visible. These qualities and traits create a gulf of difference between the make-up of one man and another.

These ideas, and the objections to them, all contain an element of truth, but they do not go so far as to explain man.

To reach the unity of humanity which is revealed in history, we must pass beyond the biologico-psychological plane of consideration. . . .

The unity toward which man lives, if he becomes authentically historical, cannot have its basis in a unity of biological derivation, but only in the higher origin that causes man to become directly out of the hand of the Deity. This unity of origin is not the continuance of a *status quo*. It is rather historicity itself. This is evident from the following:

(1) The unity of man in the movement of his metamorphoses is not a static unity of persisting, and merely alternately realised, qualities. Man has become man in his-

tory through a movement that is not a movement of
his natural make-up. As a natural being he is given his
make-up in the area open to the play of its variations, as
an historical being he reaches out beyond this natural
datum. From this origin he must press on toward the unity
that links all. This is a postulate: Without this unity understanding would not be possible, there would be a chasm
between those of disparate natures, an understanding history would be impossible.

(2) The manifestation of individual men is of a self-
exclusive character in its particular reality. Man as an individual cannot unite what he realises out of essentially disparate origins, for instance, the hero and the saint.

Man, even the individual man, is from his origin potentially everything, but in reality a single thing. In this he
is not a restricted part, however, but historical, an origin
of his own, turned to the other historical origin in the consciousness of the one historical fundament that links all.

The individual man is never a complete, never an ideal
man. The complete man cannot, in principle, exist; for
everything which he is and realises, can be, and is, broken
through again, is open. Man is not a finished and not a
perfectible being.

(3) In history, that which is unrepeatable and irreplaceable comes to light in unique creations, break-throughs and
realisations. Because these creative steps cannot be in any
way conceived causally, nor deduced as necessary, they are
like revelations from some other source than the mere
course of happening. But once they have come into existence, they lay the foundations of the humanity that
comes after. From them man acquires his knowledge and
volition, his prototypes and antitypes, his criteria, his
thought-patterns and his symbols, his inner world. They are
steps toward unity, because they appertain to the one self-
understanding spirit and address themselves to all.

## 2. The universal

The unity of mankind is impressively evident in the fact
that similar basic traits of religion, forms of thought, im-

plements, and social forms recur all over the earth. The simplicity of man is great, despite his diversity. Psychological and sociological facts are such that comparison is possible everywhere, and a multitude of regularities can be noted, which demonstrate fundamental structures of humanity in the psychological and sociological provinces. Precisely through observation of the common element, however, does that which is divergent become clear, whether it is to be comprehended from specific types of human make-up, or from historical situations and events. If we turn our gaze upon the universal, we shall find congruence in that which is essential, and comprehend particularities as local, attaching them to place and time.

It is precisely this universal, however, which cannot constitute the true unity of mankind. Just the reverse. If we turn our gaze upon the depths of the truth that is manifested, we shall find the historically great within the particular, but in the universal the commonplace, the unhistorically constant, which is, so to speak, the fluid medium of the factual and the correct.

If, between the most distant cultures, a common possession forms the substratum of humanity, it is quite especially surprising and important to note that there are always divergences as well, where we thought we had found an absolute universal—that somewhere something is missing which is otherwise typical of man, and also that the absolutely universal always possesses an abstract character, a uniformity.

That which, by the yardstick of the universal, is a mere particularisation, may be precisely the fulfilment of true historicity. The unity of mankind can take root only in the relationship of these historical particulars to one another, which is not essentially divergence, but rather a positively original content, not the instance of a universal, but a link in the one comprehensive historicity of mankind.

## 3. *Progress*

The road leads forward in knowledge and technological ability, one step succeeds the other, that which has been acquired may be passed on in the identical shape and become the property of all. As a result, there passes through the history of individual cultures, and of all cultures, a line of growing acquisitions, which is, however, confined to the impersonal, universally valid knowledge and ability of consciousness in general.

In this domain, world history may be conceived of as a development in an ascending line, with retrogressions and standstills it is true, but on the whole with perpetual augmentation of the possession to which men and peoples make their contribution, and which, by nature accessible to all men, also becomes the possession of all. Historically we see the stages of this advance, and in the present we stand at the highest point. This is only a line in the whole, however. Humanity itself, the ethos of man, his goodness and wisdom, make no progress. Art and poetry are indeed comprehensible to all, but not typical of all; they are bound to peoples and their epochs, each one at a unique and unsurpassable height.

Hence there is progress in knowledge, in technology, in the prerequisites for new human possibilities, but not in the substance of humanity. Progress in substance is refuted by the facts. The peoples which had reached the highest levels perished, succumbing to those inferior to them. Cultures were destroyed by barbarians. The physical annihilation of the highest types of men by the oppressive realities of the mass is a fundamental phenomenon of history. The average that multiplies the most, the growth of the thoughtless populace, triumphs without a struggle through mere existence *en masse* over that which is spiritually higher. There is a constant counter-selection of those who are inferior, e.g. in conditions under which cunning and brutality promise lasting advantages. One inclines toward the proposition: Everything exalted perishes, everything inferior endures.

Against such a generalisation, we can point to the recurrence of the great, even if it remains silent for centuries and longer. But how fragile, how dubious and uncertain is this endurance!

These are said to be only setbacks, only contingent ruin.

In the long run there is reason to believe in substantial progress. But precisely these contingencies, these destructions are, at any rate in the foreground, the overwhelming basic happening of history.

It is said things need not continue to be as they have been till now. It is up to us to guide the course of events better. But this is the Utopian idea that everything can be fabricated, the principle of 'breeding' applied to the realm of man, where the object can never be known, surveyed and manipulated.

It is said ruin is the consequence of guilt. If we only expiate our sins and prove ourselves in a pure life, things will be different. Indeed, this has been the exhortation since the ancient prophets—but we do not know upon what route, when or how, the good of a world order will follow from the ethically pure life. We may not deny the reality that the ethically good as such is by no means crowned with success—nor is it done for the sake of success. But the ethically good that assumes responsibility for success and the consequences remains the one great chance.

Progress will indeed bring a unity of the knowable, but not the unity of mankind. The unity of universally valid truth which, wherever it is found, remains the same in its unending advance, appears only in science and technology. This universally communicable and transferable truth, which addresses itself to the understanding alone, is not the unity of mankind. This progress brings a unity of the understanding. It links men in the understanding, so that they discuss rationally with one another; but it leaves them capable of annihilating each other with the same weapons of technology. For the understanding only links understanding as a whole, not men. It brings no genuine communication and no solidarity.

## 4. Unity in space and time

The unity of man springs from life on the common natural soil (unity of the planet), and from existence in the one common time.

In the course of history intercourse developed—with setbacks. The multiplicity of the naturally given, the manifoldness of peoples and countries, existed for a long time in unrelated contiguity. The path of intercourse linked them, caused tribes to amalgamate into peoples, peoples into groups of peoples, countries into continents, and then to fall apart again. It enabled men of different peoples to catch sight of one another and then forget each other again, until the moment of conscious and factual connexion of all to all began, and intercourse became uninterrupted—either in real consummation, or in the rupture of warfare. The history of mankind as perpetual mutual exchange in the unity of intercourse commenced.

Men had long ago taken possession of the surface of the earth, with the exception of the polar regions, deserts and high mountain-chains, in the course of many thousands of years of migration. Mankind was always mobile. Amazing journeys were made at the threshold of history. The Northmen came to Greenland and America, the Polynesians crossed the whole Pacific, the Malays reached Madagascar. The languages of Negro Africa and of America are each so closely related amongst themselves as to indicate continual intercourse within these continents. Inventions, tools, ideas, legends travelled long distances across the earth in primeval historical times, always in short stages, as though passed from one hand to the other. Only Australia, and perhaps America, remained in isolation for a long time; but even they were not absolutely isolated (there are striking parallels between Eastern Asia and Mexico). Isolation does not mean that no man of another country was ever carried to their shores, but that they were never subjected to any perceptible foreign influence.

In the course of history great empires were formed, which, for a while, increased the contact between men within their domains. Then they disintegrated again, the highways of intercourse were interrupted, relations broken off, knowledge of the existence of the others forgotten. There were peoples which, from time to time, shut themselves off from the outer world—such as Egypt, Japan and China; but every wall erected was ultimately broken through again.

During the last five hundred years, the Europeans have drawn the whole earth into their communications net. They have carried their civilisation to all parts of the world and have taken for themselves goods of civilisation which they did not possess. They brought their domestic animals, useful plants and weapons, their manufactures and machines, their customs and their beliefs and all the evils of their world; they fetched potatoes, maize, quinine, cocoa, tobacco, the hammock, etc. It was they who first made the unity of the earth conscious, intercourse systematic, lasting and reliable.

This intercourse between peoples has meant a continual growing together of mankind, the creation of unity through the planet's becoming one to the consciousness, and ultimately to the actions, of men. . . .

Unity through the one terrestrial soil, through common enclosure in space and time, is nevertheless the most superficial unity, which is certainly not identical with the unity of history. It is common to all reality and not the portion of man alone. The mere co-existence of men on the closed surface of the earth, which they fill, does not of itself constitute the unity of mankind. This unity is made possible by intercourse. It is by no means this intercourse *per se*, however, but only the outcome of that which takes place in this intercourse. . . .

## 5. *Particular unities*

In the movement of human affairs there are, to our cognition, many lines which run separately from one another and subsequently meet—or particular lines which, although they recur typically, represent only features of the whole, not the whole itself.

Thus there is the circumscribed sequence of a particular set of cultural phenomena. A few generations cohere in typical stylistic sequences or developments of thought, from their origin to their disintegration.

There are unities of cultures as *de facto* common worlds of life-forms, dispositions, ideas, units of faith, the peoples in their provenance, their language, their destiny—the re-

ligions as 'world religions', which disseminate transcenden-
tally procured attitudes to life in ethos, faith and outlook
over wide areas—the States as power units which mould
everything else.

These unities lack universality. They are individual unities alongside others, cultures alongside cultures. There are
many peoples, religions, States. These stand in relation to
one another, cultures in silent exchanges, States in warfare
and the mutual acceptance of politics, religions in mission
and disputation. All of them undergo transformation, are
not finally fixed, run into one another. . . .

## B.  UNITY THROUGH MEANING AND GOAL

If the manifold facts which represent a unity, or point
to unity, do not suffice to constitute the unity of history,
a different starting-point is perhaps possible. Unity is not a
fact, but a goal. The unity of history is perhaps produced
by men's ability to understand each other in the idea of the
One, in the one truth, in the world of the spirit, in which
all things are meaningfully related to one another and belong together, however alien to each other they may be at
the outset.

Unity springs from the meaning in the direction of which
history occurs, a meaning that lends significance to that
which, without it, would remain nugatory in dispersion.

This goal may appear as a concealed meaning, which
no one intended, but which the observer tries out inter-
pretively, or then apprehends as conscious purpose, as will
to unity. The meaning is expressed as the goal of history:

(1) The goal is taken to be *civilisation* and the *human-
isation* of man. What this may be, beyond the ordering of
existence is, however, by no means clearly determined, but
itself historical. As the ordering of existence, however, the
goal is legal world order. The path of history leads out of
dispersion *via* merely *de facto* contact in peace and war to
cohabitation on earth in a real unity achieved through the
rule of law. This unity would, through the ordering of ex-

istence, give scope to all the potentialities of the human soul and spirit.

(2) The goal is taken to be *liberty* and the consciousness of liberty. Everything that has happened up to now is to be construed as an attempt to attain liberty.

But the process that will reveal to us what liberty is has no end.

The will to a world order of law does not make its immediate goal liberty, but only political liberty, which gives human existence scope for all the possibilities of genuine liberty.

(3) The goal is taken to be the *noble man* and the creation of the spirit, the production of culture in communal conditions; it is taken to be the genius.

The urge is to the most lucid consciousness. The unity of meaning originates from the point at which man becomes most decisively conscious of himself in extreme situations—where he puts the most profound questions—where he finds the creative answers by which his life is guided and which give it its characteristic stamp. This unity in the nobility of humanity does not consist in the diffusion of implements and knowledge, not in the extent of conquests and imperial jurisdiction, not in extreme formations such as killing asceticism or the sort of training imposed on the Janizaries—not in the permanence and stability of institutions and fixations—but in the radiant moments of the most profound lucidity of consciousness, of essential revelations.

This most essential element may then be a minute speck in the stream of history. But it may begin to work like a ferment in the totality of events. Or it may remain ineffectually in memory, ready to take effect, a question put to the future. Or it may find in the world no echo to its unique nobility, vanish without recollection, and exist only for transcendence.

That such peaks appear irreplaceably valuable to us, rests upon the fact that they fall within the province of a unity which we have always presupposed and never really known, a unity without which, as its goal, origin and justification, there would be no history.

(4) The goal is taken to be the *manifestation of Being*

*in man,* the perception of being in its depths, that is, the manifestation of the Godhead.

Such goals are attainable in every present, and indeed are attained—up to a point; they are regained in a perennial process of loss and devaluation. They are realised by every generation in its own way.

This does not mean that the single, overall goal of history is achieved, however. The imaginary goal of the future tends rather to turn our attention back to the present, which must not be let slip.

The unity of history *per se* is not laid bare by any interpretation of meaning. Every formulation, even if it hits the highest target, remains at a goal which is not the Comprehensive, at least not in the sense that all other goals could be derived from one particular concept, so that the unity of the goal would lay open to view the one meaning of history. Hence all supposed goals do indeed become factors within history, if they are desired or if faith is bestowed on them, but they are never anything that covers the whole of history. . . .

At all times, however, the craving to know and believe one meaning as single and all-embracing is satisfied. And if every meaning that is absolutised is bound to come to grief, new generations in their turn immediately seek, through their philosophers, an all-embracing meaning that has governed, and is governing, history, and which, once it has been conceived, can also be assimilated into their own will as an intended meaning and taken as a guide (as in the Christian philosophy of history, as in Hegel, in Comte, etc.).

This unity is brought into view in an interpretive total conception of history.

### C.   UNITY FOR THE THINKING TOTAL CONCEPTION

To comprehend the unity of history, i.e. to think of universal history as a whole, is the urge of historical knowledge in search of its ultimate meaning.

Philosophical consideration of history has therefore en-

quired after the unity that holds mankind together. Men
settled the globe, but they were scattered and did not know
of one another, lived in the most diverse guises and spoke
thousands of languages. In earlier times, anyone who
thought of universal history, because of the narrowness of
his horizon, constructed a unity at the expense of restriction; amongst ourselves, for instance, he restricted himself
to the West, in China to the Central Empire. That which
lay beyond had no part in it and was regarded as a life of
barbarians, primitive peoples, which were certainly an object of ethnological interest, but not of history. Unity consisted in the presupposition of the tendency to cause all
the still unknown peoples of the earth to participate, stage
by stage, in the one—namely, one's own—culture, to bring
them into one's own sphere of order.

If faith presupposed one fundament and one goal, the
idea sought to recognise these in real history. Assumptions
of a knowledge of unity, either given by divine revelation
or intelligible to reason, were attempts at constructing the
one history of mankind.

God's passage through history became visible in the
West in the succession of His acts running from Creation,
*via* expulsion from Paradise, announcement of His will
through the prophets, redemption through His appearance
in person at the turning-point of the ages, to the end in the
anticipated Last Judgement. That which was first thought
of by the Jewish prophets, then assumed Christian form
through St. Augustine, which was repeated and inflected
from Joachim Fiore to Bousset, secularised from Lessing
and Herder to Hegel, was always this knowledge of the
one whole history, in which everything has its place. A
series of fundamental principles of human existence made
their appearance which, apprehended in their depths,
taught what truly is and happens.

Such a construction, however—magnificently as it has
been believed and expressed throughout two millennia—
breaks down:

(*a*) If I know the whole, every human existence has its
place in the whole. It is not for itself, but serves a path.
It is not immediate to transcendence, but through the me-

dium of a position in time, which narrows it and makes it a part. Every human existence, every period, every people, is mediatised. Against this the original relationship to the Godhead, the infinitude of the Comprehensive, which can be whole at any time, revolts.

(b) In the knowledge of the whole, the greater proportion of human reality, whole peoples, epochs and cultures, fall to one side as of no account. They are no more than chance and incidental products of natural happening.

(c) History is not closed and does not reveal its origin. For this construction, however, it is closed. The beginning and end are invented as an addition in the shape of an alleged revelation. . . .

We have drawn up a long list of negations: The unity of history is not to be apprehended by knowledge. It cannot be construed as the unity of man's biological origin. As the unity of the earth's surface and as common enclosure by real time it is a purely external unity. The unity of the all-embracing goal cannot be demonstrated. The idea of a world order of law is directed toward the substrata of human existence, not toward the meaning of history *in toto*, and is itself still a query. Unity cannot be comprehended by reference to the identity of a universally valid truth, for this unity relates only to the understanding. It is not progress toward a goal or in a process that goes on into infinity. Unity does not consist in the most lucid consciousness, nor in the nobility of spiritual creation. It is not contained in a meaning toward which everything happens or ought to happen. Nor is unity to be discerned as the articulated organism of a totality of mankind. The totality of history is not truly present in a visual image either as reality or as meaning. . . .

Every line of development, every typical form, all facts of unity are simplifications within history that become fallacious when they are used as a means of seeing through history in its totality. The important thing is to apprehend the manifoldness of these lines, forms, unities, but to remain open to that which lies beyond them, in which these phenomena occur, to remain open to man and to the always present whole of humanity.

# A BIBLIOGRAPHICAL POSTSCRIPT

In place of a formal bibliography, which would be incomplete at best, I shall append a few bibliographical comments against the background of the selections included in this volume.

## I

Most of the standard works on the European tradition of historicism are not available in English. The most important are those by F. Meinecke and K. Heussi cited in Mr. Barraclough's essay above. Additional titles of general interest include: Ernst Troeltsch, *Der Historismus and seine Überwindung* (Berlin, 1924), translated as *Christian Thought: Its History and Application* (London, 1923); Carlo Antoni, *Dallo storicismo alla sociologica* (Florence, 1940), translated into German as *Vom Historismus zur Soziologie;* Pietro Rossi, *Lo storicismo tedesco contemporaneo* (Turin, 1956); and Raymond Aron, *La sociologie allemande contemporaine* (Paris, 1936), translated as *German Sociology* (Glencoe, Ill., 1957).

Maurice Mandelbaum, *The Problem of Historical Knowledge* (New York, 1938), is a critical study of this European movement by a philosopher. H. Stuart Hughes, *Consciousness and Society* (New York, 1958), is a sympathetic study by an intellectual historian.

H. A. Hodges, *The Philosophy of Wilhelm Dilthey* (London, 1952), is a systematic interpretation; a shorter work by the same author, *Wilhelm Dilthey: An Introduction* (New York, 1944), includes selections from Dilthey's writings; but the reader interested in Dilthey must still consult the collected works in German, especially the following two volumes: *Der Aufbau der geschichtlichen Welt in den Geisteswissenschaften* and *Das geschichtliche Bewusstsein und die Weltanschauungen,* vols. VII and VIII, respectively, of the *Gesammelte Schriften.*

A late restatement of Croce's views on history may be found in *History as the Story of Liberty* (Meridian Books: New York, 1955). *An Autobiography* by R. G. Collingwood (London, 1936) is an interesting human document and throws light upon his theory of history, as does *An Essay on Philosophical Method* (Oxford, 1950) by the same author.

Part I lacks a contribution by Max Weber, who was

perhaps the most powerful mind in the recent European tradition combining historicism, neo-idealism, and scholarly, empirical research. Owing to the work of Talcott Parsons, H. H. Gerth, C. Wright Mills, and others, Weber is now a familiar figure in American social thought as well. Some of his most important theoretical essays may be found in Max Weber, *On the Methodology of the Social Sciences,* translated and edited by Edward A. Shils and Henry A. Finch (Glencoe, Ill., 1949).

## II

In the debate between historians and philosophers in Part II, the case for either side could have been strengthened by references to other works in the field.

The Social Science Research Council has published two monographs by its Committee on Historiography: Bulletin 54, *Theory and Practice in Historical Study* (New York, 1946), and Bulletin 64, *The Social Sciences in Historical Study* (New York, 1954). A more important source, however, for the views of eminent historians is the *American Historical Review,* especially the articles reproducing the annual presidential address delivered before the American Historical Association. On these occasions, historians have frequently taken time out for philosophical reflections upon their craft.

References to the major works by Charles A. Beard appear in the above selections. *Everyman His Own Historian* by Carl Becker (New York, 1935) has become a slogan. J. B. Bury, *Selected Essays,* edited by Harold Temperly (Cambridge, 1930), includes "The Science of History" and "The Place of History in the Perspective of Knowledge." An elegant defense of the opposite point of view may be found in George Macaulay Trevelyan, *Clio, A Muse* (new ed., London, 1930). Epistemological and general issues of philosophical interest come up in the following works: Sir L. B. Namier, *Avenues of History* (London, 1952); F. M. Powicke, *Modern Historians and the Study of History* (London, 1955); or, on a more popular level, A. L. Rowse, *The Use of History* (London, 1946). H. R. Trevor-Roper, *Men and Events* (New York, 1957), includes essays on Burckhardt and Toynbee.

Marc Bloch, *Apologie pour L'Histoire* (Paris, 1952), translated as *The Historian's Craft* (New York, 1953), is a posthumous fragment by a great historian whom the Germans shot during the last war. Henri Berr, *La Synthèse en Histoire* (Paris, 1953), and Lucien Febvre, *Combats pour L'Histoire* (Paris, 1953), are other important statements by French historians. The thoughtful essays by Pieter Geyl are now collected under the title of *Debates with Historians* (London, 1955); unfortunately there is no such collection in English of the theoretical writings by Jan Huizinga and Jan Romein.

On the side of the philosophers, there are several omissions that should be noted. First, the "analytic" movement may feel short-changed despite the selections from Nagel and White. Thus I list a few additional references frequently cited in recent literature: Alan Donagan, "Explanation in History," *Mind*, LXVI (1957); William Dray, *Laws and Explanation in History* (London, 1957); Patrick Gardiner, *The Nature of Historical Explanation* (London, 1952); Carl G. Hempel, "The Function of General Laws in History," *Journal of Philosophy*, XXXIX (1942), reprinted in *Readings in Philosophical Analysis*, edited by H. Feigl and W. Sellars (New York, 1949); A. M. MacIver, "The Character of a Historical Explanation," *Proceedings of the Aristotelian Society*, suppl. vol. XXI (1947); A. I. Melden, "Historical Objectivity, A 'Noble Dream'?", *Journal of General Education*, VII (1952); Morton White, "Historical Explanation," *Mind*, LII (1943), and "Toward an Analytic Philosophy of History," in *Philosophic Thought in France and the United States*, edited by M. Farber (Buffalo, 1950).

Another group of philosophers who may feel slighted, despite the selection from John Dewey, belong to a movement loosely labeled "naturalism." The following works, therefore, are worth noting: Morris R. Cohen, *The Meaning of History* (La Salle, Ill., 1947); Sidney Hook, *From Hegel to Marx* (New York, 1935) and *The Hero in History* (Beacon paperback: Boston, 1955), two works by a philosopher who has written extensively on the theory of history; and John H. Randall, Jr., *Nature and Historical Experience* (New York, 1958), a basic volume comprising the author's numerous contributions to the philosophy of naturalism and history. G. J. Renier, *History: Its Purpose and Method* (Boston, 1950), also falls into this general category, as does the collective volume, *Naturalism and the Human Spirit*, edited by Yervant H. Krikorian (New York,

1944), which includes an essay, "The Materials of Historical Knowledge," by Edward W. Strong.

Finally, there is no selection that represents the Marxist view of history. This is due primarily to the fact that, in this field, there is no substitute for reading the works of Marx and Engels, and both belong to the nineteenth century. From an enormous literature by their sucessors, I cite two substantial works: Karl Kautsky, *Die materialistische Geschichtsauffassung* (Berlin, 1927), and George Lukacs, *Geschichte und Klassenbewusstsein* (Berlin, 1923). *Marxism and Modern Thought*, edited by N. I. Bukharin and others (New York, 1935), is worth mentioning because it includes a long essay, "Marxism and Bourgeois Historical Science," by A. I. Tiumeniev which deals specifically with the historical tradition represented in this anthology. Leon Trotsky is a special case if only for *The History of the Russian Revolution* just reissued by the Michigan University Press. His pamphlet, *Their Morals and Ours* (New York, 1940), is an analysis of the moral issue from a revolutionary perspective.

## III

The topics discussed in Parts III and IV may be treated in a more summary fashion, because both enter, in one form or another, into most writings on the theoretical foundations of history.

Thus references to the subject of morality and history would merely duplicate most of the works cited so far. It is worth mentioning, however, that the problem of moral judgments in history is often treated as a special case of a more general problem known as the "sociology of knowledge." *Ideology and Utopia* by Karl Mannheim (New York and London, 1936) was an early and influential text in the literature on this subject. The same author's *Essays on the Sociology of Knowledge,* edited by Paul Kecskemeti (New York, 1952), includes a special chapter on modern historicism. The same connection between historicism and sociology is noted in some of the titles listed in Part I of these bibliographical comments.

Of the two authors debating the issue in this volume, Herbert Butterfield first criticized the moral and pragmatic attitude in *The Whig Interpretation of History* (London, 1931 and 1950). Sir Isaiah Berlin, *The Hedgehog and the Fox* (New York, 1953), dealing with Tolstoy's philosophy of history in *War and Peace*, also touches upon the moral problem as well as upon the problem of the meaning of history.

## IV

Most of the literature on the "meaning of history," in the traditional sense, is written from a religious point of view. I cite a few titles in addition to those mentioned in the text: Rudolf Bultmann, *History and Eschatology* (Edinburgh, 1957); Herbert Butterfield, *Christianity and History* (London, 1943); Romano Guardini, *The End of the Modern World* (New York, 1956); Jacques Maritain, *On the Philosophy of History* (New York, 1957); Reinhold Niebuhr, *Faith and History* (New York, 1949); and Paul Tillich, *The Interpretation of History* (New York, 1936).

On the secular side, it must be remembered that the problem of "meaning," from an empirical and/or analytic point of view, is primarily an epistemological question belonging to the logic of explanation and interpretation in history. In this sense it is discussed in the works cited in Part II of these bibliographical notes.

I add a few miscellaneous titles bearing upon the same subject: Karl Popper, *The Poverty of Historicism* (Boston, 1958), is another critique of metaphysical and teleological laws in history. Hugh Miller, *The Community of Man* (New York, 1949) is a restatement of an evolutionary theory of history. Pierre-Henri Simon, *L'Esprit et L'Histoire* (Paris, 1954), is a study from an existentialist point of view. The essay "Man and History," by Max Scheler in *Philosophical Perspectives*, translated by Oscar A. Haac (Boston, 1958), is a sketch for an interpretation of history according to a typology of man. Finally, the collective volume *Philosophy and History*, edited by R. Klibansky and H. J. Paton (Oxford, 1936), includes an essay, "The Philosophic Character of History," by R. Klibansky which is in the neo-Kantian tradition.